Paint Shop Pro™ 7
fast&easy®

Check the Web for Updates:

To check for updates or corrections relevant to this book and/or CD-ROM visit our updates page on the Web at http://www.prima-tech.com/updates.

Send Us Your Comments:

To comment on this book or any other PRIMA TECH title, visit our reader response page on the Web at **http://www.prima-tech.com/comments**.

How to Order:

For information on quantity discounts, contact the publisher: Prima Publishing, P.O. Box 1260BK, Rocklin, CA 95677-1260; (916) 787-7000. On your letterhead, include information concerning the intended use of the books and the number of books you want to purchase. For individual orders, turn to the back of this book for more information.

Paint Shop Pro™ 7
fast&easy®

Diane Koers

A Division of Prima Publishing

A Division of Prima Publishing

Prima Publishing and colophon and Fast & Easy are registered trademarks of Prima Communications, Inc. PRIMA TECH is a registered trademark of Prima Communications, Inc., Roseville, California 95661.

Publisher: Stacy L. Hiquet

Marketing Manager: Judi Taylor Wade

Associate Marketing Manager: Heather Buzzingham

Managing Editor: Sandy Doell

Acquisitions Editor: Jawahara K. Saidullah

Technical Reviewer: Sonja Shea

Cover Design: Prima Design Team

Editorial and Book Production: Argosy / West Newton, MA

Paint Shop Pro 7 is a trademark of Jasc Software.

Important: Prima Publishing cannot provide software support. Please contact the appropriate software manufacturer's technical support line or Web site for assistance. This book is an independent publication of Prima Publishing and is not affiliated with or sponsored by Jasc Software or any other manufacturer mentioned herein.

Prima Publishing and the author have attempted throughout this book to distinguish proprietary trademarks from descriptive terms by following the capitalization style used by the manufacturer.

Information contained in this book has been obtained by Prima Publishing from sources believed to be reliable. However, because of the possibility of human or mechanical error by our sources, Prima Publishing, or others, the Publisher does not guarantee the accuracy, adequacy, or completeness of any information and is not responsible for any errors or omissions or the results obtained from use of such information. Readers should be particularly aware of the fact that the Internet is an ever-changing entity. Some facts may have changed since this book went to press.

ISBN: 0-7615-3241-2

Library of Congress Catalog Card Number: 00-109081

Printed in the United States of America

00 01 02 03 04 DD 10 9 8 7 6 5 4 3 2 1

To my family:
Vern, Tim, Chris, Trina, Drew, Alex, Mom, and Ira

Contents at a Glance

Contents

PART IV
WORKING WITH TEXT 201

PART VI
SPECIAL PHOTO PROJECTS 327

PART VII
APPENDIXES. 361

Acknowledgments

I am deeply appreciative to the many people who assisted with this book. Thank you for all the time you gave and for your assistance.

To Jawahara Saidullah for the opportunity to write this book and her confidence in me. Jawahara, it has been a bona fide pleasure working with you. Thank you to Caroline Roop for her assistance (and patience) in the book development; to Suzanne Goraj for help making this book grammatically correct; to Sonja Shea for checking all the technical angles; to Bob LaRoche for his proofreading skills, and to all those at Prima who are working behind the scenes whose names I don't know. I really appreciate your fine work.

A special recognition goes to all those on the various Paint Shop Pro newsgroups, especially Sonja Shea (aka Bonesy), Kathy Guthe (aka Bluegenie2), Bill, Ron, Joe, and all the "regulars." Thanks for letting me bug you with my questions and for all the special assistance you provided. I learned and laughed with all of you! To Nancy, Kris, Joe, and everyone at Jasc software; you are the nicest group of people I've ever worked with.

To my husband, Vern. Thank you again, for all your support and never-ending faith in me. Your help at deadline time is immeasurable.

Finally, and most importantly, I give praise and thanks to God above for all the blessings He's bestowed on me. Without Him, I can do nothing.

About the Author

Diane **Koers** owns and operates All Business Service, (www.allbusinessservice.com), a software training and consulting business formed in 1988 that services the central Indiana area. Her area of expertise has long been in the word-processing, spreadsheet, and graphics areas of computing as well as providing training and support for Peachtree Accounting Software including co-authoring *Peachtree for Dummies*. Diane's other authoring experience includes 10 other Prima Publishing *Fast & Easy* books (including *Windows ME Fast & Easy*, *WordPerfect 9 Fast & Easy*, *Office 2000 Fast & Easy*) and co-authored Prima's *Essential Windows 98*. She has also developed and written software training manuals for her clients.

Active in her church and civic activities, Diane enjoys spending her free time traveling and playing with her grandsons and her three Yorkshire Terriers.

Introduction

Welcome to the world of Paint Shop Pro.

First, let me say I'm not a graphic or digital artist. I'm not any type of an artist. I'm a teacher and I've written this book from the perspective that most of us are not graphic artists. We're simply computer users who want to use our computer to create amazing graphic images. Paint Shop Pro can help you create such graphics.

But, creating terrific graphics is not just a matter of drawing something on your screen. It's many steps put together. Most images are created out of several different objects, each with its own special effect, then assembled together to create the final image. Sound complicated? I first thought so, but it's really not; in fact, the Paint Shop Pro application makes it very simple. This book, *Paint Shop Pro 7 Fast & Easy* takes you through each process one step at a time.

The *Fast & Easy* series uses a step-by-step approach and is written in an easy-to-understand common lingo. Each step is accompanied by a visual representation of your screen so that you can follow along to make sure you are on the right track.

This book is divided into six parts and three appendixes. In Part I, I show you how to control the tools used to create the basic objects. While it's not the most exciting part of the book, it's certainly the most practical. Look out then! Things start to be lots of fun! In Parts II, III and IV, you learn how to assemble the objects and add special effects. Part V illustrates the very basics of creating graphic elements for publication to the Web, and Part VI includes steps for a couple of particular photographic projects such as removing red eye from photos. Finally, the appendixes show you how to install Paint Shop Pro, list examples of some wonderful special effects, and include lists of Web sites you can go to for cool Paint Shop Pro accessories.

Through this book you learn *how* to create images, however *what* you create is totally up to you! Your imagination is the only limit to what you can do with them after that. This book cannot begin to teach you everything you can do with Paint Shop Pro 7, nor will it give you all the different ways to accomplish a task. What I *have* tried to do is give you the fastest and easiest way to get started with this fun and exciting graphics program.

WHO SHOULD READ THIS BOOK?

This book can be used as a learning tool or as a step-by-step task reference. The easy-to-follow, highly visual nature of this book makes it the perfect learning tool for a beginning computer user as well as those seasoned computer users who are new to graphics applications. No prerequisites are required from you, the reader, except that you know how to turn your computer on and how to use your mouse.

By using this *Paint Shop Pro 7 Fast & Easy* book, any level of user can quickly look up steps for a task without having to plow through pages of descriptions.

ADDED ADVICE TO MAKE YOU A PRO

You'll notice that this book focuses on the steps necessary for a task and keeps explanations to a minimum. Included in the book are elements that provide some additional information to help you master the program, without encumbering your progress through the steps:

- **Tips** offer shortcuts when performing an action, and they describe a feature that can make your work in Paint Shop Pro quicker and easier.
- **Notes** give you a bit of background or additional information about a feature; they also give advice about how to use the feature in your day-to-day activities.

This book truly is the *fastest and easiest* way to learn Paint Shop Pro 7. Enjoy!

—Diane Koers

PART I

Getting Started with the Basics

1

Exploring Paint Shop Pro Basics

Welcome to Paint Shop Pro Version 7. If this is your first opportunity to use Paint Shop Pro, you may be a little intimidated by the vast array of tools on the opening screen. Just remember that although Paint Shop Pro is a powerful program, it's also easy to use, which is why many people are choosing it. Don't worry! You'll be creating your first image after just a couple of mouse clicks. In this chapter, you'll learn how to:

- Start the Paint Shop Pro application
- Identify toolbars and tool palettes
- Manage files
- Change views

Starting Paint Shop Pro

If you have not yet installed Paint Shop Pro, refer to Appendix A for instructions. Once you install the product, you're ready to begin.

1. **Click** on **Start**. The Start menu appears.

2. **Click** on **Programs**. The Programs submenu appears.

3. **Click** on **Jasc Software**. The Jasc Software submenu appears.

4. **Click** on **Paint Shop Pro 7**. The program begins.

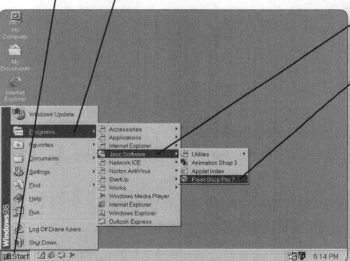

Setting File Associations

The File Format Associations dialog box appears the first time you use Paint Shop Pro. The File Format Associations determine which files your computer opens automatically using the Paint Shop Pro application.

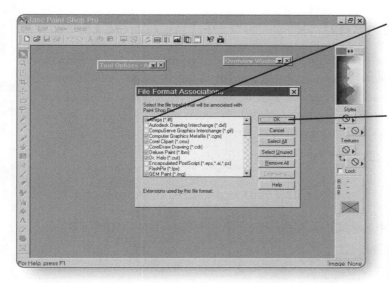

1. **Click** on any **file type** to add or remove the check mark. Items with a check mark will be associated with Paint Shop Pro.

2. **Click** on **OK**. The File Format Associations dialog box closes.

TIP

To later review or change file associations, click on File, select Preferences, and then select File Format Associations.

Viewing Tips

When you start Paint Shop Pro, a Tip of the Day dialog box appears. Take a moment to read the tip. The tips contain some very useful information. Each time you launch the program a new tip appears.

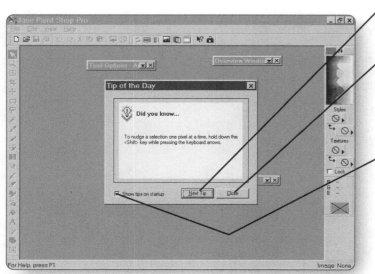

1. **Click** on **Next Tip**. Paint Shop Pro displays other tips.

2. **Click** on **Close**. The Tip of the Day dialog box closes.

TIP

If you prefer not to display the dialog box when you launch Paint Shop Pro, remove the check from Show tips on startup.

The tips are available anytime by clicking the Help menu and choosing Tip of the Day.

Examining Screen Objects

The Paint Shop Pro window is full of tools, toolbars, and palettes. Each has a specific purpose to assist you in creating or editing images. As you read through this book, you'll use and learn more about each of these objects.

Identifying Screen Objects

The minitable below describes each of the screen objects.

Object Name	Function
Standard Toolbar	Displays tools to manage files and commonly used menu functions.
Tool Palette	Displays image-editing tools.
Status Bar	Displays image details.
Color Palette	Contains a selection of available colors and styles and displays the current foreground and background colors and styles.

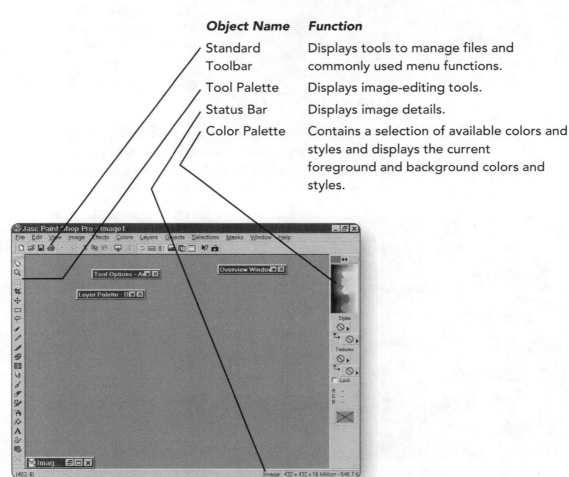

Object Name	**Function**
Tool Options Palette	Displays options for the currently selected tool.
Layer Palette	Lists each layer in the current image.
Overview Window	Displays entire image when zooming in to a small area.

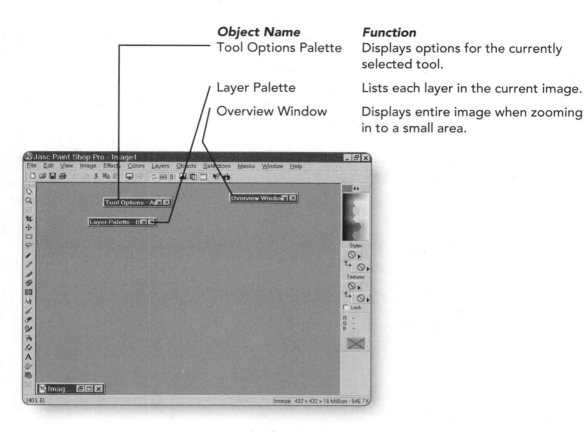

(Not displayed)

Object Name	**Function**
Browser Toolbar	Displays useful tools when browsing images.
Histogram Window	A graph showing the distribution of color and light in an image.
Web Toolbar	Displays commonly used tools when working with Web graphics.
Photo Toolbar	Displays commonly used tools when working with photographs.
Effects Toolbar	Displays commonly used effects.

Three objects—the Overview Window, the Tool Options Palette, and the Layer Palette—are floating objects, which means they are in the middle of your screen. You'll learn how to manage floating objects in the next several sections of this chapter.

Working with Automatic Rollup

The four floating-screen objects have a feature called automatic rollup. The Tool Options Palette, the Overview Window, the Histogram Window, and the Layer Palette all open automatically as you hover your mouse in their area, but then close up again when you move your mouse out of their vicinity.

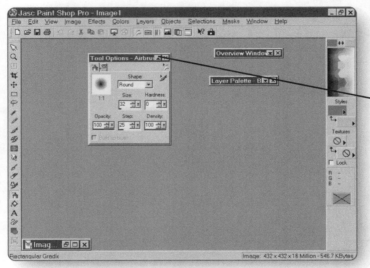

You can disable the automatic rollup on any of these four windows and lock the window so it remains open at all times.

1. **Click** on the **down arrow** on the title bar of the window you want to lock. The down arrow turns into an up arrow and the rollup window remains open.

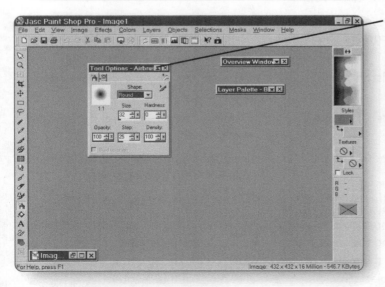

2. **Click** on the **up arrow** on the title bar of the window you want to unlock. The up arrow turns into a down arrow and the automatic rollup feature is reactivated.

Moving a Floating Screen Object

If a floating screen object is in the way of your work, you can easily move it to a new location.

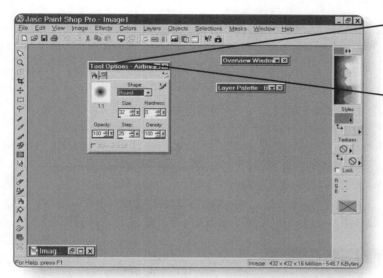

1. Position the **mouse** over the title bar of the object you want to move.

2. Drag the **window** to a desired location. You see an outline of the window.

3. Release the **mouse button**. The window moves to the new position.

Closing a Screen Object

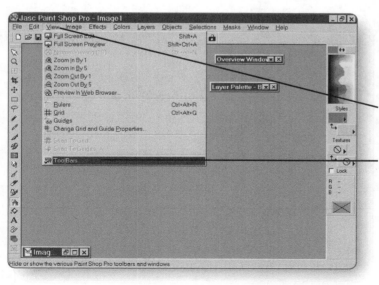

If you don't use a particular screen object (although I think you'll find them all very useful), you can close it.

1. Click on **View**. The View menu appears.

2. Click on **ToolBars**. The Toolbars dialog box opens. All the screen objects are considered toolbars.

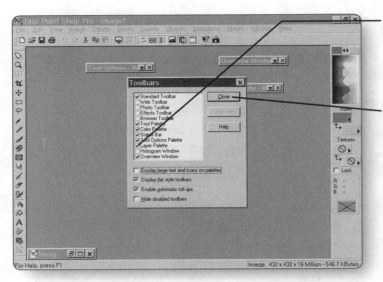

3. Remove the **check mark** next to any screen object you want to hide. The object disappears from your screen.

4. Click on **Close**. The Toolbars dialog box closes.

TIP

To quickly close one of the floating objects, click on the Close button.

Redisplaying Screen Objects

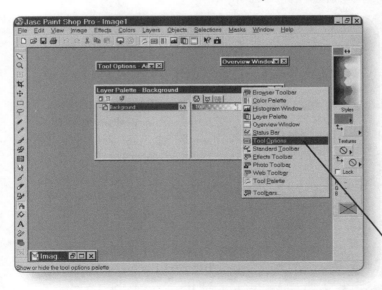

Whether you closed a screen object accidentally or intentionally, it's very easy to redisplay the object. You can redisplay the Toolbar dialog box by clicking on View, Toolbars, or using the Toolbar shortcut menu.

1. Press the **right mouse button** (*right-click*) on **any screen object**. A list of objects appears.

2. Click on the **screen object** you wish to redisplay. The screen object reappears onscreen.

TIP

Press the Tab key to hide or redisplay all floating screen objects or press Shift+Ctrl+T to view all toolbars in the center of the screen.

Working with Files

If you've worked with other Windows applications, you're probably familiar with file names and other characteristics.

Creating a New File

Unlike some programs you may use, Paint Shop Pro doesn't automatically open with a blank document for you. If you want to create a document from scratch, Paint Shop Pro requires several pieces of information before you begin.

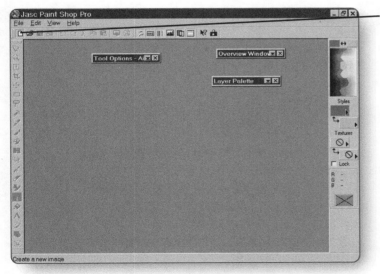

1. **Click** on the **New button**. The New Image dialog box opens.

TIP

You can also create a new file by pressing Ctrl+N or by choosing New from the File menu.

Paint Shop Pro requires you to predetermine the size of the new image.

By default, the working screen is measured in pixels; however, you can specify the measurement in inches or centimeters as well.

NOTE

What's a pixel, you ask? *Pixel* stands for *picture element*, which means absolutely nothing to many of us. In reality, a pixel is the individual square used to make up an image—in particular, a raster image. You'll learn about raster images in later chapters. In terms of measurement, a pixel is the smallest element that can be assigned a color.

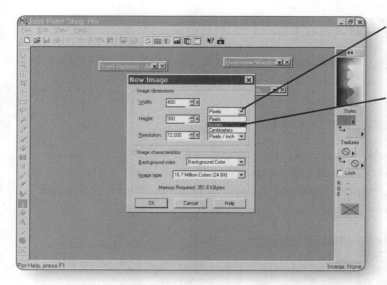

2. Click on the **down arrow** ↓ in the Image Dimensions section. A selection list appears.

3. Click on your preferred **unit of measurement**. The selection displays in the list box.

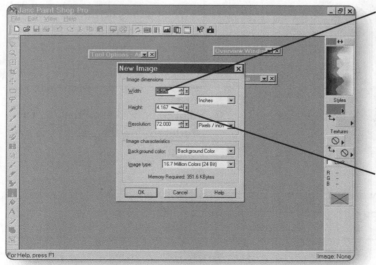

4. Double-click the **current width** displayed in the list box. The width is highlighted.

5. Type the desired **measurement**. Typing a new measurement replaces the existing measurement.

6. Double-click on the current height. The height is highlighted.

7. Type the desired **measurement**. Typing a new measurement replaces the existing measurement.

Now let's talk about resolution. Resolution measures the number of pixels in a specific unit of measurement. The higher the resolution, the more detail gets displayed.

A general rule of thumb is this: If you're designing a graphic for onscreen use or for posting to the Web, set your resolution to 72dpi. That's the resolution of most Web browsers and e-mail applications. If you're going to print the image, go with a higher resolution—for example, 600 or 1200, depending on your printer.

TIP

Large image dimensions combined with high resolutions can result in very large file sizes.

---

8. Optionally, **highlight** the current **resolution** and **type** a new **measurement**. The new resolution displays.

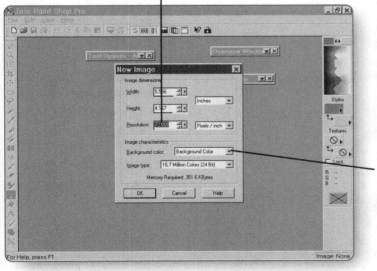

The lower section in the New Image dialog box deals with the background color and the number of available colors. Typically the background color, which is like the color of a canvas, is black or white. Other selections are also available.

9. **Click** on the **down arrow** ↓ next to the background color box. A list of choices appears.

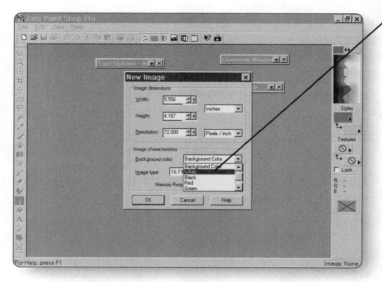

10. Click on your choice of a **background color**. The selection appears in the list box.

Unless you know your image is to be in black and white or grayscale, I recommend you start an image with the maximum number of colors, which is 16.7 million colors. (Whew! That's a LOT of colors!) Many of the Paint Shop Pro special effects aren't available if you set your maximum colors to a lower number.

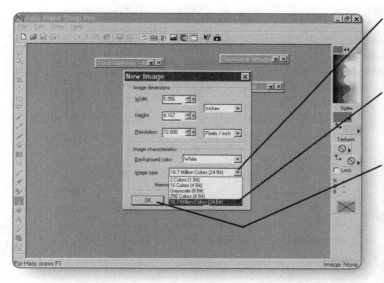

11. Click on the **down arrow** ↓ next to Image type. A list of options appears.

12. Select an **option**. The selection appears in the Image type list box.

13. Click on **OK**. You're ready to begin creating an image.

Saving a File

Saving a file in Paint Shop Pro is identical to saving a file in most Windows applications. Don't make the mistake many people do by waiting until you've finished working on a project to save it. Save your file early in its creation. Saving your work early and often can save you lots of grief should your computer lock up or a power failure occur.

Saving a File the First Time

When you first create a file, it has no name. If you want to use that file later, it must have a name so Paint Shop Pro can find it. Paint Shop Pro asks for a name the first time you save the file, and after that, the name you give it appears in the title bar at the very top of the screen.

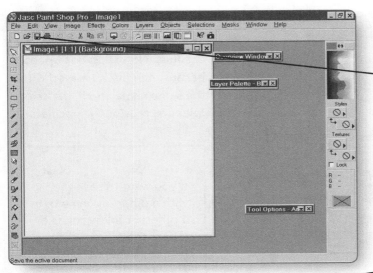

1. Click on the **Save button**. The Save As dialog box appears.

TIP

You can also save a new file by pressing Ctrl+S or by choosing Save from the File menu.

---

2. Type a **name** for your file in the File name: text box. The file name displays.

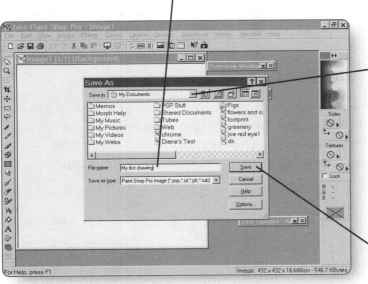

NOTE

The Save in: drop-down list box lists folder options where you can save the file. I recommend you save the files to your "My Documents" folder. Click on the down arrow to browse for a different folder.

---

3. Click on **Save**. Paint Shop Pro saves your file and the name you specified appears in the title bar.

Resaving a File

As you continue to work on your file, you should resave it every ten minutes or so to help ensure that you do not lose any changes.

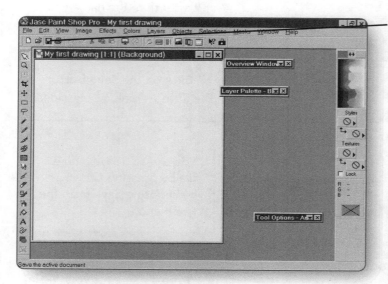

1. Click on the **Save button**. The file will be resaved with any changes. No dialog box opens, because the file is resaved with the same name and in the same folder as previously specified.

> **TIP**
>
> If you want to save the file with a different name or in a different folder, or as a different file type, click on File, then choose Save As. The Save As dialog box will prompt you for the new name or folder. The original file will remain as well as the new one.

Closing a File

When you are finished working on an image, you should close it. Closing is the equivalent of putting it away for later use. When you close a file, you are only putting the file away—not closing the program. Paint Shop Pro is still active and ready to work for you.

1a. **Click** on **File**. The File menu appears.

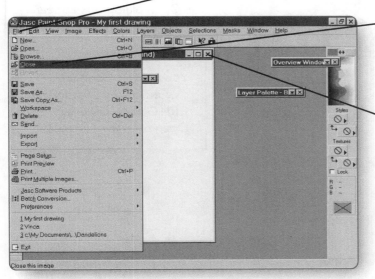

2a. **Click** on **Close**. The file is put away.

OR

1b. **Click** on the **Close button** ☒. The file is closed. By choosing this method, you combine steps 1 and 2.

NOTE

If you close a file with changes that have not been saved, Paint Shop Pro prompts you with a message box. Choose Yes to save the changes or No to close the file without saving the changes.

Opening an Existing File

To work on a previously created file, whether it be a file you created from scratch, a photograph, or a piece of clip art from another program, use the Open dialog box to locate your file.

Opening an image is putting a copy of that image into the computer's memory and onto your screen so that you can work on it. If you make any changes, be sure to save the file again.

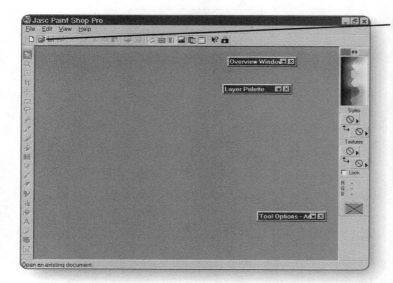

1. **Click** on the **Open button**. The Open dialog box appears.

TIP

You can also open an existing file by pressing Ctrl+O or by choosing Open from the File menu.

2. **Click** on the **image** you want to open. The file name is highlighted.

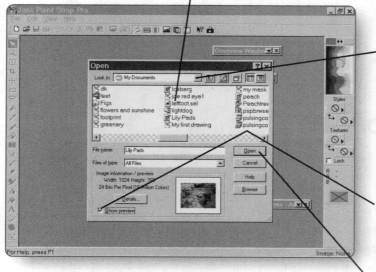

NOTE

If your file is located in a different folder than the one displayed in the Look in: list box, click on the drop-down arrow to navigate to the proper folder.

3. **Click** on the **Show Preview** check box. A thumbnail (small illustration) of the image appears.

4. **Click** on **Open**. The image is placed on your screen, ready to edit.

Browsing Images

A very useful feature provided with Paint Shop Pro is the Browse feature. Browsing lets you view thumbnails of your images. Browsing the thumbnails allows you to look at many images at the same time to quickly select the image you're looking for.

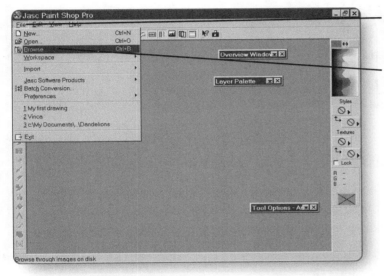

1. **Click** on **File**. The File menu appears.

2. **Click** on **Browse**. The Browse window opens.

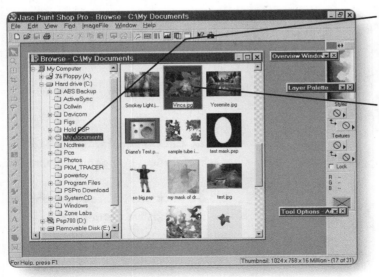

3. **Click** on the **folder** you wish to browse. Thumbnails of graphic files located in the selected folder appear.

4. **Double-click** on the **image** you want to open. The image appears onscreen.

5. The Browse window stays open in the background. **Click** on the **Close button** to close it.

Setting Autosave

Paint Shop Pro has a feature called Autosave, which periodically saves a temporary version of your document for you. After a crash, when you boot up and reopen Paint Shop Pro, the program opens a recovered version of the files you were working on at the time of the crash. You can then save them. I highly recommend you activate this feature.

1. Click on **File**. The File menu appears.

2. Click on **Preferences**. The Preferences submenu appears.

3. Click on **Autosave Settings**. The Autosave Settings dialog box opens.

4. **Click** on **Enable Autosave**. The option appears with a check mark.

Paint Shop Pro allows you to specify the time intervals for the Autosave to save your work.

5. Optionally, **click** on the **up/down arrows** to increase or decrease the amount of time between each Autosave.

6. **Click** on **OK**. The Autosave Settings dialog box closes.

Changing Your Perspective

As you work on an image, Paint Shop Pro includes several tools to change screen appearance.

Viewing the Ruler

Paint Shop Pro includes horizontal and vertical rulers. Using the rulers helps line up image elements.

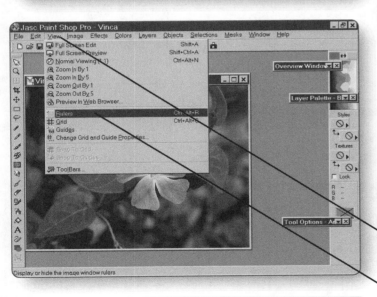

1. **Click** on **View**. The View menu appears.

2. **Click** on **Rulers**. The rulers display with measurements in pixels.

Repeat the above steps to hide the rulers.

TIP

Change the rulers unit of measurement by clicking on File, Preferences, General Program Preferences and clicking on the Rulers and Units tab.

Displaying the Grid

Displaying the grid places nonprinting, equally spaced vertical and horizontal lines on the screen. Use the gridlines to help you align image elements.

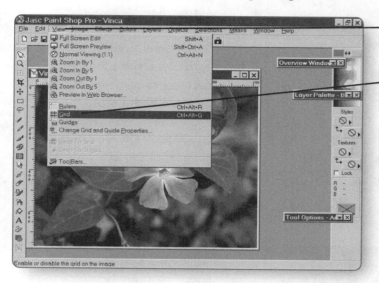

1. **Click** on **View**. The View menu appears.

2. **Click** on **Grid**. The grid appears onscreen.

Repeat the above steps to hide the grid.

TIP

Change the spacing between the lines of the grid by selecting Change Grid and Guide Properties from the View menu.

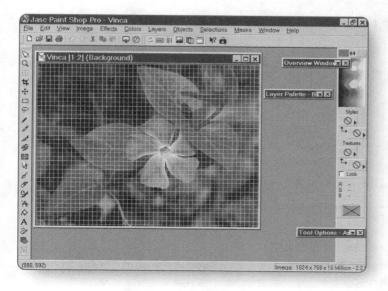

Zooming In and Out

Use the zoom feature to zoom in and magnify portions of your image for close-up detail work. You can also zoom out to see your entire image.

The zoom feature is available under the View menu, but you'll find it easiest to use the Zoom tool on the Tool Palette.

You'll learn about other Tool Palette tools in Chapter 2.

1. **Click** on the **Zoom tool**. As you move your mouse over your image, the mouse pointer turns into a magnifying glass.

2. **Click** on the **image**. The image zooms in. Each click of the mouse zooms the image closer.

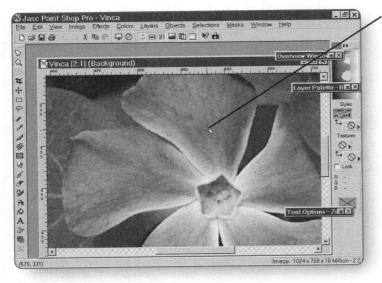

3. **Click** the **right mouse button**. The image zooms out. Each click of the mouse zooms the image out.

Seeing the Overview Window

New to Paint Shop Pro Version 7 is the Overview Window. When you have zoomed in on a small area for a detailed operation, you may find it useful to see the entire image while you work. That's the purpose of the Overview Window.

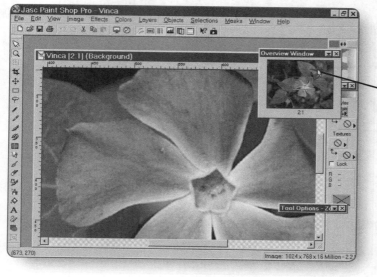

1. Zoom in on an image.

2. Position the **mouse pointer** over the Overview Window. The Overview Window opens.

> ## NOTE
> Paint Shop Pro may operate more slowly when the Overview is open.

When an image is too large to fit in its window, its visible area is enclosed by a rectangle.

> ## TIP
> To move from one area of the image to another, move the cursor over the rectangle. When the cursor changes to the Hand icon, click the mouse button, drag to the new area you want to view, and release the button.

Using Keyboard Shortcuts for Screen Objects

In this chapter, you've seen how to hide, display, and move the various toolbars, palettes, and windows on the Paint Shop Pro window. Here are a few shortcuts you might like to know about. Press the keyboard letter listed below to display or hide a screen object:

Screen Object	Keyboard Shortcut
Tool Options Palette	O
Color Palette	C
Layer Palette	L
Tool Palette	P
Overview Window	W
Toolbar	T

2

Discovering Paint Shop Pro Tools

In Chapter 1 you discovered many of the different screen objects provided by Paint Shop Pro. The object you'll probably use the most is the Tool Palette. The Tool Palette contains tools you'll need to create and edit images, whether you create the image from scratch or edit a photograph or other artwork. In this chapter, you'll learn how to:

- Identify commonly used tools
- Draw with the Paintbrush and Airbrush
- Set Paintbrush options
- Draw lines and preset shapes
- Use Undo
- Discover keyboard shortcuts

Identifying the Tool Palette Tools

The minitable below lists some of the tools on the Tool Palette and their functions. In the interest of space, I've listed only the tools used in this *Paint Shop Pro 7 Fast & Easy* book.

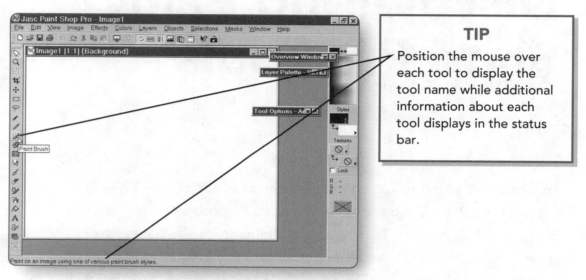

TIP

Position the mouse over each tool to display the tool name while additional information about each tool displays in the status bar.

Tool	Function
Zoom tool	Increases or decreases the magnification of the displayed image.
Crop tool	Eliminates areas of an image.
Mover tool	Moves a selection to a different area of an image.
Selection tool	Selects a shaped area for modification.
Freehand tool	Makes selections with irregularly shaped borders.
Magic Wand tool	Makes selections based on content.
Dropper tool	Selects a foreground and background color.

Tool	Function
Paintbrush tool	Paints an image.
Eraser tool	Replaces colors in an image with the background color or with a transparency.
Picture Tube tool	Similar to the Paintbrush, but instead of painting lines, paints images and shapes.
Flood Fill tool	Fills an area with a color, pattern, or gradient.
Text tool	Creates text areas and objects.
Drawing tool	Draws freehand, lines, and curves.
Preset Shapes tool	Draws rectangles, squares, ellipses, circles, and fun shapes such as clocks, keys, butterflies, and more.
Vector Object Selection tool	Lets you move, resize, skew, stretch, and rotate vector objects.

Changing Tool Options

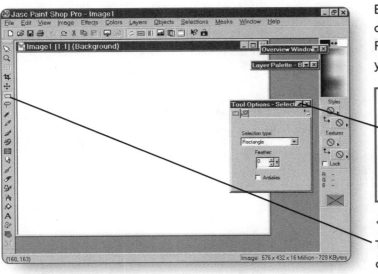

Each tool has its own set of options. Use the Tool Options Palette to set the options before you actually use the tool.

TIP

To quickly view tool options, lock the Tool Options Palette open by clicking on its lock arrow.

1. Click on the **Selection tool**. The Tool Options Palette displays selection options.

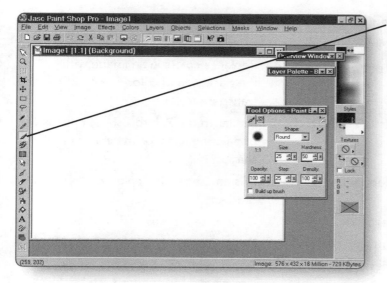

2. Click on the **Paintbrush tool**. The Tool Options Palette shows paintbrush options.

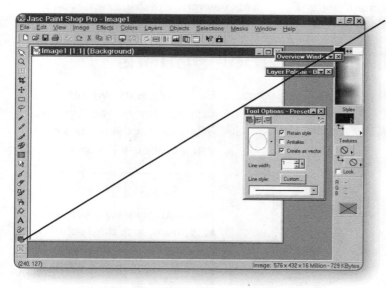

3. Click on the **Preset Shapes tool**. The Tool Options Palette displays preset shape options.

Drawing with the Tools

For the samples in this chapter, start with a new image six inches by six inches, using a white background.

TIP

Refer to "Creating a New File" in Chapter 1 for instructions on creating a new image.

Painting with a Paintbrush

You can draw and paint freehand style using the Paintbrush.

Drawing with the Paintbrush

Begin by using the Paint Brush tool to draw a line across your image.

1. Click on the **Paintbrush tool**. The mouse pointer turns into a paintbrush tip.

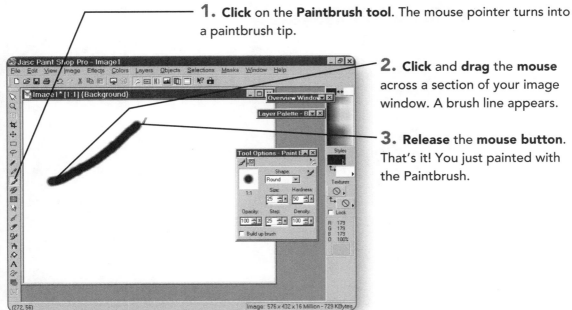

2. Click and **drag** the **mouse** across a section of your image window. A brush line appears.

3. Release the **mouse button**. That's it! You just painted with the Paintbrush.

Choosing a Brush Shape

Use the Tool Options Palette to select the shape and angle of
your brush. Brush shape controls the shape of the brush tip.

1. Click on the **down arrow** ↓ next to the Shape list box. A list
of selections appears. The choices are round, square, vertical,
horizontal, right slash, and left slash.

2. Click on a **selection**. A
sample appears in the preview
box.

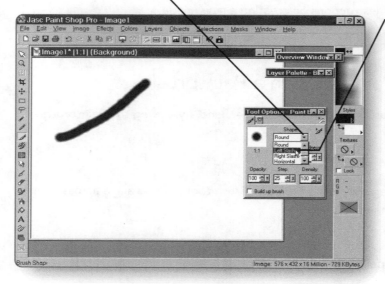

3. Draw another **line**. See how changing the brush shape changes the effect of the paintbrush stroke.

Try changing other Paintbrush options and redrawing a line to see what happens.

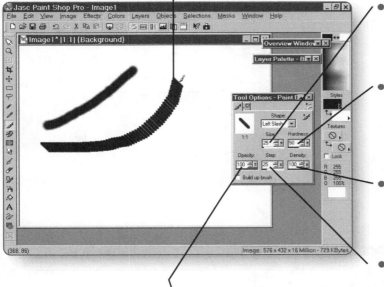

- **Size**. A higher value results in a larger, wider brush stroke while a lower value produces a thinner line.

- **Hardness**. A higher value or "harder" brush stroke will have a crisper edge while a lower value produces a softer edge.

- **Density**. A higher value paints a more solid line, while a lower value produces a speckled stroke effect.

- **Step**. A higher value decreases the frequency of the drops of paint as the brush tip touches the image, while a lower value produces a smoother and more dense effect.

- **Opacity**. A higher value applies a more solid color effect while a lower value results in softer, more transparent color.

Setting the Brush Type

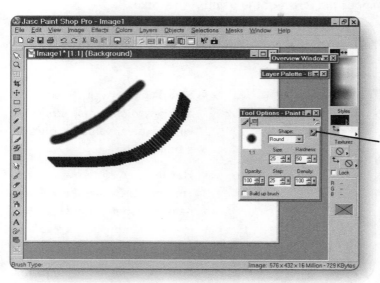

A really cool feature of Paint Shop Pro is the ability to select a brush type. Use the Paintbrush tool to simulate other drawing utensils, such as crayon, chalk, or charcoal.

1. **Click** on the **Brush Types button**. A list of options appears.

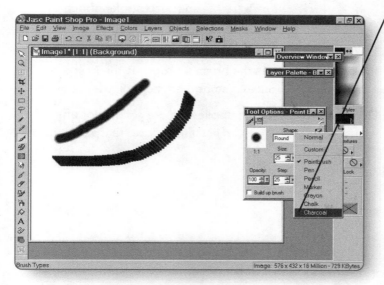

2. **Select** a **brush type**. A sample appears in the preview window.

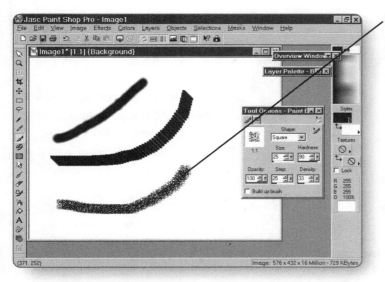

3. Draw another **line**. See how changing the brush type changes the effect of the paintbrush stroke.

Operating the Airbrush Tool

Although using the Airbrush tool is very similar to using the Paint Brush tool, you'll also find that using the Airbrush tool is similar to painting with a spray can. When spray painting, if you stay in one place for a moment, the paint builds up. The same reaction occurs when using the Airbrush tool. You'll notice this behavior even more if you set the Opacity fairly low in the Tool Options Palette.

But there's one difference from spray painting—the Airbrush tool doesn't drip!

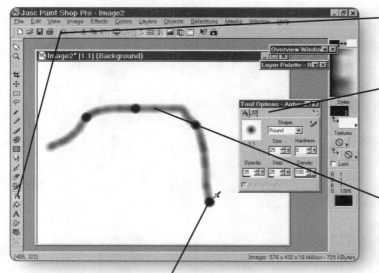

1. **Click** on the **Airbrush tool**. The mouse pointer turns into an airbrush tip.

2. **Set** any desired **options** from the Tool Options Palette. You'll find the same options for the Airbrush that you have with the Paintbrush.

3. **Click** and **drag** the **mouse** across a section of your image window, **pausing every few seconds**. A line appears.

4. **Release** the **mouse button**. That's it! You just painted with the Airbrush.

In the example you see here, I set the opacity to 35. You can see where I stopped moving the mouse by the thickening of paint.

Using the Draw Tool

While the Paintbrush tool you used earlier allowed more freedom in drawing by emulating a real drawing tool, the Draw tool is more like a drafting tool, drawing straighter, more distinctive lines.

1. Click on the **Draw tool**. The mouse pointer looks like a pencil.

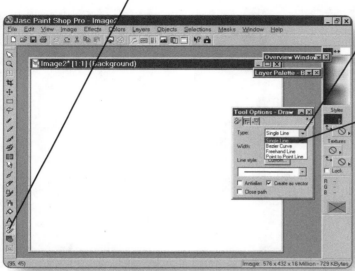

2. Click on the **Type: drop down list** on the Tool Options Palette. A list of line types appears.

3. Click on a **line type**. The option appears in the Type: list box.

Line type choices include single lines, Bezier curves, freehand, and point-to-point.

NOTE

A Bezier curve (pronounced **bez'-zee-ay**) is a type of curved line that is calculated mathematically to connect separate points into curves.

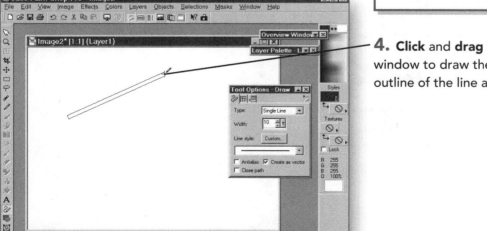

4. Click and **drag** in the image window to draw the line. An outline of the line appears.

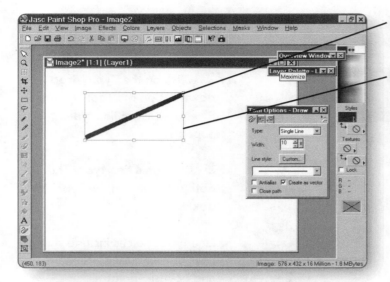

5. **Release** the **mouse button**. The line appears in the image.

The box surrounding the line indicates the line is selected. You'll learn about selections in the next chapter.

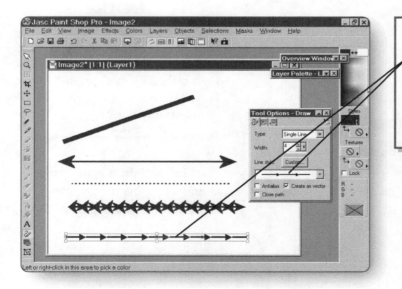

TIP

Try drawing lines with some of the different line styles such as dotted, dashed, arrowheads, and so forth.

Drawing a Preset Shape

Paint Shop Pro includes many preset shapes from the common shapes such as rectangles, triangles, stars, and ellipses to fun shapes such as flowers, happy faces, telephones, and musical notes.

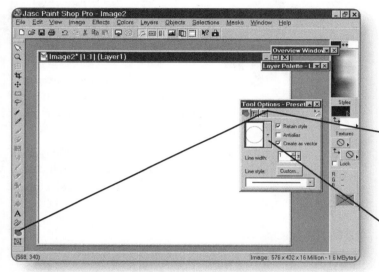

Drawing a Rectangle

Draw a box using the Rectangle tool. You'll learn in Chapter 4 how to fill the interior of the box.

1. **Click** on the **Preset Shape tool**. The mouse pointer turns into a black cross with a square and circle on it.

2. **Click** on the **down arrow** ↓ next to the shape box on the Tool Options Palette. A list of shapes appears.

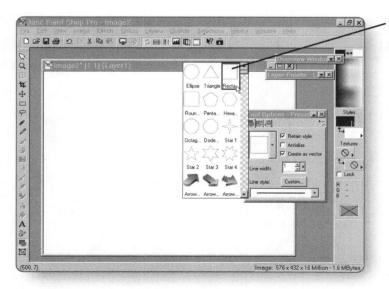

3. **Click** on **Rectangle**. The option appears in the shape box.

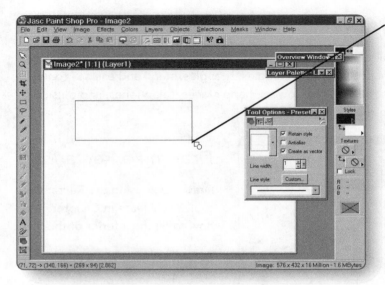

4. **Click** and **drag** in the image window. A shape of a rectangle appears.

TIP

If you click and drag from the bottom to the top, the image draws upside down.

5. **Release** the **mouse button**. The rectangle appears on the screen.

Like the line you drew earlier, the rectangle has a box with handles around it indicating it is selected.

Creating the Perfect Circle

Who says you can't draw a perfect circle? With Paint Shop Pro's ellipse tool you can. You can draw not only perfect circles, but perfect squares, perfect stars, and perfect lots of other shapes!

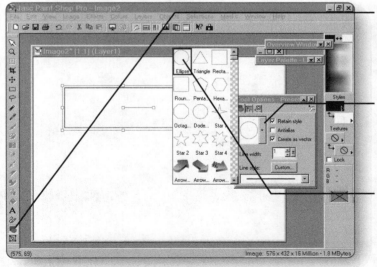

1. **Click** on the **Preset Shape tool**. The mouse pointer turns into a black cross with a square and circle on it.

2. **Click** on the **down arrow** ↓ next to the shape box on the Tool Options Palette. A list of shapes appears.

3. **Click** on **ellipse** (or any desired shape). The option appears in the shape box.

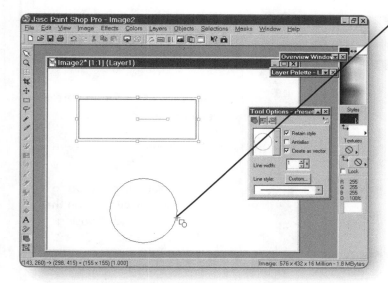

4. **Press** and **hold down** the **Shift key** on your keyboard WHILE you **click** and **drag** in the image window. The shape appears on your document.

5. **Release** the **mouse button,** then **release** the **Shift key**. The perfect shape appears on the screen.

Going Backward with Undo

Paint Shop Pro includes an Undo command that reverses the command made to the current image. It can remove painting or drawing operations, color alterations, filter effects, etc. It cannot undo any modification that has been closed or any changes to the file name or file format.

NOTE

The number of operations you can undo depends on the settings in the Undo tab in the File, Preferences, General Program Preferences. It is limited only by the disk space in your computer.

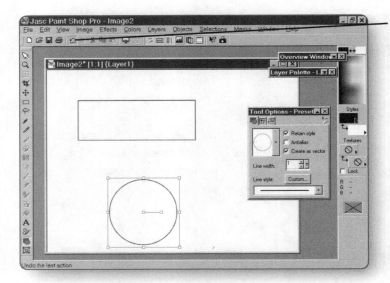

1. Click on the **Undo button**. Paint Shop Pro reverses the previous step.

Each click of the Undo button reverses another step.

TIP

Optionally, use the Undo function by clicking on the Edit menu and choosing Undo or pressing Ctrl+Z.

Saving Time with Keyboard Shortcuts

You've seen how to choose tools from the toolbar by clicking on them, but you can save yourself time by using keyboard shortcuts for many tools.

Press the keyboard letter listed below:

Tool or Brush	Keyboard Shortcut
Arrow	J
Zoom (Magnifier)	G
Deform	D
Crop	R
Selection	S
Freehand Selection	A
Magic Wand Selection	M
Dropper	Y
Paintbrush	B
Clone	N

Tool or Brush	*Keyboard Shortcut*
Color Replacer	, (comma)
Retouch	Z
Scratch Remover	K
Eraser	E
Picture Tube	. (period)
Airbrush	U
Flood Fill	F
Text	X
Drawing	I
Preset Shape	/ (slash)
Vector Object Selection	Q

3

Working with Selections

In order to make changes to a portion of an image—whether the image is one you've created, a photograph, or another type of art-work—you need to tell Paint Shop Pro *what* you want to change before you can specify *how* you want to change it. This is called *making a selection*. You can then make your change to the isolated selected area without affecting the rest of the image.

Paint Shop Pro includes several different selection tools. In this chapter, you'll learn how to:

- Use the selection tools
- Understand feathering
- Discover the Magic Wand
- Add, subtract, and remove selections

Selecting with the Shape Selection Tool

"The Selection tool" is what Paint Shop Pro calls the easiest to use of the three tools used to make selections. For the sake of distinguishing between the terms "Selection tool" and "selection tools," we'll call the Selection tool the *Shape* Selection tool. (The other two are the Freehand and Magic Wand tools—more about them later in this chapter.)

> **TIP**
>
> Begin practicing selections by creating a new blank image window. Even though the image is blank, you can still see the selections.

Choosing a Selection Shape

The Shape Selection tool allows you to select a portion of your image in any one of 15 different shapes including rectangles, triangles, circles, stars, and arrows.

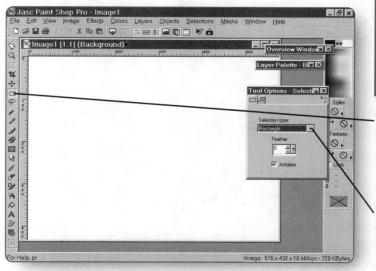

> **TIP**
>
> At any time, you can press Ctrl+A to select the entire image

1. Click on the **Shape Selection tool**. The mouse pointer turns into a white cross with a dotted box beside it.

2. Click on the **down arrow** ↓ next to Selection type: on the Tool Options Palette. A list of selection shapes appears.

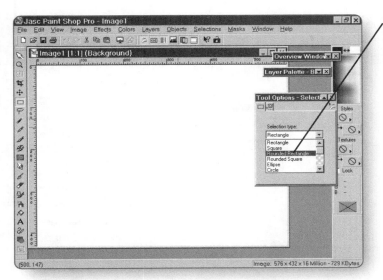

3. Click on a **shape**. The selection appears highlighted in the list box.

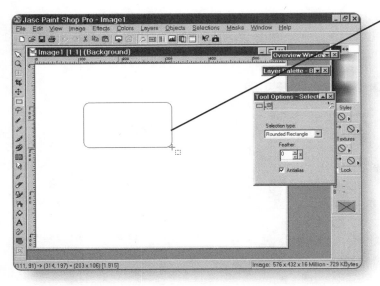

4. Click and **drag** the **mouse** across a portion of your image window. A solid line appears around the area you draw.

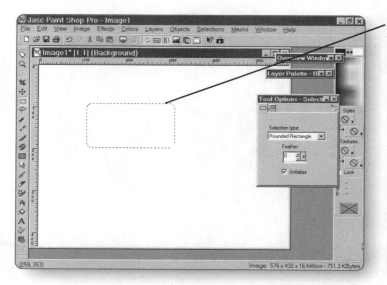

5. **Release** the **mouse button**. The drawn area is surrounded with a marquee of "marching ants"—moving dashed lines. The area within the marching ants is your selected area.

> ### TIP
> If you do not see selection lines, click on Selections and click on Hide Marquee to remove the check mark.

Adding Feathering

Feathering is a process that expands your selection and softens the edges of your selection. You won't notice its effect on a blank image, but take a look at this image.

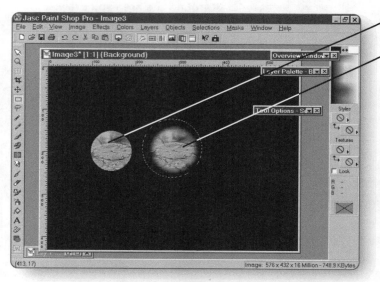

No feathering

Feathered selection

The image on the left was selected without feathering, while the image on the right was selected with feathering set to 10. Notice the softer edges as well as the extension of the selection area.

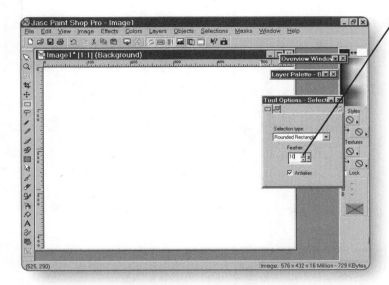

1. Click on the **up** ↑ or **down arrow** ↓ next to Feather: box on the Tool Options Palette. The higher the feathering value, the softer the edges.

You can now draw your selection as you learned in the previous section.

Antialiasing

Antialiasing—my oh my, is that a mouthful of word! Antialiasing is a graphic term used by digital artists pertaining to mathematical calculations and pixels on a screen. When an image is aliased, it has a somewhat jagged edge. Therefore, using *anti*aliasing reduces the jagged edges of an image or selection, giving a smoother appearance.

Actually, you see the antialias feature not only when you select portions of an image but also when you are using some of the tools, such as the Preset Shapes tool or Draw tool.

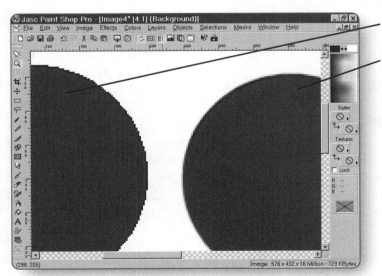

— Drawn without antialias checked

— Drawn with antialias checked

I've zoomed in on the figure you see to show the effects of using antialias. The circle on the left is drawn without the antialias feature, while the circle on the right is drawn with the antialias feature.

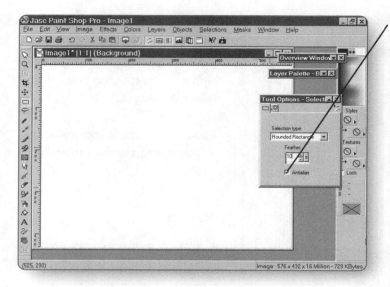

1. **Click** the **check box** next to Antialias. A check appears in the check box and Paint Shop Pro activates the antialias feature.

You can now draw your selection.

Removing All Selections

If you've selected an area in error, or when you've completed whatever you wanted to do to a selection, you need to remove the selection marks "the marching ants."

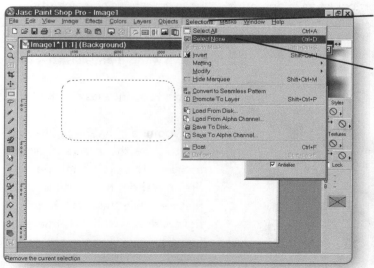

1. **Click** on **Selections**. The Selections menu appears.

2. **Click** on **Select None**. The marching ants disappear and the area is no longer selected.

TIP

Optionally, press Ctrl+D to remove all selection marks.

Using the Freehand Tool

Selecting with the Freehand tool gives you a great amount of freedom in drawing the area you want to select. Use this tool to select irregularly shaped areas of an image.

Using your mouse with the Freehand tool may feel a little clumsy at first. You'll find out later in this chapter how to add to and subtract from your selection if you didn't get it just quite right with the Freehand tool.

TIP

Selecting with the Freehand tool is much easier if you are zoomed in on the area you want to select.

---

1. **Click** on the **Freehand tool**. The mouse pointer turns into a cross with a "lasso" beside it.

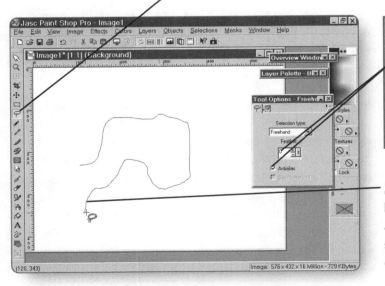

TIP

You can choose both the feathering and antialias features from the Tool Options Palette for use with the Freehand tool.

---

2. **Click** and **hold** the **mouse button** down **as you draw** around the area you want to select. A line appears as you draw.

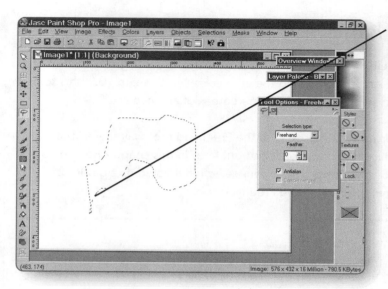

3. Release the **mouse button**. The selected area appears with marching ants.

Making Magic Wand Selections

The third selection tool, the Magic Wand, works differently from the other two selection tools. The Shape and Freehand selection tools allowed you to select an area of the image, but the Magic Wand works by selecting pixels of equal or similar colors or brightness.

The selections are made based on one of four values: With RGB Value, the Magic Wand selects pixels based on the amount of color they contain. With Hue, it selects pixels based on the position in the color wheel. (You'll learn about the color wheel in Chapter 4.) With Brightness, it selects pixels based on the amount of white they contain. With All Pixels, it selects only areas containing pixels; no transparent areas are selected. I use the RGB value selection frequently. You'll learn about RGB in Chapter 4, "*Understanding RGB.*"

As an example, I've drawn a pink circle and in the pink circle I've drawn a black musical note. I need to select the musical note in order to modify it.

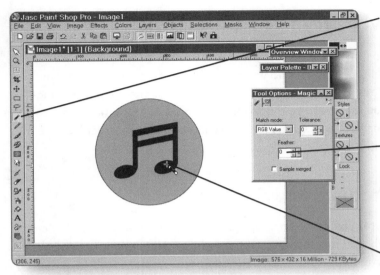

1. Click on the **Magic Wand tool**. The mouse pointer turns into a black cross with a magic wand beside it.

TIP

You can select the feathering option for the Magic Wand from the Tool Options Palette.

2. Click the **mouse** (at the cross) on the **area of the image** you want to select. In this example, click anywhere in the black musical note.

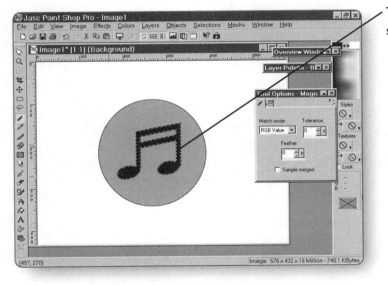

The musical note appears selected with marching ants.

Modifying Selections

For whatever reason—whether you have multiple objects to select, or your hand wasn't quite steady enough when you made the initial selection, or you've just changed your mind— you may need to modify a selection. You don't need to deselect and start over. You can add to or subtract from your initial selection.

Adding to a Selection

After you make an initial selection, you can add to it. You can mix and match between the Freehand Selection tool and the Shape Selection tool when adding to a selection.

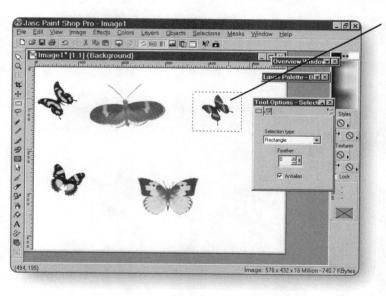

1. **Select** an **area**.

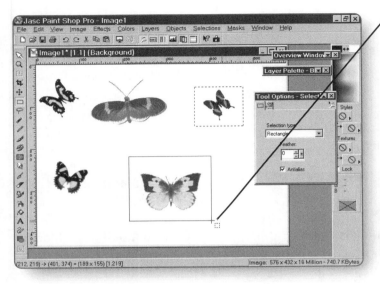

2. Hold down the **Shift key** and **select** a second **area**. The mouse pointer adds a plus sign to the mouse pointer icon.

3. Release the **Shift key**. Both the original selection and the newly selected area appear with marching ants.

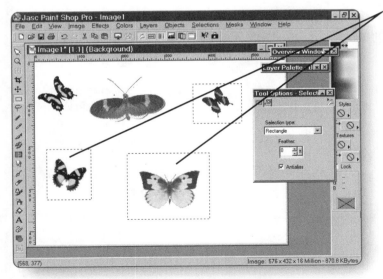

Repeat to add as many additional areas to a selection as needed.

Expanding a Selection Area

Did you make a complex selection only to find you made it too tight or forgot to feather it? Paint Shop Pro includes a feature to expand your selection.

1. **Make** a **selection**. The selection appears with marching ants.

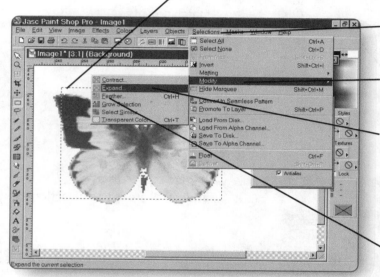

2. **Click** on **Selection**. The Selection menu appears.

3. **Click** on **Modify**. The Modify submenu appears.

4. **Click** on **Expand**. The Expand Selection dialog box opens.

TIP

Instead of clicking on Expand, you can click on Feather to expand the selection area *and* add feathering or click on Contract to shrink the selection area.

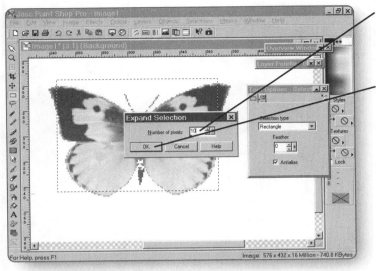

5. **Enter** the **number of pixels** you want to expand the selection.

6. **Click** on **OK**. The selection expands.

Subtracting from a Selection

Just as easily as you can add to a selection, you can subtract areas from a selection. This function works with selections you made using either the Shape Selection tool or the Freehand Selection tool.

1. **Select** an **area**. In the example shown, I've used the Freehand tool to select the shape of a butterfly, but the selection went too far on one of the wings.

2. **Hold down** the **Ctrl key** and **select** a second **area**. The mouse pointer adds a minus sign to the mouse pointer icon.

3. **Release** the **Ctrl key**. The original selection appears without the newly selected area.

Repeat to subtract as many areas from a selection as needed.

4

Understanding the Color Palette

Color and style are probably *the* most important element when creating and working with graphics. Even minor changes to color settings can dramatically alter your image. Style takes into account special combinations such as gradients, patterns, and textures including the appearance of brick, wood, leather, or sand.

Paint Shop Pro provides all these options on the Color Palette. In this chapter, you'll learn how to:

- Understand color models
- Make background and foreground color selections
- Change patterns and gradients
- Create color special effects
- Work with greyscale
- Control transparency

Defining Color Models

Before selecting colors, you should have a basic understanding of how Paint Shop Pro determines colors. Although there are several, Paint Shop Pro uses two main methods or models of defining color: RGB and HSL.

Understanding RGB

RGB stands for Red, Green, and Blue, the colors used by most monitors and video output devices. Remember when you had to adjust your TV color because the people's faces were too red or too green? You were working with RGB settings. All colors on the screen, whether on your television or computer screen, are a combination of red, blue, and green.

Appreciating HSL

The second color model, HSL, illustrates Hue, Saturation, and Lightness. HSL uses RGB values but allows you, the user, to modify the RGB values even further.

- **Hue**. The shade or tint of an RGB color.
- **Saturation**. The amount of grey in a hue. The higher saturation produces more vivid color while a lower saturation produces more grey.
- **Lightness**. The quantity of light in a color. The higher the lightness value, the whiter the image becomes while at a low value the image becomes darker or black.

Making Color Selections

Within every tool are two defined areas: foreground and background. For example, if you are just creating a box with a perimeter around it, Paint Shop Pro uses just the foreground color. If the box has a filled-in center, Paint Shop Pro uses the background color.

The two color swatches at the top of the Color Palette represent the current foreground and background colors. The first box (the one to the left) is the foreground color, while the box on the right is the background color.

NOTE

The foreground color is sometimes called the *line color* or *stroke color* and background color is sometimes called *fill color*.

Choosing from the Color Panel

The fastest way to choose a color is by using the Available Color Panel provided on the Color Palette.

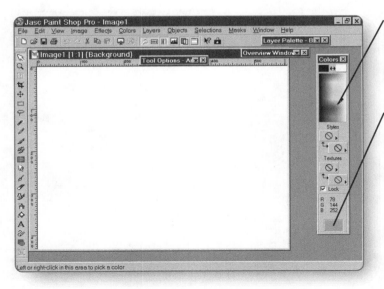

1. Position the **mouse pointer** over the color you want to select. The mouse pointer appears as an eyedropper.

The color and its RGB values appear in the preview box.

2a. Click the **left mouse button**. The color you select becomes the new foreground color.

OR

2b. Click the **right mouse button**. The color you select becomes the new background color.

Selecting from the Color Dialog Box

To finely tune the color, saturation, lightness, and hue of your selection, use the Color dialog box.

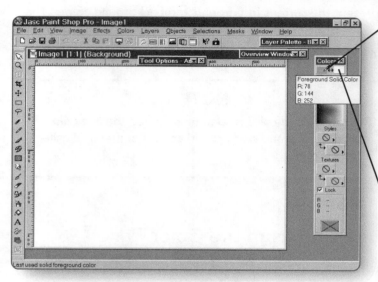

1. Position the **mouse pointer** over the foreground color box. The mouse pointer appears as an eyedropper and the current color specifications appear.

2. Click on the foreground **color box**. The Color dialog box opens.

TIP

To select a background color, click on the background color box (the second box).

The Color dialog box consists of several elements:

Basic colors palette. This palette represents some of the more common colors in a color palette.

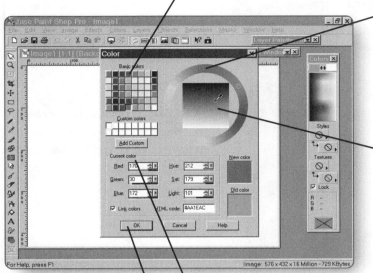

The color wheel. The color wheel represents various Hue values. Click on a color or drag the little white circle to select a color and then you'll need to select a saturation/lightness.

Saturation/Lightness box. Once you've selected a color, adjust the saturation and lightness by clicking the mouse or dragging the little black circle until the sample box represents the color you want.

RGB and HSL values. Here you can see the RGB and HSL values of your selected color, or enter and adjust the values of the color you want displayed.

3. **Click** on a **color**. The New Color box displays the newly selected color.

4. **Click** on **OK**. The Color dialog box closes and the newly selected color appears in the foreground (or background) color box.

Reversing Color Selections

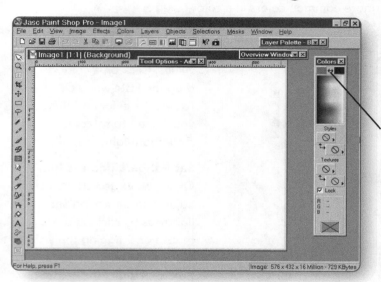

Paint Shop Pro provides an easy way to reverse your foreground and background colors without having to select them both again.

1. **Click** on the **double arrow** between the foreground and background color. The two color boxes reverse.

Adding a Border

Give your image a colored border. Paint Shop Pro uses the background color to create a straight-edged border around the perimeter of the canvas.

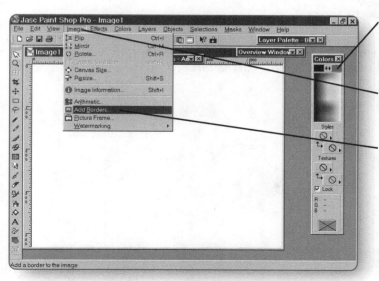

1. **Select** a **background color**. The color appears in the background color box.

2. **Click** on **Image**. The Image menu appears.

3. **Click** on **Add Borders**. The Add Borders dialog box opens.

TIP

If you want all four edges to have the same size borders, be sure there's a check mark in the Symmetric check box.

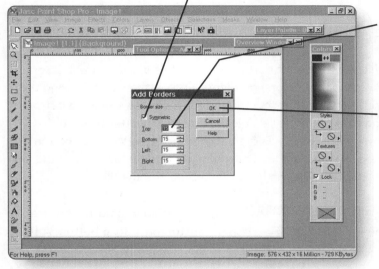

4. Select a **size** (in pixels) for each border. The higher the value, the thicker the border appears.

5. Click on **OK**. The Add Borders dialog box closes.

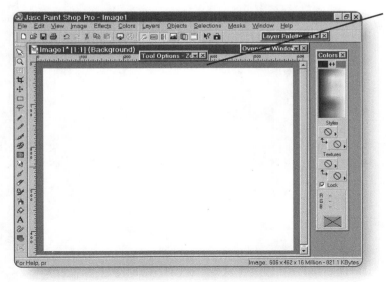

The border appears around the canvas.

Working with Styles

There's certainly more to life—excuse me, I meant images—than color. The bottom half of the Color Palette works with patterns, gradients, and textures. There are two separate sets of buttons: Styles and Textures.

Selecting Styles

Use the top set of buttons on the Style section of the Color Palette to set colors, gradients, and patterns. When using the Airbrush, Paintbrush, or Flood Fill tools, the top Style button is the foreground style (color, gradient, or pattern), while the lower Style button is the background style. When using the Text, Shapes, or Line Draw tool, the top Style button is the line or stroke, while the lower Style button is the fill.

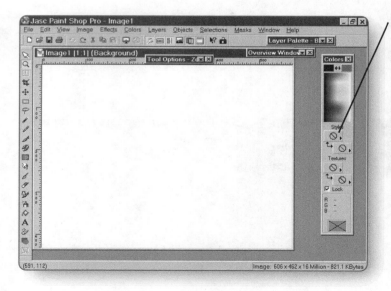

1. **Click** and **hold** the **mouse button** on a Style button. A fly-out selection appears.

> **TIP**
>
> Click on the arrow to keep the fly-out selection open.

The fly-out selection has four icons from which to select:

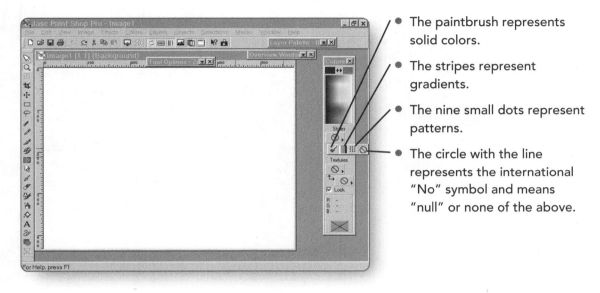

- The paintbrush represents solid colors.

- The stripes represent gradients.

- The nine small dots represent patterns.

- The circle with the line represents the international "No" symbol and means "null" or none of the above.

Choosing Colors

Selecting the solid colors option from the Styles fly-out selection displays the currently selected color.

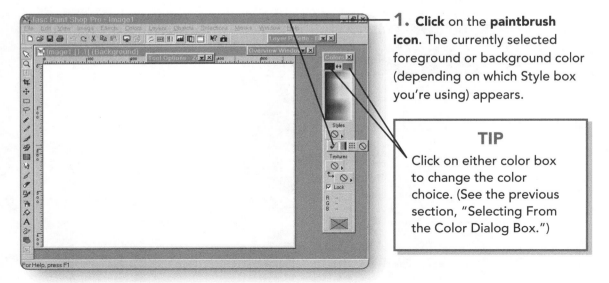

1. **Click** on the **paintbrush icon**. The currently selected foreground or background color (depending on which Style box you're using) appears.

TIP

Click on either color box to change the color choice. (See the previous section, "Selecting From the Color Dialog Box.")

Generating Gradients

Gradients are created from the gradual blending of colors together. Paint Shop Pro includes multiple predesigned gradients. Many more gradient designs are available free from the Web—and if you're really creative, you can even design your own.

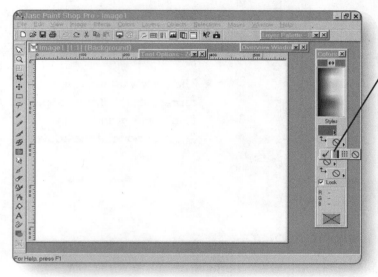

1. Click on the **gradient icon**, the one with the stripes. The Style button turns into stripes.

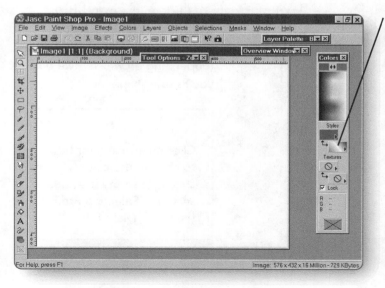

2. Click on the **Style button**. The Gradient dialog box opens.

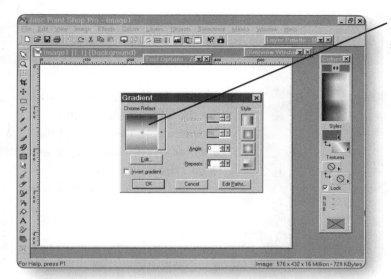

3. Click on the **preview box**. A selection of gradients appears.

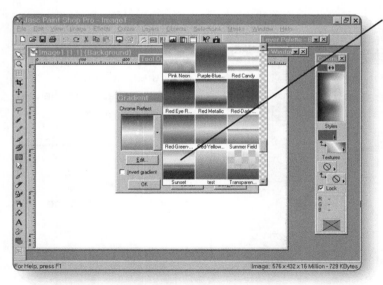

4. Click on the **gradient** of your choice. The selection box closes and a sample gradient appears.

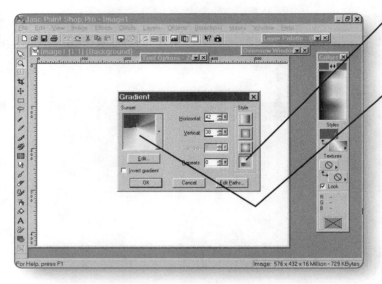

5. **Click** on a gradient **style**. A sample appears in the preview box.

6. **Position** the **mouse pointer** on the white marker in the preview box. The shape of the marker varies with the gradient style. The mouse pointer turns into a black four-headed arrow.

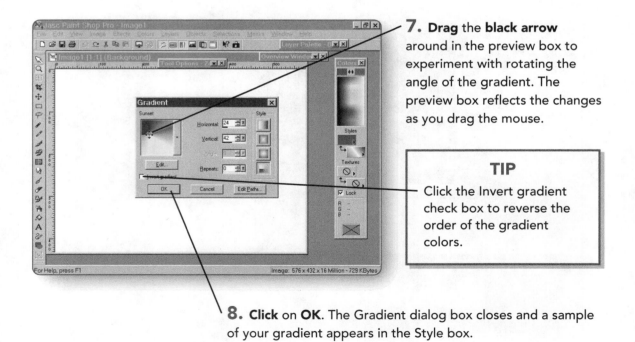

7. **Drag** the **black arrow** around in the preview box to experiment with rotating the angle of the gradient. The preview box reflects the changes as you drag the mouse.

TIP

Click the Invert gradient check box to reverse the order of the gradient colors.

8. **Click** on **OK**. The Gradient dialog box closes and a sample of your gradient appears in the Style box.

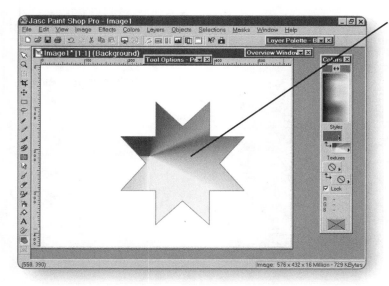

This figure illustrates a star drawn using a gradient fill style.

Picking Patterns

In addition to gradients, Paint Shop Pro includes many different patterns to use in the foreground or background of images.

In this section, we'll take a look at selecting an existing image to use as a pattern, as well as look at some of the patterns included with the software.

1. Open an **image**, whether it's a photo or drawing. The image appears on the screen.

In this example, you see a photograph of a flower.

2. Click on the **pattern icon**, the one with the nine dots. The Style button reflects a pattern.

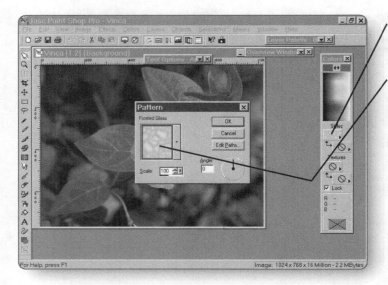

3. Click on the **Style button**. The Pattern dialog box opens.

4. Click on the **pattern preview box**. A selection of patterns appears.

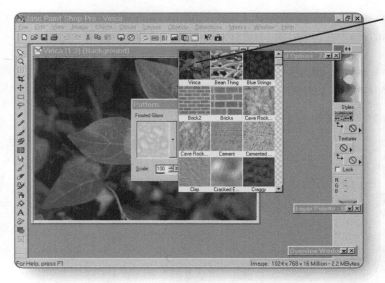

Notice the currently open image also appears as a pattern choice.

5. Click on the **pattern** you'd like to use. A sample appears in the preview box.

6. Click on **OK**. The Pattern dialog box closes and the pattern appears in the Style box.

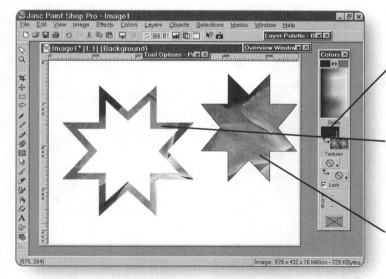

TIP

Click on the color switcher to reverse the foreground and background styles.

This image represents a star drawn using the preset shape tool with the flower pattern as the foreground (stroke) pattern.

This image represents a star drawn using the preset shape tool with the flower pattern as the background (fill) pattern.

Tinkering with Textures

Using texture effects gives an image a three-dimensional appearance as though the image were created on a textured surface.

Similar to using the Style boxes, when using the Airbrush, Paintbrush, or Flood Fill tools, the top Texture box is the foreground texture while the lower Texture box is the background texture. When using the Text, Shapes, or Line Draw tool, the top Texture box is the line or stroke while the lower Texture box is the fill.

Textures, however, rely on the Style boxes. In order to use the tools with textures, you'll need to have a "non-null" selection in the Style boxes.

1. **Click** and **hold** the **mouse button** on a Textures button. A fly-out selection appears.

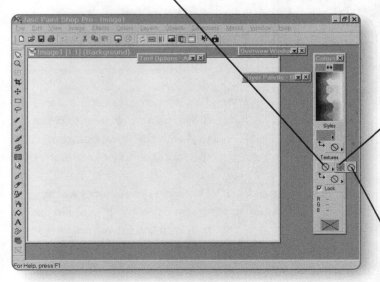

TIP

Click on the arrow to keep the fly-out selection open.

2. **Click** on the **Texture icon**, the fuzzy looking one. The Texture button reflects a texture.

TIP

The circle with the line represents the international "No" symbol and means "null" or no texture.

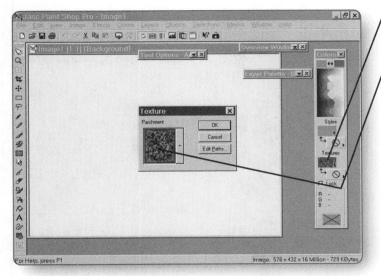

3. Click on the **Texture button**. The Texture dialog box opens.

4. Click on the **preview box**. A selection of textures appears.

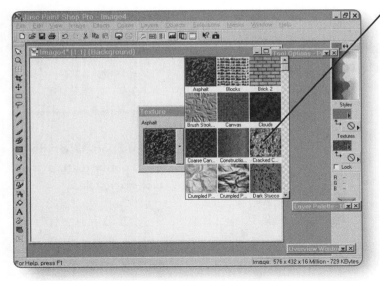

5. Click on a **texture**. The selected texture appears in the preview box.

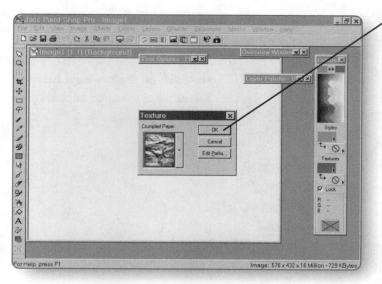

6. Click on **OK**. The Texture dialog box closes and the selected texture appears in the Texture box.

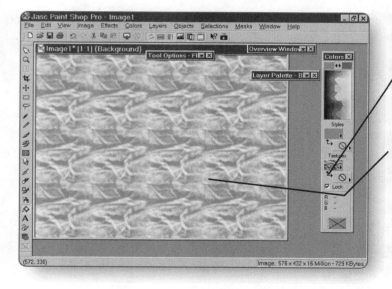

TIP

Click on the color switcher to reverse the foreground and background textures.

A background flood-filled with the crumpled paper texture and a solid color grey style.

Locking Color Choices

Towards the bottom of the Color Palette is a Lock checkbox. When the Lock checkbox is unchecked, the colors and styles are unlocked. This means that each tool you use can have its own combinations of colors and styles. If you switch tools, for example from the Paintbrush to the Flood Fill tool, the color and style selections change to the same color or style in effect the *last time you used that particular tool.*

If you lock the colors, the current settings are used for all tools.

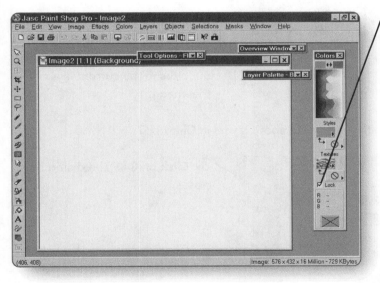

1. If not already checked, **click** the **Lock check box**. A check mark appears in the box and all tools use the current settings.

Counting Colors

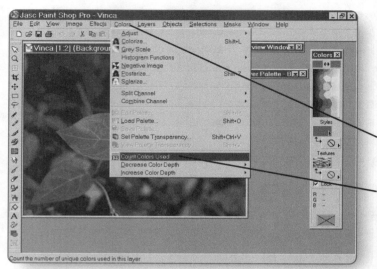

When you create a new image you have to select the maximum number of colors to be in that image. Want to know how many actually are in a particular image?

1. **Click** on **Colors**. The Colors menu appears.

2. **Click** on **Count Colors Used**. An information dialog box appears stating the total number of colors in the current layer of the image.

You'll learn more about layers in Chapter 7.

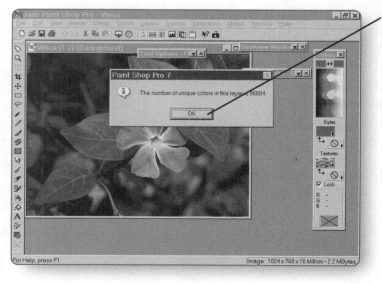

3. **Click** on **OK**. The dialog box closes.

Creating a Negative Image

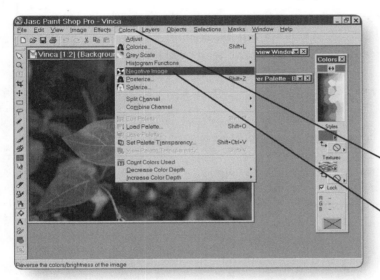

Just like a negative you get when you take your photos to the drugstore for processing, you can create a negative of any image. Creating a negative reverses all the color values in an image to their exact opposite.

1. **Click** on **Colors**. The Colors menu appears.

2. **Click** on **Negative Image**. Paint Shop Pro reverses all color values in the current image.

TIP

Choosing Solarize from the Colors menu produces the same effect as the Negative Image command, except you can control the lightness levels.

Introducing Greyscale

Another color model used by Paint Shop Pro is greyscale, which is what you use with black-and-white images. The images are not purely black and white, they are made up of 256 shades of grey. Any image you create can be in greyscale and any existing image can be converted to greyscale.

Creating a New Greyscale Image

When you create a new image, you're required to specify the number of colors. Instead of the 16 million colors you've been working with so far, for a new greyscale image, you'll specify greyscale as the image type.

1. **Click** on the **New button**. The New Image dialog box appears.

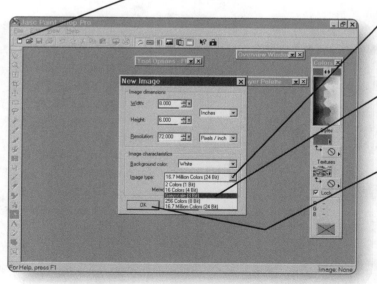

2. **Click** on the **Image Type: down arrow**. A list of selections appears.

3. **Click** on **Greyscale**. The option appears in the drop-down list.

4. **Click** on **OK**. A new image window appears.

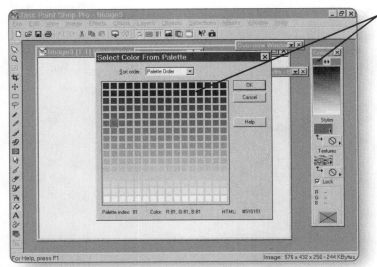

Take a look at your color selections. Only shades of grey appear.

Converting an Image to Greyscale

If you have an existing color image, whether a photograph or drawing, you can easily convert it to greyscale.

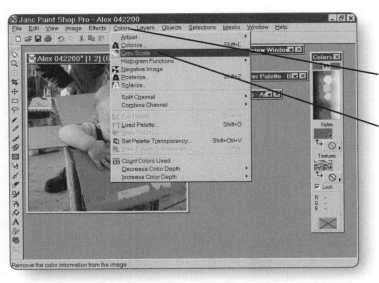

1. Open an **existing image**. The image appears on the screen.

2. Click on **Colors**. The Colors menu appears.

3. Click on **Grey Scale**. The image is converted to greyscale.

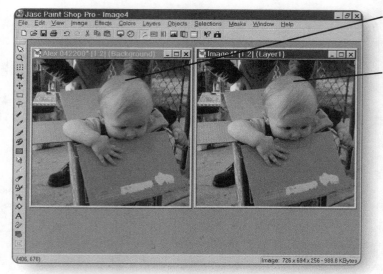

The image before conversion to greyscale.

The image after conversion to greyscale.

5

Printing Images

Many projects created in Paint Shop Pro are for electronic production. There are times, however, when you'll want to print your image to paper. You'll find printing in Paint Shop Pro very similar to other Windows programs, but Paint Shop Pro includes several handy options you can benefit from. In this chapter, you'll learn how to:

- Change page settings
- Preview and print your work
- Print thumbnails
- Print multiple images on a page

Setting Options with Page Setup

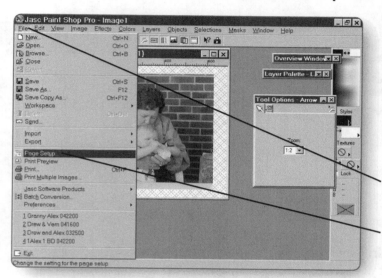

As you prepare to print your image, you can determine several typical printing options, including margins, paper size, and orientation, as well as some image placement options. Use the Page Setup dialog box to set all of these options.

1. Click on **File**. The File menu appears.

2. Click on **Page Setup**. The Page Setup dialog box opens.

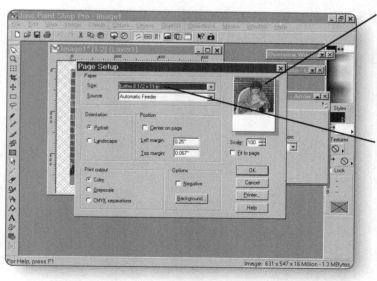

The preview window displays the image with the currently selected print options. As you change any option, the preview box displays the image with the changes.

- **Paper.** You can tell Paint Shop Pro what size paper to use and from where the paper is being fed. The options you see vary with the currently selected printer.

- **Orientation**. You can print the image in portrait and if your printer supports the function (most do), you can print it lengthwise in landscape.

- **Position**. By default, the image prints in the upper-left corner of the page. To have Paint Shop Pro automatically center it to the page, click the Center on page check box. The manual margin settings are unavailable when this box is checked, because Paint Shop Pro automatically determines margins for a centered image.

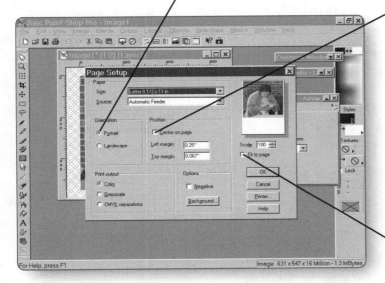

- **Scale**. You can change the size of the image by changing the scale, or to have the image print on the full page (without losing proportions), click the Fit to Page check box.

● **Print output**. If you are working on a color image and printing to a color printer, but want to print the image in black and white, click the Greyscale option. Paint Shop Pro replaces the colors in the image with greys of equal lightness, giving the effect of a black-and-white image.

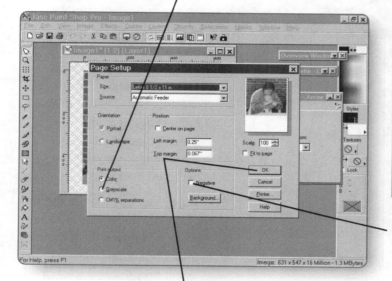

NOTE

If you are printing a color image to a non-color printer such as a laser printer, you don't need to check the Greyscale option. Paint Shop Pro automatically prints the image in greyscale.

● **Options**. From the options section you can opt to print a photograph image as a negative, or you can click on Background and select a color to print on the page around the image.

3. Select any desired **settings**. The preview window reflects your changes except for choices made in the Options section. (You can only see those changes by using Print Preview.)

4. Click on **OK**. The Page Setup dialog box closes.

Using Print Preview

Most users want to scope out how the image will look before it actually prints to the printer. Print Preview saves time and natural resources and prevents any unexpected surprises at printing time.

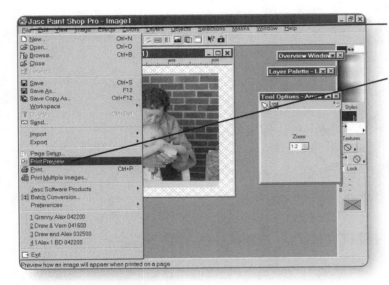

1. Click on **File**. The File menu appears.

2. Click on **Print Preview**. The current image appears onscreen as it will print.

You can zoom in to look at the print page in greater detail. Notice the mouse pointer is a magnifying glass.

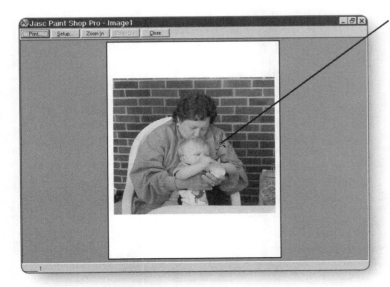

3. Click anywhere on the **image**. The image zooms in.

Click again and the image zooms in closer; click again and the image zooms out.

4a. **Click** on **Close**. The Preview window closes and the image returns to the normal editing screen.

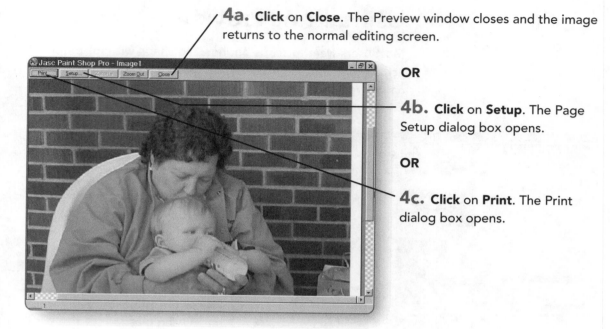

OR

4b. **Click** on **Setup**. The Page Setup dialog box opens.

OR

4c. **Click** on **Print**. The Print dialog box opens.

Printing a Single Image

Printing an open image in Paint Shop Pro is identical to printing in other Windows applications.

1. **Click** on the **Print button**. The Print dialog box opens.

TIP

Optionally, press Ctrl+P or click on File and choose Print.

2. **Select** a **printer** to print the image. The printer name appears.

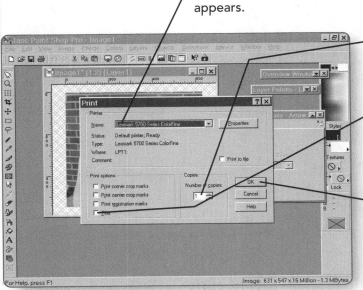

3. **Enter** the **number of copies** to print. The number appears in the Number of copies: box.

4. Optionally, **click** the **Title check box** to print the file name on the page. A check mark appears in the Title check box.

5. **Click** on **OK**. The image prints to your selected printer.

Producing Thumbnails

In Chapter 1, you learned about the Paint Shop Pro Browse feature that allowed you to view thumbnails of your images. You can print the thumbnail images you see in the Browse window.

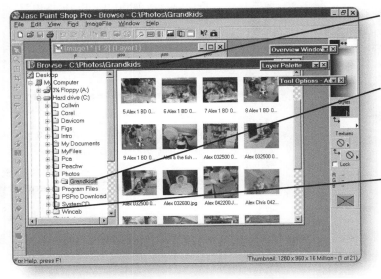

1. **Open** the **Browse window**. (Hint: Click on File, Browse.) The Browse window opens.

2. **Locate** and **click** on the **folder** with the images you want to print. The images appear in the Browse window.

3. **Click** on the **Print button**. The Print dialog box opens.

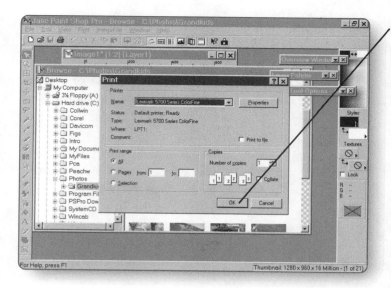

4. Click on **OK**. The thumbnails print with up to 30 images per page.

Printing Multiple Images

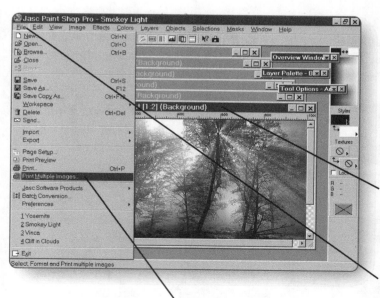

Printing multiple images on a single sheet of paper can save you money, especially if you're printing photographs on photo paper. Printing multiple images is different than thumbnails in that you get to select which images to print as well as their size and placement on the page.

1. Open any **images** you want to print. The open images appear in cascading windows in the Paint Shop Pro window.

2. Click on **File**. The File menu appears.

3. Click on **Print Multiple Images**. Paint Shop Pro switches to Print Preview mode.

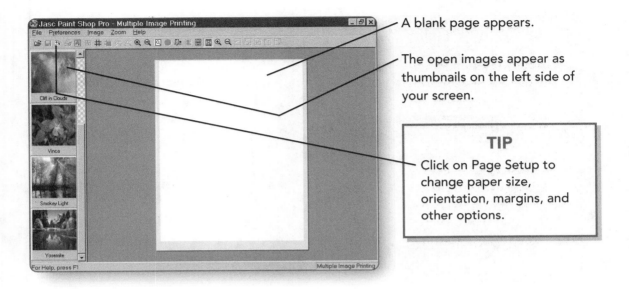

A blank page appears.

The open images appear as thumbnails on the left side of your screen.

TIP

Click on Page Setup to change paper size, orientation, margins, and other options.

Placing the Images on the Page

Next, you need to lay out the images on the page. You can determine where you want them and resize them if desired.

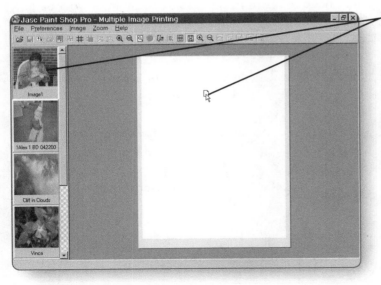

1. **Drag** the first **image** you want to place on the page. The mouse pointer turns into an arrow with a small white box.

2. **Release** the **mouse button**. Depending on the original size of the image, you may be prompted to scale the image.

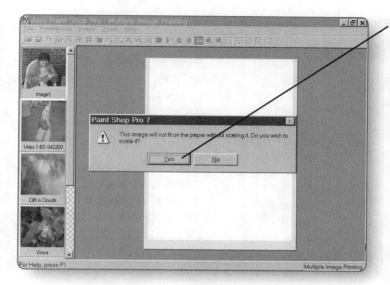

3. **Click** on **Yes**. Paint Shop Pro places the image on the page.

4. **Repeat steps 1 through 3** for each image you want to place on the page.

Resizing Images for the Page

You may need to resize the images to better fit on your page.

1. **Click** on a **placed image**. Four sizing "handles" appear around the selected image corners.

2. **Position** the **mouse pointer** over any of the handles. The mouse pointer turns into a white double-headed arrow.

3. **Click** and **drag** the **handle** to resize the image. A set of dashed outlines indicates the new size as well as the original size.

> **TIP**
>
> Look in the lower-right corner of the status bar for exact size dimensions.

4. **Release** the **mouse button**. The image adjusts to the new size.

5. **Repeat steps 1 through 4** for each image you want to resize.

Moving Images on the Page

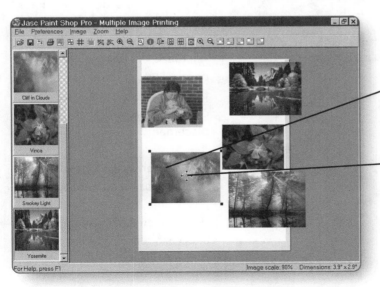

Use your mouse to easily move the images to any position on the page.

1. **Click** on the **image** you want to move. The image appears with selection handles.

2. **Place** the **mouse pointer** anywhere in the body of the image. The mouse pointer appears as a cross with four arrowheads.

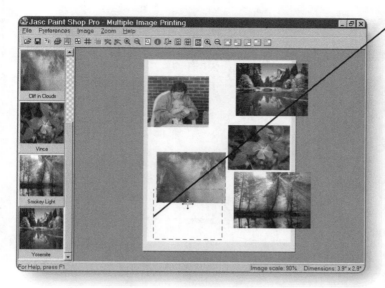

3. **Click** and **drag** the **mouse** until the image is at the desired position. A dashed outline indicates both the new position and the original position.

4. **Release** the **mouse button**. The image moves to the new location.

Using Auto Arrange

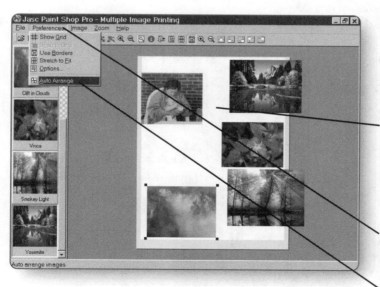

Don't want to take the time to do all that moving and resizing? Let Paint Shop Pro's Auto Arrange feature do the work for you.

1. **Place** the **images** on the page as you learned earlier in this chapter, but don't be concerned about size or exact placement.

2. **Click** on **Preferences**. The Preferences menu appears.

3. **Click** on **Auto Arrange**. Paint Shop Pro rearranges the images to fit the page.

Auto Arrange divides the paper into sections of equal size and places an image in each section.

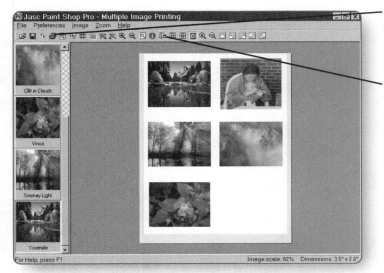

Click on the Print button when you're ready to print the multiple images.

Click on the Close button to return to the standard Paint Shop Pro editing window.

6

Getting Help and Assistance

Although you'll find many answers to your questions in this book, sometimes you need additional assistance. Paint Shop Pro supplies you with several types of support. In this chapter you'll learn how to:

- Use the Help Topics
- Obtain Context Help
- Locate Help on the Web
- Contact Jasc Software

Searching the Program for Help

If you get stuck and don't know what to do next, you'll find online help just a mouse-click away.

Using the Help Topics

The Help Topics feature presents help information in a folder-like format, making it easy for you to browse available topics.

1. **Click** on **Help**. The Help menu appears.

2. **Click** on **Help Topics**. The Help window opens with the Contents tab on top.

TIP

Optionally, press F1 to open the help window.

Available topics are listed on the left.

3. Double-click on a **general topic**. The general topic folder opens and a list of other specific topics or other general topics appears beneath it.

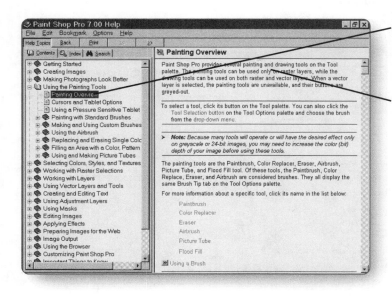

4. Click on the **specific topic** you want to view. The specific topic becomes highlighted.

Paint Shop Pro displays the information on that topic in the help window on the right.

Using the Help Index

If you don't find what you need in the Help topics, try looking through the extensive alphabetical help index.

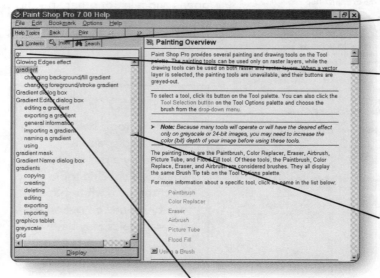

1. **Click** on the **Index tab**. The Help Index window appears.

2a. **Type** the **first characters** or **word** of your keyword. The keywords list jumps alphabetically to the word that you typed.

OR

2b. **Scroll** through the **list of keywords** until you find your keyword.

3. **Click** on the **topic** you're interested in. The information displays in the help window.

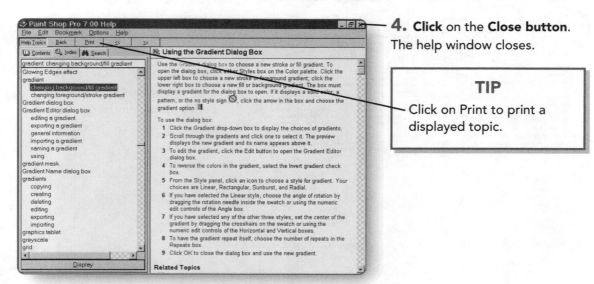

4. **Click** on the **Close button**. The help window closes.

> **TIP**
>
> Click on Print to print a displayed topic.

Obtaining Context Help

There are so many objects on a Paint Shop Pro screen, it's hard to remember what each item is or does. Use the Context Help feature to identify the various buttons and components.

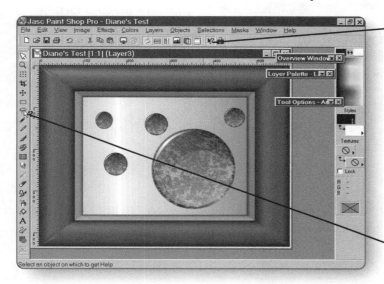

1. Click on the **Help button**. The mouse pointer changes to a pointer with a question mark.

TIP

Optionally, press Shift+F1 or choose Context Help from the Help menu to access the Context help feature.

---

2. Position the **pointer** over any button, item, or menu selection on the screen.

3. Click the **mouse**. A detailed help window opens explaining the function of the item you clicked on.

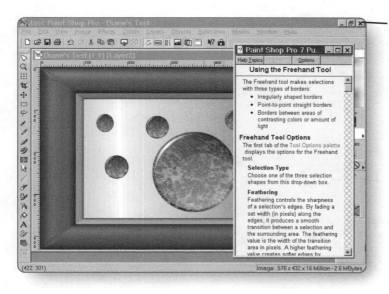

4. Click on the help window **Close button** ☒. The help window closes.

Getting Assistance with a Dialog Box

Paint Shop Pro provides help with the dialog boxes used in its application.

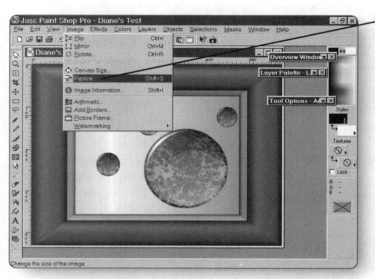

1. **Click** on a **menu selection** that results in a dialog box. (Hint: Any menu selection ending with an ellipsis (...) results in a dialog box.)

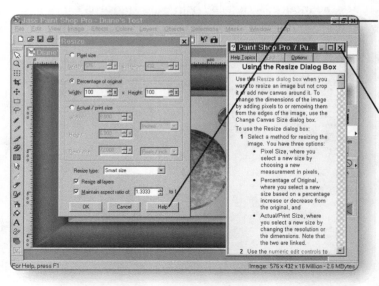

2. **Click** on **Help** in the dialog box. A help window opens with information specific to the open dialog box.

3. **Click** on the help window **Close button** ✕. The help window closes.

Getting Help on the Web

With Internet access, you'll find lots of help on the Jasc Software Web site. Its site provides the answers to many frequently asked questions (FAQs), as well as tips, tutorials, updates, and patches, a chat room, and a search engine.

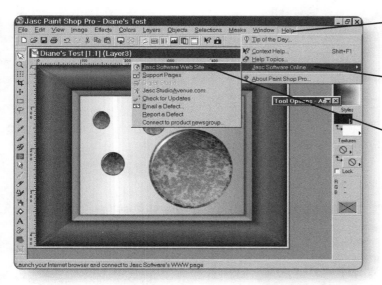

1. **Click** on **Help**. The Help menu appears.

2. **Click** on **Jasc Software Online**. A submenu appears.

3. **Click** on **Jasc Software Web Site**. Your default Web browser launches and takes you to the Jasc Software home page.

You'll find the Jasc Software home page at www.jasc.com.

NOTE

You may be prompted to connect to your Internet Service Provider.

Web pages change frequently so the ones you see may not look like the ones shown.

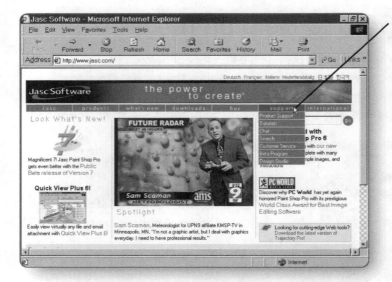

4. Click on **Support**. The Support menu appears.

From the Support menu, you have options to choose:

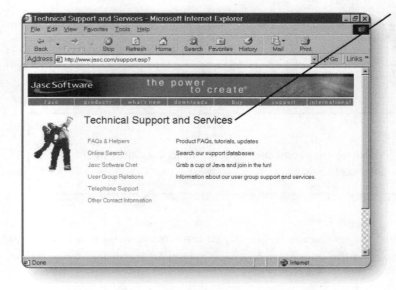

• **Product Support**. Takes you to the Technical Support and Services page. From there you can browse through the FAQs, do an online search, or participate in a Jasc chat room.

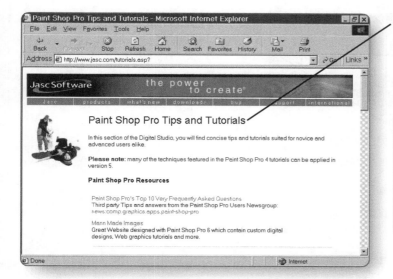

● **Tutorials**. Takes you to the Paint Shop Pro Tips and Tutorials page, where you'll find other Paint Shop Pro resources.

TIP

You might also take a look at Appendix B for a list of helpful Web sites relating to Paint Shop Pro.

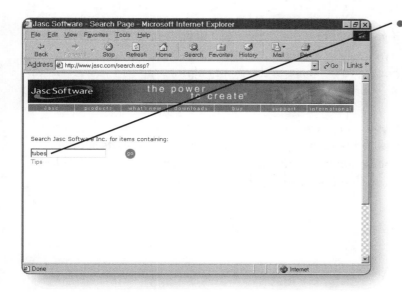

● **Search**. Takes you to the Jasc search engine, where you can search the Jasc software database for articles containing words you specify.

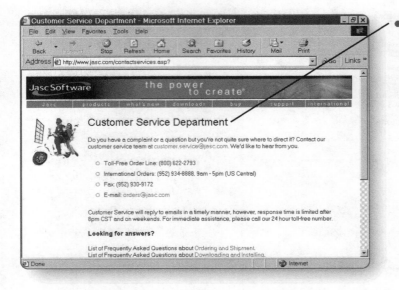

- **Customer Service**. Takes you to the Customer Service page where you'll find phone numbers and other Jasc information.

Contacting Jasc Software

If you don't find the answer you need from the Jasc Web site, try e-mailing it your question. I've found its tech support people to be some of the most helpful support I've ever used. You can e-mail Jasc tech support at techsup@jasc.com.

If you don't have Internet access, or just prefer to talk with a real live person, try contacting Jasc Software at its support phone number, (952) 930-9171. Support is available Monday through Friday, 8am–6pm Central Standard Time.

Part I Review Questions

1. What does the File Format Associations dialog box determine? See *"Setting File Associations"* in Chapter 1.

2. What four screen floating objects have automatic rollup? See *"Working with Automatic Rollup"* in Chapter 1.

3. How do you draw a perfect circle using the ellipse tool? See *"Creating the Perfect Circle"* in Chapter 2.

4. When working with the shape selection tool, where do you determine which shape you use? See *"Choosing a Selection Shape"* in Chapter 3.

5. What does antialiasing reduce? See *"Antialiasing"* in Chapter 3.

6. What key do you press to add to a selection? See *"Adding to a Selection"* in Chapter 3.

7. What does HSL stand for? See *"Appreciating HSL"* in Chapter 4.

8. What do the four symbols on the Style fly-out button represent? See *"Selecting Styles"* in Chapter 4.

9. What options can you modify in the Page Setup dialog box? See *"Setting Options with Page Setup"* in Chapter 5.

10. What key can you press to quickly open the Help window? See *"Using the Help Topics"* in Chapter 6.

PART II

Working with Raster Graphics

7

Developing Layers

Up to this point you've learned how to use the tools to create simple objects. Now we're going to step to the next level of graphics, which is called layering. You have the option of creating a layer for each object you create in Paint Shop Pro.

Layering is like putting each portion of your graphic image on a separate transparent sheet of paper. You can then shuffle the order of the layers (sheets)—layering makes it much easier to edit or move any particular portion of the image. As you edit one portion of the image, you won't disturb the other portions of the image. In this chapter, you'll learn how to:

- Create, duplicate, and delete layers
- View and hide layers
- Change layer opacity
- Rename layers

Creating Layers

Every Paint Shop Pro image consists of at least one layer, usually the background layer—similar to the canvas of a painting. Paint Shop Pro supports up to 100 layers per image if not limited by the memory in your computer. Images created with a transparent background don't have a background layer.

1. **Create** a **new image** with a non-white background. (Creating a new layer doesn't require a non-white background. Using a non-white background makes it easier to demonstrate the concept of layers.)

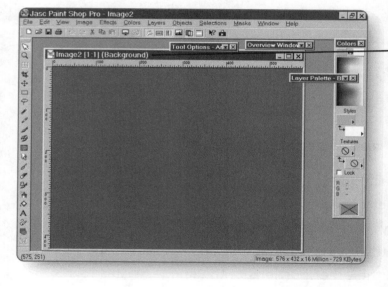

TIP

Notice that the image title bar displays the current layer, which in the case of a new image is the background layer.

In addition to the background layer that Paint Shop Pro provides, you can create three other types of layers in Paint Shop Pro: raster, vector, and adjustment layers. Raster layers contain pixel-based information while vector layers contain instruction data for drawing vector lines, shapes, and text.

NOTE

The next several chapters in this book deal primarily with raster layers. You'll learn more about vector images in Part III. Adjustment layers are beyond the scope of this book and will not be addressed.

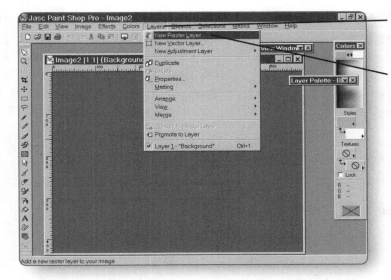

2. **Click** on **Layers**. The Layers menu appears.

3. **Click** on **New Raster Layer**. The Layer Properties dialog box opens.

For now, don't make any changes to the Layer properties.

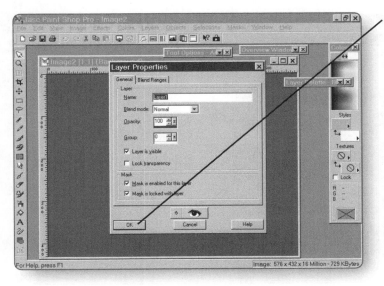

4. **Click** on **OK**. A new layer appears on the image.

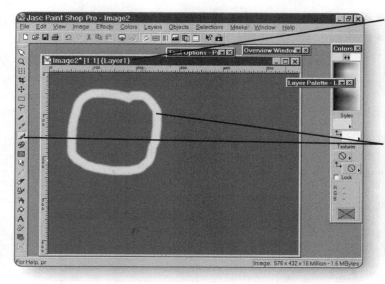

Although nothing appears to have changed, take a look at the image window title bar. The title bar displays the name of the new layer, which by default is Layer1 unless you specify another name.

5. **Use** the **Paintbrush tool** and **draw** something on the screen. Make sure you draw it in a color different from the background color. This gives you something to see on the new layer.

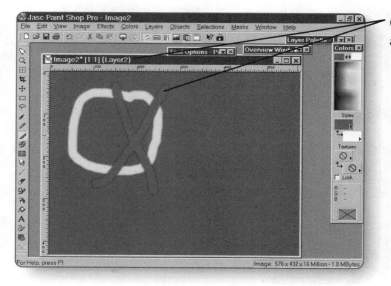

6. **Repeat steps 2 through 5** to add another layer and drawing.

Viewing Layers

The Layer Palette displays each layer and its order in the layer stack.

1. Position the **mouse** over the Layer Palette. The Layer Palette opens and reveals a list of the different layers.

Paint Shop Pro reveals quite a bit of information in the Layer Palette, including:

- **Type of layer**. Each type of layer represents a different layer type. In our example, you see a circle with red, blue, and green, indicating this is a raster layer.

- **Layer name**. When you start adding lots of layers, you'll want to give each layer a unique name to quickly identify what each layer holds.

- **Visibility**. The eyeglass icon indicates that the layer is visible. You'll see later in this section how to hide layers.

- **Opacity**. Opacity is the measure of an object's ability to block light transmission—the opposite of transparency. You'll see how to change opacity in the next section, "Changing Layer Opacity."

- **Blend Mode**. This feature uses methods of combining the pixels of the current layer with the pixels of the underlying layers. Blending layers is beyond the scope of this book and will not be covered.

- **Lock Transparency**. This option lets you lock transparent pixels in an image so that only the non-transparent pixels can be edited.

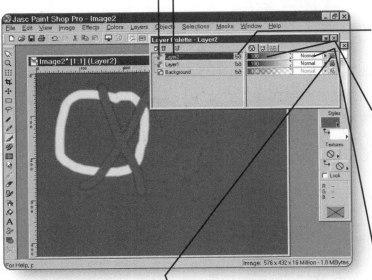

You may want to hide particular layers to more easily view and edit objects on the remaining layers. Let's experiment with hiding and redisplaying layers.

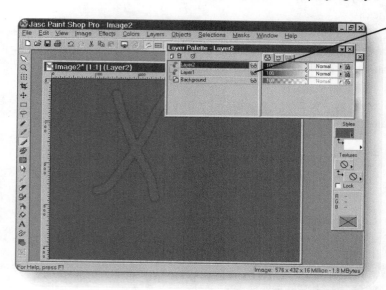

2. Click on the **visibility icon**. The eyeglass icon changes to eyeglasses with a red "X" and the layer hides.

In this example, Layer1 is hidden. Notice the yellow circle disappeared.

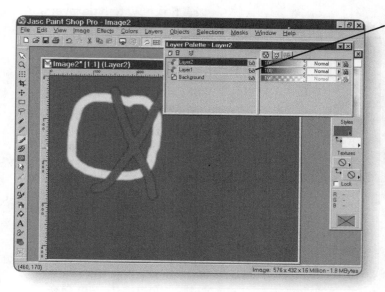

3. Click on the same **visibility icon** again. The hidden layer redisplays.

NOTE

At any time, you can hide as many of the layers as you'd like.

Changing Layer Opacity

When the opacity is lower, the resulting image is more transparent. When the opacity is higher, the image is fully opaque or visible.

> **NOTE**
>
> You cannot change the opacity of the background layer. If you need to change opacity in a background, you need to promote the background to a layer.

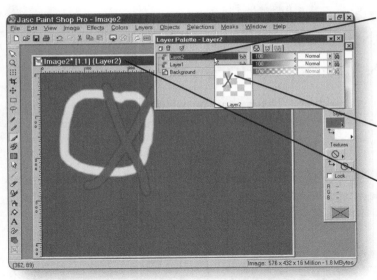

1. On the Layer Palette, **click** on the **layer** you want to modify. The layer name becomes highlighted, indicating it is the active layer.

A miniature representation of the layer displays.

The active layer name appears in the image title bar.

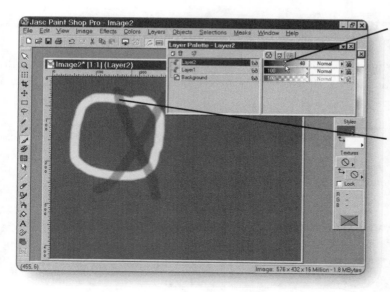

2. Drag the layer opacity **handle** to the left or right. The opacity value displays and the layer image changes as you slide the opacity handle.

In the example, decreasing the opacity makes the red "X" more transparent.

Naming Layers

As you add more layers, you may want to more easily identify what each layer represents. Use the Layer Name feature to clearly name each layer.

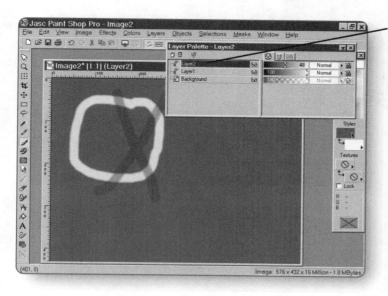

1. From the Layer Palette, **double-click** on the **layer name** you want to rename. The Layer Properties dialog box opens.

TIP

Optionally, choose Properties from the Layers menu to open the Layer Properties dialog box.

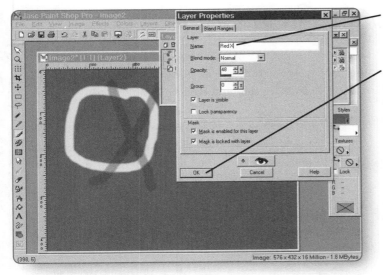

2. **Type** a new **descriptive name** in the Name: text box.

3. **Click** on **OK**. The Layer Properties dialog box closes.

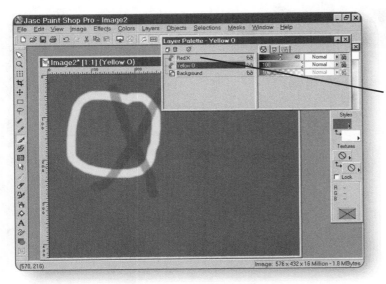

4. **Repeat steps 1 through 3** for each layer you want to rename.

The Layer Palette reflects the new layer names.

Duplicating Layers

If you created a layer just the way you want it and need another similar layer, rather than re-create the layer, you can duplicate the existing one and modify the new one.

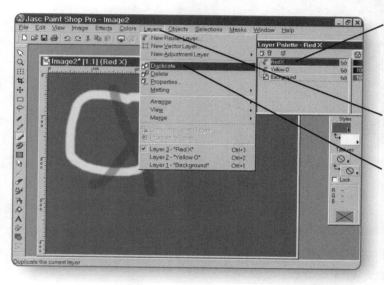

1. From the Layer Palette, **click** on the **layer name** you want to duplicate. The layer name appears in the image title bar.

2. Click on **Layers**. The Layers menu appears.

3. Click on **Duplicate**. Paint Shop Pro duplicates the layer. The new layer appears on the Layer Palette.

Moving a Layered Image

Can't see the new duplicated layer? That's because its image is lying directly on top of the layer it was duplicated from. You'll probably want to move the new image.

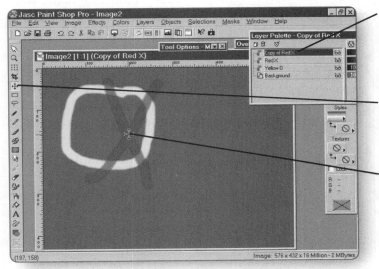

1. From the Layer Palette, **click** on the **layer name** you want to move. The layer name appears in the image title bar.

2. Click on the **Mover tool**. The mouse pointer turns into a four-headed arrow.

3. Position the **mouse pointer** over the image.

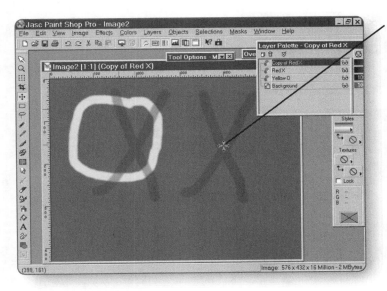

4. Click and **drag** the **image** to a new position. The image moves onscreen to its new position.

5. Release the **mouse button**. The image remains in the new position.

Deleting Layers

If you've created a layer you no longer want, you can easily delete it from the Layer Palette.

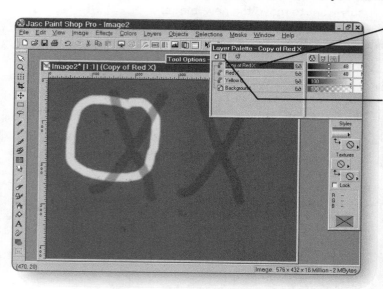

1. Click on the **layer name** you want to delete. The layer name appears in the image title bar.

2. Click on the **Delete Layer icon** (which looks like a trash can) on the Layer Palette. A confirmation box appears.

TIP

Optionally, click on the Layers menu and choose Delete.

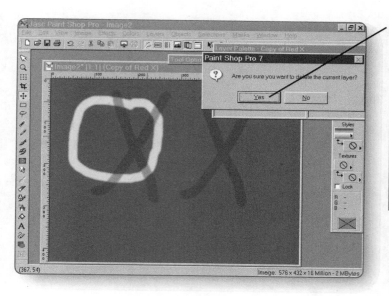

3. Click on **Yes**. Paint Shop Pro deletes the layer and its contents.

TIP

If you delete a layer in error, click on Edit, Undo (or press Ctrl+Z) to reverse your last action.

8

Designing with Picture Tubes

If you run down to Wal-Mart and look in the school supplies section, you're bound to see lots of ink stamps. You know...the kind where you just touch the end of the stamp to a paper and it creates an image and you can stamp the image on the paper over and over again. Well, Paint Shop Pro's picture tubes are similar to those stamps—but even better. You can actually paint images with these tubes. Plus, while the stamps you find at the store can each produce only a single image, that's not necessarily the case with tubes. Some tubes may contain only a single image, but many tubes produce several variations of a single image or several different images with a common theme. In this chapter, you'll learn how to:

- Use picture tubes
- Modify picture tube size
- View and install additional picture tubes

Using Picture Tubes

If there were such a prize, picture tubes would win the Gold Medal as the "Most Fun Feature" of Paint Shop Pro. Picture tubes are small, instant pictures that you can create with a click of your mouse button.

Creating a Tube Layer

I strongly advise placing the picture tubes on layers for easier editing. For ease in editing the image itself after it is drawn on the screen, place each tube on its own layer. Picture tubes are raster images, so place them on a raster layer.

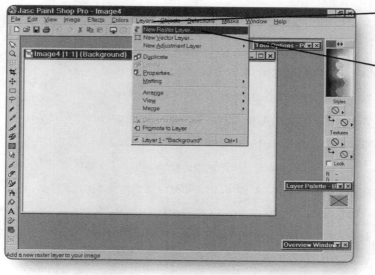

1. Click on **Layers**. The Layers menu appears.

2. Click on **New Raster Layer**. The Layer Properties dialog box opens.

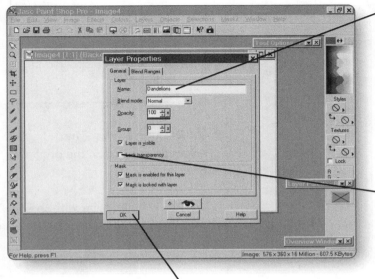

3. Optionally, give the layer a discriptive name by, **typing** a new **name** for the layer in the Name: text box. Since, in the example, we're going to paint dandelions, we've called the layer "Dandelions."

TIP

Be sure the Lock Transparency is *NOT checked*. You won't be able to paint with tubes if the option is checked.

4. Click on **OK**. The Layer Properties dialog box closes.

5. Click on the **Picture Tube tool**. The mouse pointer looks like a paintbrush with a stamp next to it.

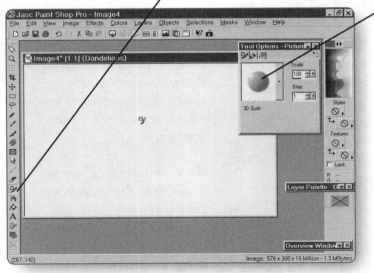

6. From the Tool Options Palette, **click** on the **preview box**. A selection of tubes displays.

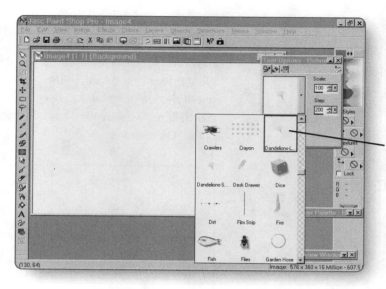

NOTE

Your selections may vary from the ones displayed in this figure.

7. Click on a **tube**. The selection appears in the preview box.

You're ready to paint with the picture tube.

Painting with a Picture Tube

Use the Picture Tube tool similarly to the Paintbrush tool.

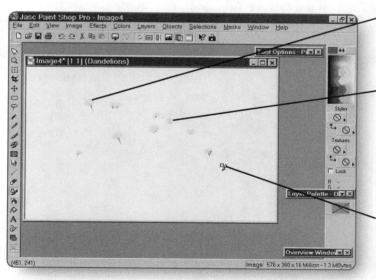

1. Click the **mouse** where you want the image to appear. The image appears.

2. Click the **mouse** at a different position on the canvas. Depending on the tube you select, another identical image appears or a similar image appears.

3. With the mouse button down, **drag** the **mouse** over the canvas. Depending on the selected tube, the screen may begin to fill with your tube images.

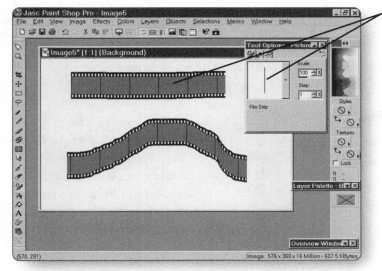

Try drawing with the different tubes. Many are much more exciting than they appear in the preview box. The Film Strip and Lightning tubes are perfect examples of the actual tube looking tremendously different than the sample in the preview window.

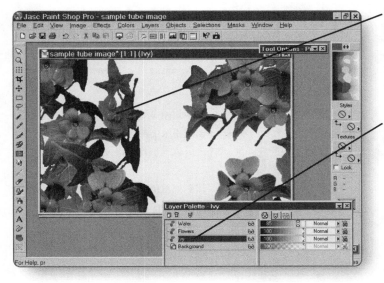

This image was created with just a few mouse clicks using three different tubes: an ivy tube, a flower tube, and the water drop tube.

Each tube was drawn on a different layer.

Modifying Picture Tube Size

If you find a picture tube is painting an image too large or too small, you can edit the scale. You must change scale size before you paint the image.

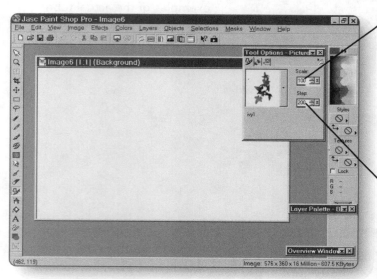

1. From the Tool Options Palette, after you select the tube you want to use, **click** in the **Scale box** and **select** the picture tube size. You can reduce and enlarge it from 10% to 250% of its original size.

TIP

As you decrease the step size, the distance between the intervals at which the tubes appear in the image decreases.

2. Paint with the picture tube. Paint Shop Pro creates the images at the new size.

This image reflects the ivy drawn at 100% on the left, and drawn at 50% on the right.

Previewing Picture Tubes

A picture tube is really a drawing or series of drawings created and saved in a special format. The images are created on a transparent background, so all you see is the image itself.

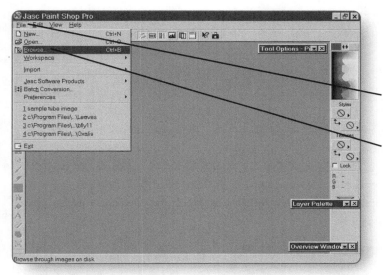

The easiest way to view your picture tubes is with the Paint Shop Pro browser.

1. Click on **File**. The File menu appears.

2. Click on **Browse**. The Browse dialog box opens.

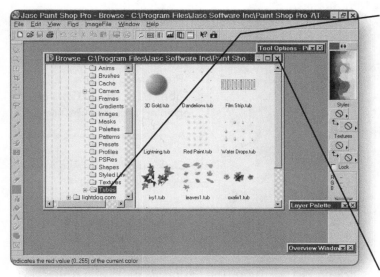

3. Locate and **click** on the **Tubes folder** or **any folder in which you have tubes**. A thumbnail representation of each tube appears.

NOTE

Don't double-click on the tube images unless you intend to open them for modification or for exporting.

---

4. Click the **Close button**. The Browse window closes.

Installing New Picture Tubes

Many tubes come with the Paint Shop Pro application and even more are available on the CD. You can even find thousands of free picture tubes on the Internet.

> **TIP**
>
> See Appendix B, "Exploring Useful Web Sites," for a few Internet tube locations.

In many cases, Paint Shop Pro automatically reads the picture tubes, provided you copy them to the locations specified in File, Preferences, File Locations. However, if the tube was created in an older version of Paint Shop Pro, the current version may not recognize it as a tube so you can run the Paint Shop Pro export procedure.

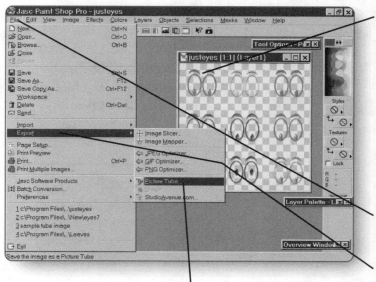

1. **Open** the **file** containing the picture tube. The picture tube appears onscreen.

> **NOTE**
>
> See the previous section, "Previewing Picture Tubes," for instructions on opening picture tube files.

2. **Click** on **File**. The File menu opens.

3. **Click** on **Export**. The Export submenu opens.

4. **Click** on **Picture Tube**. The Export Picture Tube dialog box opens.

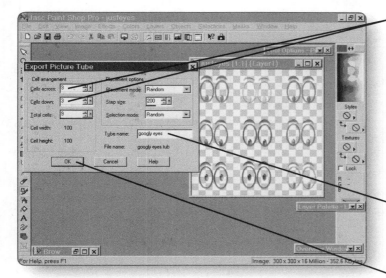

5. Specify the **number of rows** and **columns** in an image. In this example image, the image consists of 3 cells across and 3 cells down.

6. Click in the Tube **name: text box**. A blinking insertion point appears.

7. Type a **name** for the tube. The name appears in the text box.

8. Click on **OK**. Paint Shop Pro adds the picture tube to its list.

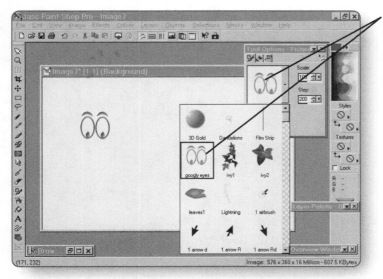

9. Click on the **picture tube preview box** in the Tool Options Palette to see the latest addition.

Happy tubing!

9

Forming Masks

Masking is probably the most powerful feature of Paint Shop Pro. A mask is a greyscale image that you use to hide and display parts of a layer. Masks hide portions of the layer without actually deleting them or modifying them. Think of a mask like a stencil that you place over an image to let only part of the image show through. In this chapter, you'll learn how to:

- Create and save masks
- Apply and remove a mask
- Edit a mask

Creating a Simple Mask

A mask can cover a layer completely or with varying levels of opacity. Where a mask is black, it completely covers the layer and where it is white, it leaves the layer uncovered. If you use a grey value between black and white, the mask produces a semi-visible effect.

Although Paint Shop Pro includes a number of masks and hundreds more are available on the Internet, you may want to design your own mask.

For an example, we'll create a mask with a simple oval shape.

TIP

It's easier to create a mask if you don't have any other images open when creating.

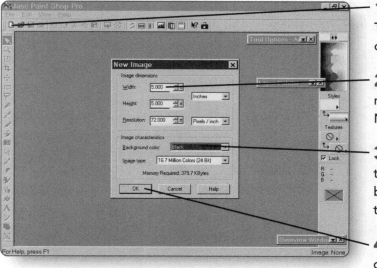

1. **Click** on the **New button**. The New Image dialog box opens.

2. **Select** the **image size**. The measurements appear in the New Image dialog box.

3. **Set** the **image background** to black. When applied, the black portion of a mask blocks the image from showing.

4. **Click** on **OK**. The blank canvas appears.

Now we need to delete the center of the black layer so that when the mask is applied, part of our image can show through.

5. Click on the **Selection tool**. The tool is selected.

6. Choose Ellipse from the Tool Options Palette. A preview sample appears in the Tool Options Palette.

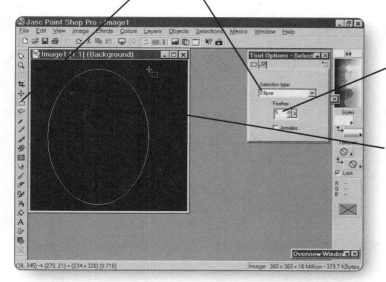

TIP

Set the feathering to 4 or 5 for a nice edge softening added effect.

7. Draw an **oval selection** in the black image. Marching ants appear around the selection.

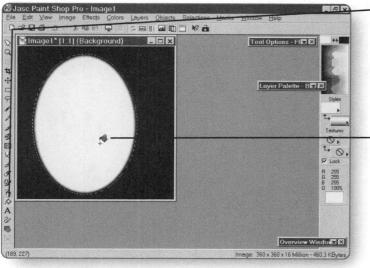

8. Click on the **Flood Fill** tool. The mouse pointer turns into a paint bucket. Select white as the foreground color. Remember that whatever you paint in white appears through the mask.

9. Click in the **oval selection**. The oval fills with white.

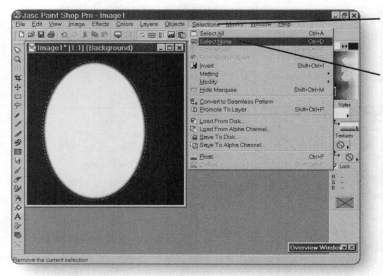

10. Click on **Selections**. The Selections menu appears.

11. Click on **Select None**. The oval is deselected and the marching ants disappear.

So far, you have an image consisting of an oval. Next, you need to tell Paint Shop Pro that the image is a mask.

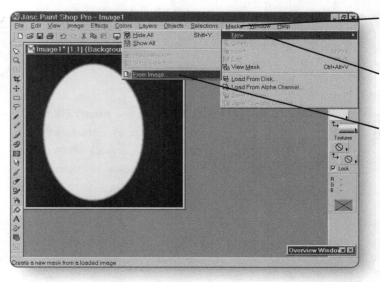

12. Click on **Masks**. The Masks menu appears.

13. Click on **New**. The New submenu appears.

14. Choose From Image. The Add Mask From Image dialog box opens.

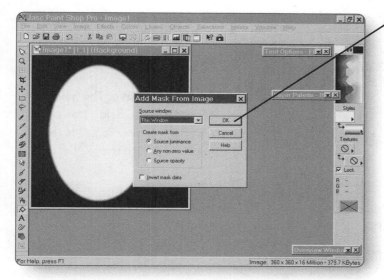

15. **Click** on **OK**. Paint Shop Pro now knows the current image is a mask. The black portion turns into a transparency (indicated by grey-and-white checks).

TIP

Click on File, Preferences, General Program Preferences, then click on the Transparency tab to determine the way Paint Shop Pro displays a transparent area on your screen.

Saving Masks

Now that you've created a mask, save it for future use. Paint Shop Pro names mask files with a .MSK extension to identify it as a mask.

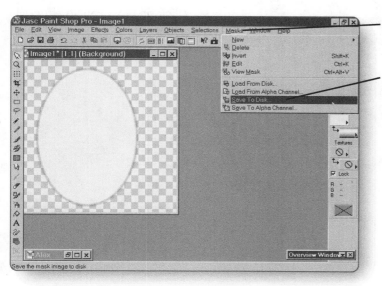

1. **Click** on **Masks**. The Masks menu appears.

2. **Click** on **Save To Disk**. The Save Mask Channel dialog box opens.

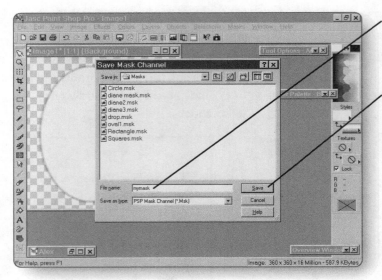

3. **Enter** a descriptive **name** for the mask. The name appears in the File name: text box.

4. **Click** on **Save**. The Save Mask Channel dialog box closes and Paint Shop Pro saves the mask for future use.

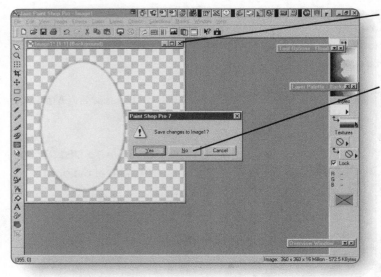

5. **Click** the **Close box** to close the mask image. A message box opens.

6. **Click** on **No**. (You've already saved the image as a mask.) The image closes from the screen.

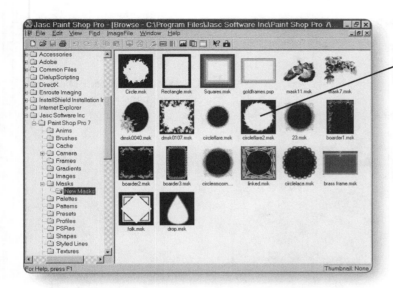

Applying a Mask

Applying a mask is a matter of opening an image and telling Paint Shop Pro which mask you want to apply.

1. Open an **image** to which you want to apply a mask. The image appears onscreen.

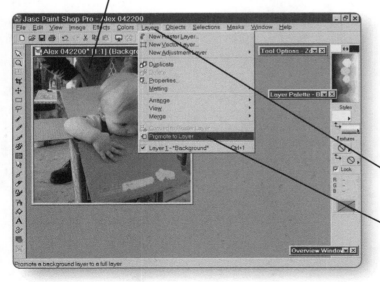

If the image contains only a background layer, promote the background layer to a "regular" layer before applying a mask. This gives you more flexibility when doing editing such as moving.

2. Click on **Layers**. The Layers menu appears.

3. Click on **Promote to Layer**. The image is no longer considered a background, it's a raster layer.

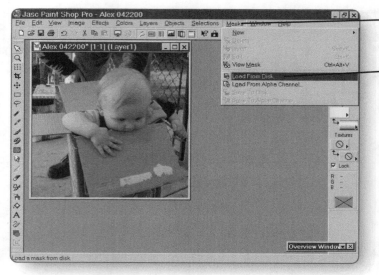

4. Click on **Masks**. The Masks menu appears.

5. Click on **Load From Disk**. The Load Mask Channel dialog box opens.

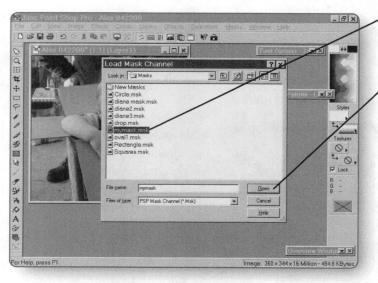

6. Locate and **click** on the **mask** you want to use. The mask name is highlighted.

7. Click on **Open**. The Load Mask Channel dialog box closes

Paint Shop Pro applies the mask to the image.

> **TIP**
>
> If the mask appears backwards, click on Masks, Invert.

Masking on Layers

If you foresee the need to further edit the image itself, you may want to create your mask on a separate layer.

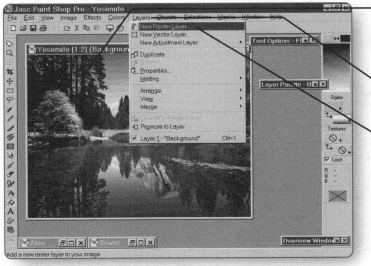

1. Open an **image** to which you want to apply a mask. The image appears onscreen.

2. Click on **Layers**. The Layers menu appears.

3. Click on **New Raster Layer**. The Layer Properties dialog box opens.

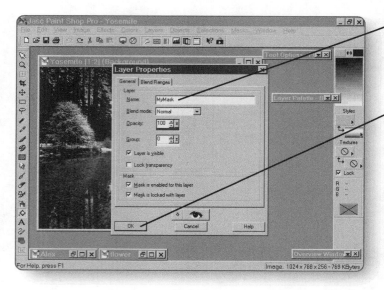

4. **Enter** a **name** for the new layer, for example "MyMask." The name appears in the Name: text box.

5. **Click** on **OK**. A new layer appears in the layer box although you see no changes on the image at this point.

Next you need to give the new blank layer a color, gradient, or pattern.

6. **Click** on the **Flood Fill tool**. The mouse pointer turns into a paint bucket.

7. **Select** a **color**, **gradient**, or **pattern** from the foreground Styles box. The options appear in the foreground Styles box.

TIP
Make sure the MyMask layer is the active layer.

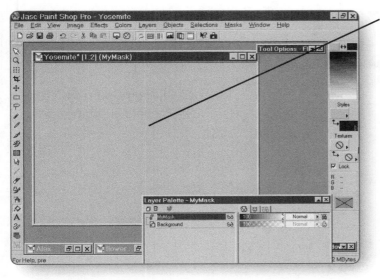

8. Click anywhere on the **blank layer**. The layer "fills" with the new color.

Don't panic! Because you activated the MyMask layer, all you've done is fill up that layer with color. Your original image is as yet untouched.

Now you can apply the mask to the MyMask layer.

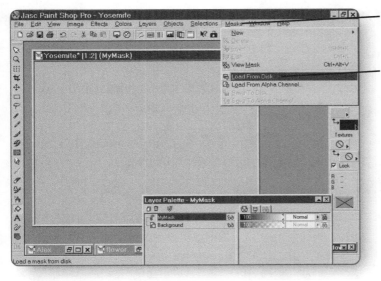

9. Click on **Masks**. The Masks menu appears.

10. Click on **Load From Disk**. The Load Mask Channel dialog box opens.

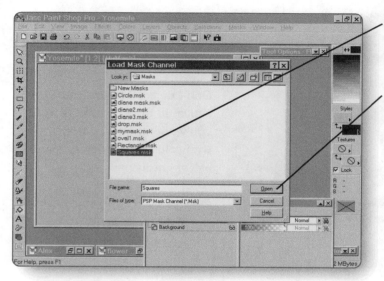

11. **Locate** and **click** on the **mask** you want to use. The mask name is highlighted.

12. **Click** on **Open**. The Load Mask Channel dialog box closes

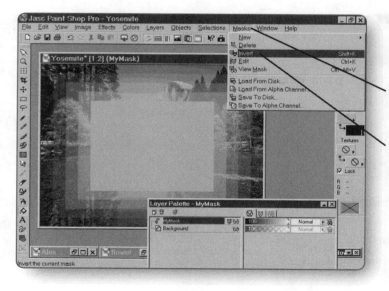

Paint Shop Pro applies the mask to the image layer, but you may need to invert the mask.

13. **Click** on **Masks**. The Mask menu appears.

14. **Click** on **Invert**. The mask areas reverse.

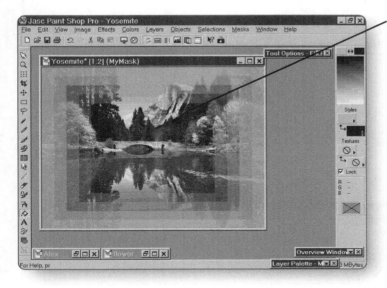

The image shows through the mask.

Moving Images in a Mask

If the mask doesn't uncover the portion of the image you want to display, you may want to move the image to a different position in the mask. If the image and mask are on separate layers, you simply activate the image layer and move it with the mover tool. If, however, the mask and image are on the same layer, the process changes.

By default, the mask and the image are linked so you use the Link Mask option to tell Paint Shop Pro whether to separate the mask from the image. When this option is active, the mask and layer move, flip, and rotate together as one unit, but when the option is not active, the layer and mask move independently.

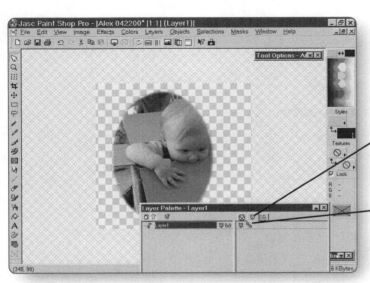

1. From the Layer Palette, **click** the **Mask tab**. The Layer Palette displays masking options.

2. Click the **Link Mask button**. The Link Mask option appears with a red X indicating the link feature is no longer active.

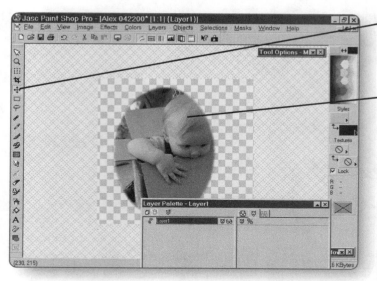

3. **Click** on the **Mover tool**. The mouse pointer turns into a four-headed arrow.

4. **Click** and **drag** the **image** until it's in the location you want. In this example, the baby in the image needs to be moved to the left.

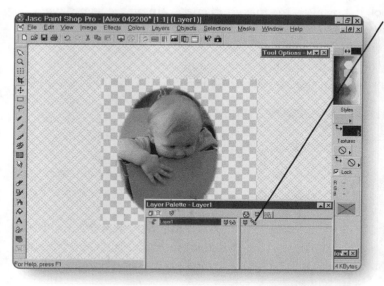

5. From the Layer Palette, **click** the **Link Mask button**. The red X disappears, indicating the mask and image are once again linked together.

Editing Masks

When you edit a mask you aren't changing the image itself. You're changing the masking area or changing the degree of masking. You must be in Mask Edit mode to edit a mask area.

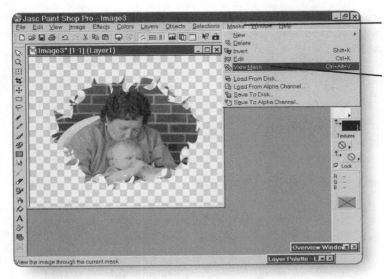

1. Click on **Masks**. The Masks menu appears.

2. Click on **View Mask**. The mask appears as a red overlay on the image.

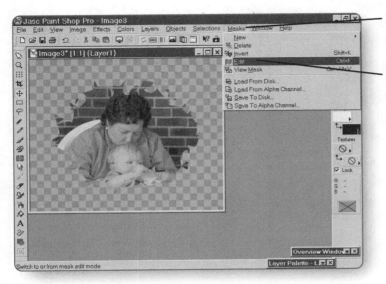

3. Click on **Masks**. The Masks menu appears.

4. Click on **Edit**. Paint Shop Pro enters Edit Mask mode.

While in Edit Mask mode, Paint Shop Pro provides only greyscale colors.

The image title bar displays Mask, indicating you are using Edit Mask mode.

> **NOTE**
>
> When you leave Edit Mask mode, the color boxes return to their previous colors.

Although you can use the painting tools to modify the masked area, you can also use the selection tools to select an area, then flood fill the selected area with white, which unmasks more of the image, or with black, to add masking.

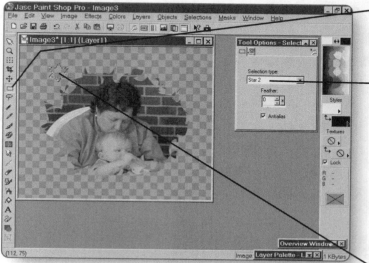

5. **Click** on a **selection tool**. The Tool Options Palette displays selection tool options.

6. From the Tool Options Palette, **select** a **Selection type**. The selection you make appears in the selection type preview box.

For this example, I'm going to add some star-shaped cutouts to the mask.

7. **Click** and **draw** the **selection area** in the image. The selection appears with marching ants.

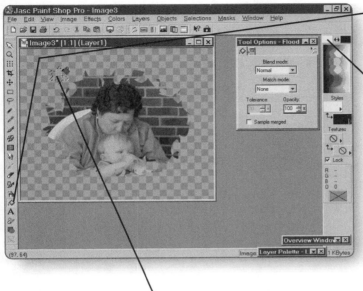

8. Click on the **Flood Fill tool** or the **Paintbrush tool**. The tool becomes selected.

9. Click on a **Foreground color** to match the task you want. For example, choose black to mask more of the image, or choose white to display more of the image. The foreground color appears in the sample box.

> ## TIP
> Use lighter and darker greys to add various levels of masking.

10. Flood fill or **paint** the **selected areas**. The image reflects the mask changes.

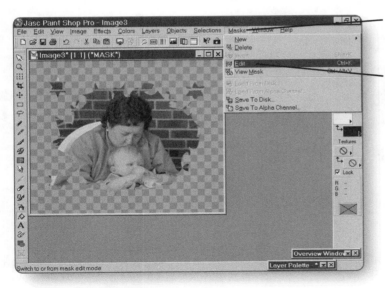

11. Click on **Masks**. The Masks menu appears.

12. Click on **Edit**. The color palette returns to normal.

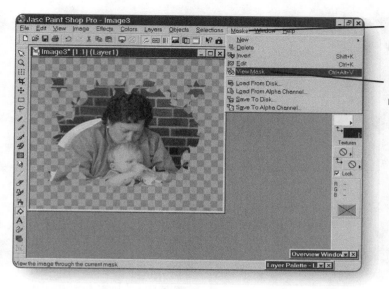

13. **Click** on **Masks**. The Masks menu appears.

14. **Click** on **View Mask**. The mask becomes hidden.

The modified masked image as it appears in Print Preview.

Removing a Mask

If you've applied a mask to an image and decide you no longer want it, or would like a different mask, you can delete it.

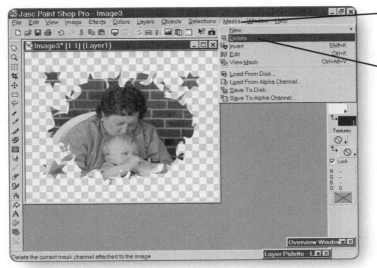

1. Click on **Masks**. The Masks menu appears.

2. Click on **Delete**. A confirmation dialog box opens.

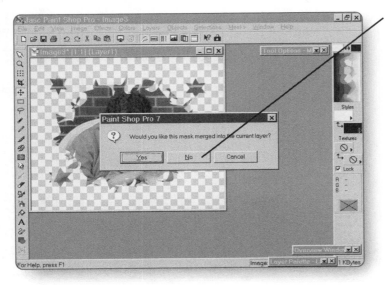

3. Click on **No**. Paint Shop Pro removes the mask from the image.

10

Adding Effects, Filters, and Deformations

The terms *effects*, *filters*, and *deformations* are basically synonymous. Earlier versions of Paint Shop Pro separated filters and deformations. As you access the Internet for tutorials on different projects, you may see them still referred to as filters or deformations, but Paint Shop Pro Version 7 combines them and refers to them as "effects." My oh my, does Paint Shop Pro have some special effects in store for you! In this chapter, you'll learn how to:

- Use the Effect Browser
- Apply an effect
- Install third-party filters

Discovering Effects

Effects work on the individual layers of an image, so you could apply a different effect for each layer. Effects work only on raster images and only if the image is full color or in certain greyscale settings.

Using the Effect Browser

The easiest way to see what an effect does to your image is to use the Effect Browser.

1. Open or **create** the **image** to which you want to apply an effect.

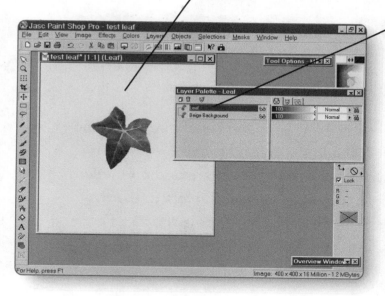

2. From the Layer Palette, **click** on the **layer** of the image to which you want to apply an effect. The layer name appears on the image title bar.

TIP

On most filters, selecting an area prior to choosing an effect applies the effect to the selected area only.

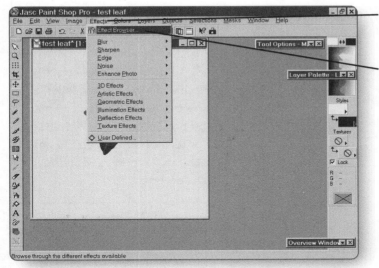

3. Click on **Effects**. The Effects menu appears.

4. Click on **Effect Browser**. The Effect Browser Window opens.

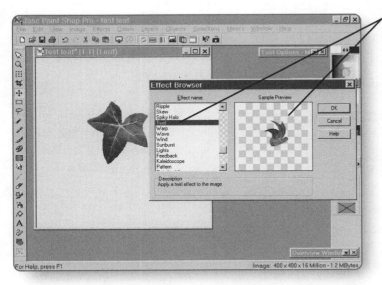

5. Click on an **effect**. The layer with the effect appears in the sample preview window.

Experiment with all the effects until you find the one you want. The image doesn't get changed until you close the Effect Browser Window.

6. **Click** on a **different effect**. The preview window reflects the layer with the new effect.

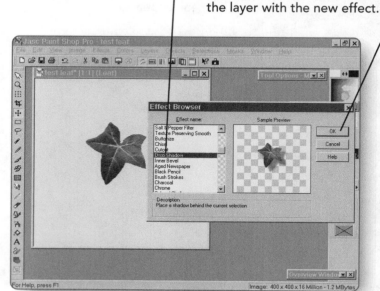

7. **Click** on **OK**. The effect applies to the current layer of the current image, or you may be prompted with a dialog box for further detail. See the next section, "Working with Effect Dialog Boxes."

> ### TIP
>
> Remember, if you select an effect you don't like, choose Edit, Undo to reverse your steps. Once a modified image is saved and closed, you cannot undo the previous step.

Working with Effect Dialog Boxes

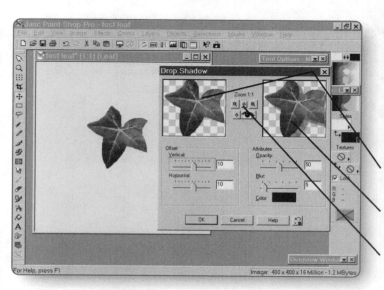

Some effects require additional input from you before the effect applies, although the options vary with individual effects.

Standard elements on Effect dialog boxes include:

- **Before preview window.** See your image before the effect.

- **After preview window.** See your image after the effect.

- **Move Image View.** Select a different area of the image to preview.

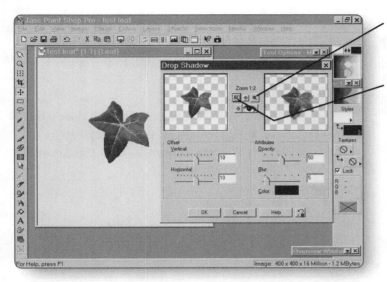

- **Zoom Out.** See the preview image in a smaller perspective.

- **Zoom In.** See the preview image in a larger perspective.

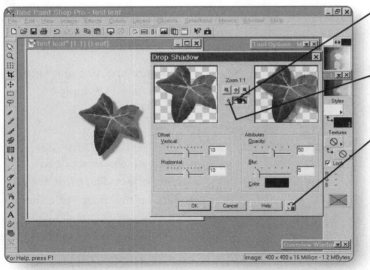

- **Proof Button.** Click here to see the current change on the entire image.

- **Auto Proof Button.** Click here to see all effect changes on the image window.

- **Reset.** Click this button to change the effect options to the default values.

The remaining options vary depending on which effect you're working with. In this figure you see the options for the Drop Shadow effect where you can adjust the distance and opacity of the shadow.

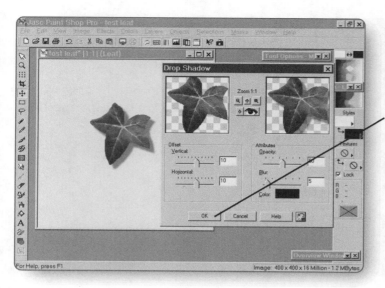

1. Make any desired **changes**. The preview windows reflect the effect change to the current layer.

2. Click on **OK**. The dialog box closes and the effect applies to the current layer of the current image.

Applying an Effect

If you know what effect you want to apply to an image, select it from the menu.

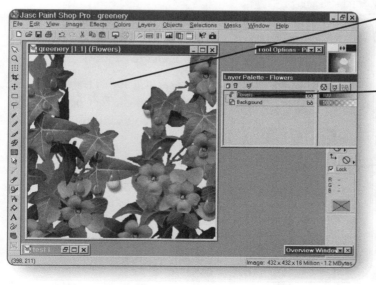

1. Open or **create** the **image** to which you want to apply an effect.

2. Click on the **layer** of the image to which you want to apply an effect. The layer name appears on the image title bar.

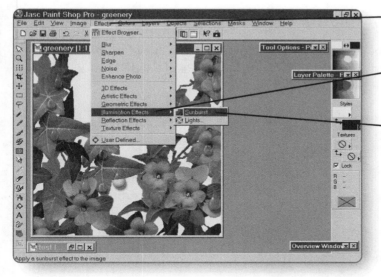

3. Click on **Effects**. The Effects menu appears.

4. Click on an **effect category**. A submenu appears.

5. Click on an **effect**. The effect applies to the current layer of the current image, or you may be prompted with a dialog box for further detail. See the previous section, "Working with Effect Dialog Boxes."

> **TIP**
>
> Effects with an ellipsis (…) display a dialog box with options. Effects without an ellipsis apply immediately upon selection.

Working with Third-Party Filters

There are hundreds of third-party suppliers of filters (also called plug-ins) that you can use with Paint Shop Pro. Some are quite pricey and others are free. Look around on the Internet and I think you'll be quite pleased with what you find. Whether you choose Flaming Pear's Blade Pro, KPT's Power Tools, Alien Skin's Eye, or one of the hundreds of others, you'll find unique special effects in each application.

The only requirement is that the filter must be Paint Shop Pro- or Adobe Photoshop-compatible and must have .8bf as the file name extension. An example might be swirleypop.8bf or bubblejets.8bf.

Installing Third-Party Filters

You install the filters according to the manufacturer's directions, but you'll need to tell Paint Shop Pro where on your computer you keep those filters.

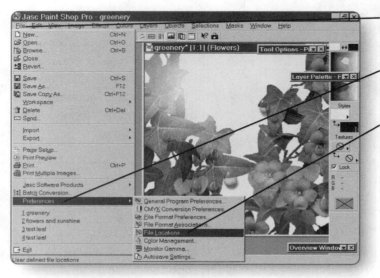

1. **Click** on **File**. The File menu appears.

2. **Click** on **Preferences**. The Preferences submenu appears.

3. **Click** on **File Locations**. The File Locations dialog box opens.

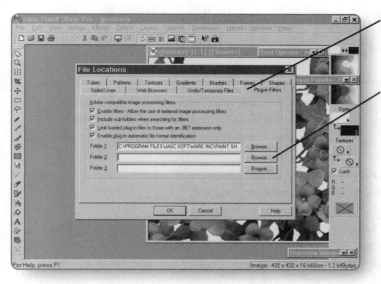

4. **Click** on the **Plug-in Filters tab**. The Plug-in Filters tab comes to the front.

5. **Click** on a **Browse button**. The Browse for Folder dialog box opens.

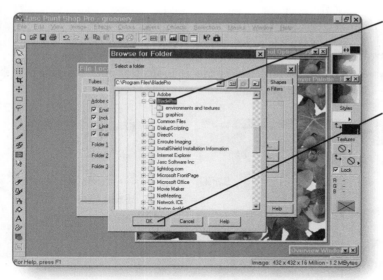

6. Locate and **click** on the **folder** where the filters are stored. The folder name becomes highlighted.

7. Click on **OK**. The file location displays in a Folder text box.

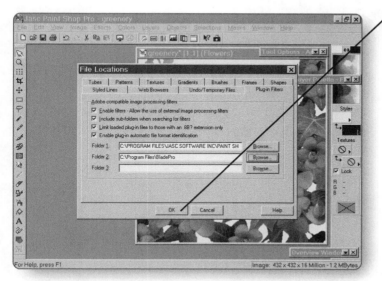

8. Click on **OK**. The File Locations dialog box closes.

Accessing Third-Party Filters

After installation of the filter and after telling Paint Shop Pro where to find the filters, new menu choices appear that allow you to access the plug-ins.

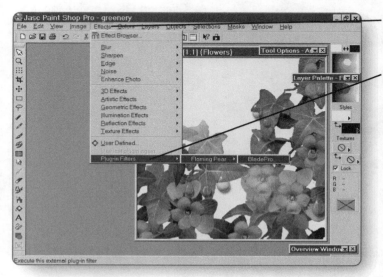

1. Click on **Effects**. The Effects menu appears.

The plug-in selections appear at the bottom of the Effects menu. The exact location varies with the individual filters.

Part II Review Questions

1. How many layers can a Paint Shop Pro image support? See *"Creating Layers"* in Chapter 7.

2. Which type of layer contains pixel-based information? See *"Creating Layers"* in Chapter 7.

3. Which palette displays each layer and its order in the layer stack? See *"Viewing Layers"* in Chapter 7.

4. When opacity is lower, is the resulting image more transparent or less transparent? See *"Changing Layer Opacity"* in Chapter 7.

5. Where do you modify the size of a picture tube? See *"Modifying Picture Tube Size"* in Chapter 8.

6. What Paint Shop Pro feature can you use to hide and display parts of a layer? See *"Forming Masks"* in Chapter 9.

7. What type of effect does a mask produce when using a grey value? See *"Creating a Simple Mask"* in Chapter 9.

8. What file name extension does Paint Shop Pro use to identify a mask? See *"Saving Masks"* in Chapter 9.

9. What's another word for third party filters? See *"Working with Third Party Filters"* in Chapter 10.

10. How do you tell Paint Shop Pro where you keep third-party filters? See *"Installing Third-Party Filters"* in Chapter 10.

PART III

Using Vector Graphics

11

Constructing Vector Objects

Up to this point, you've worked primarily with raster objects, which use pixels to store image information. The other type of Paint Shop Pro object, vector objects, on the other hand, are stored as separate items with information about each item's position, starting and ending points, width, color, and curve information. Working with vector objects gives you more flexibility in moving and editing the individual objects.

You'll find vector objects useful when designing logos and making line drawings. In this chapter, you'll learn how to:

- Create vector layers
- Draw vector shapes
- Draw vector lines

Creating a Vector Layer

An image can contain both raster objects and vector objects; however, vector objects and raster objects cannot be mixed on a layer. Vector objects must be on a vector layer. If you try to create a vector object on a raster layer, Paint Shop Pro automatically creates a vector layer for you. If the current layer is already a vector layer, Paint Shop Pro adds the new object to the current layer.

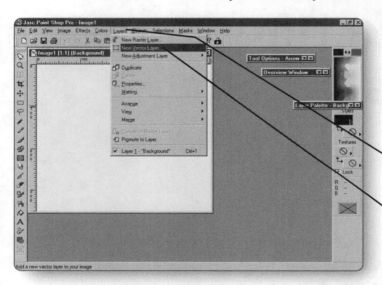

1. **Click** on **Layers**. The Layers menu appears.

2. **Click** on **New Vector Layer**. The Layer Properties dialog box opens.

The Layer Properties dialog box is the same for both vector and raster layers.

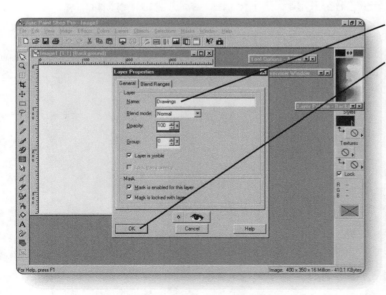

3. **Enter** a **name** for the layer.

4. **Click** on **OK**. The Layer Properties dialog box closes.

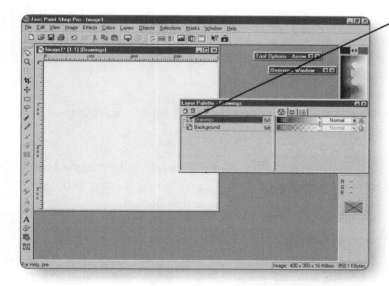

The Layer Palette displays the vector icon to the left of a vector layer button.

Drawing Vector Shapes

The Drawing, Preset Shape, and Text tools can create both vector and raster objects. Use the tools as vector tools on vector layers and raster tools on raster layers.

The paint tools are greyed out and unavailable when the current layer is a vector layer.

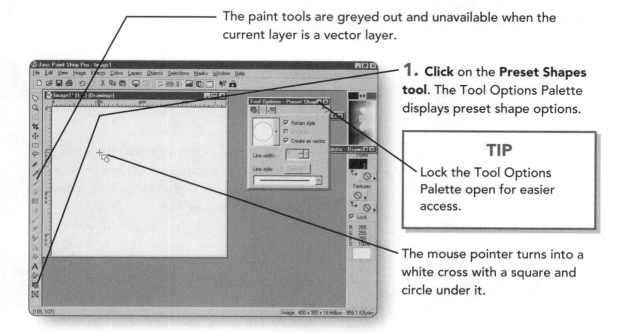

1. Click on the **Preset Shapes tool**. The Tool Options Palette displays preset shape options.

TIP
Lock the Tool Options Palette open for easier access.

The mouse pointer turns into a white cross with a square and circle under it.

Drawing a Rectangle

The rectangle and other shapes are available to assist you in drawing with accuracy.

1. Click the **Tool Selection button**. A list of preset shape tools appears.

2. Click on the **Rectangle tool**. The rectangle appears in the tool selection button.

For now, leave Retain style checked. We'll take a look at changing the style later in this chapter.

Make sure Create as vector is checked. If not, the rectangle draws as a raster object.

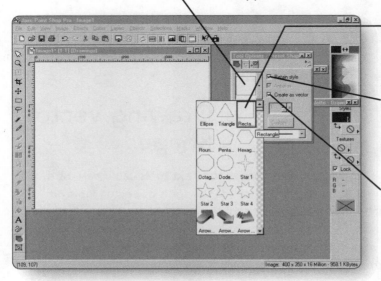

3. Position the **mouse** at the point you want the rectangle to begin.

4. Click and **drag** the **mouse** diagonally on the image. An outline of the rectangle appears as you draw.

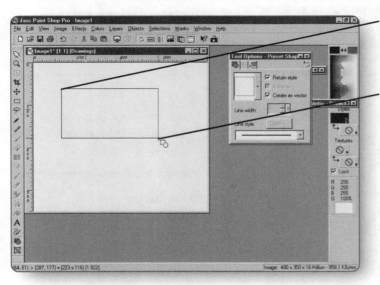

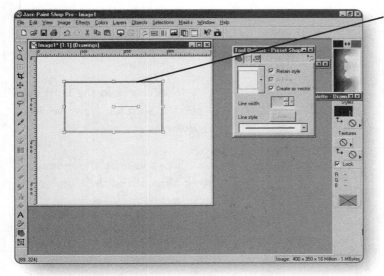

5. Release the **mouse button**. The rectangle appears on the image with handles surrounding it, indicating that the object is selected.

Drawing a Perfect Circle

Think you can't draw a perfectly round circle or a perfect square? You can with Paint Shop Pro! The secret is in the Shift key on your keyboard.

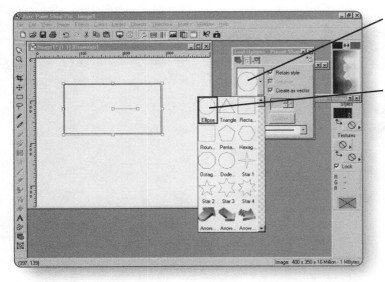

1. Click the **Tool Selection button**. A list of preset shape tools appears.

2. Click on the **Ellipse tool**. The ellipse shape appears in the tool selection button.

> **TIP**
> Select the rectangle tool to draw perfect squares.

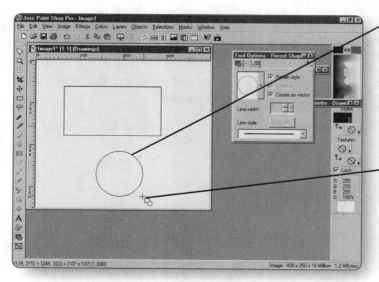

3. **Position** the **mouse** at the point you want the circle to begin.

4. **Press** and **hold** the **Shift key**. Keep the Shift key down while drawing.

5. **Click** and **drag** the **mouse**. An outline of the circle appears as you draw.

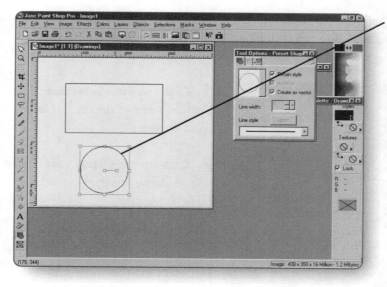

6. **Release** the **mouse button**. The circle appears on the image with handles surrounding it, indicating that the object is selected.

7. **Release** the **Shift key**.

Drawing Icons

There's much more to shapes than circles and squares. In fact, Paint Shop Pro includes almost 400 different shapes and objects, including things like traffic signs, talk balloons, buttons, and smiley faces! One of my favorites is the cat crossing sign!

Select and draw the icons exactly as you learned in "Drawing a Rectangle" earlier in this chapter.

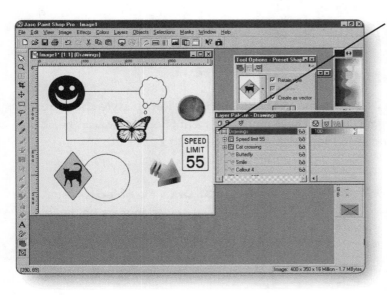

When the layer contains vector objects, a plus sign appears next to the icon. Click the plus sign next to the icon (it turns into a minus sign) to display the buttons of all the vector objects on the layer.

Drawing Shapes with Style

If, when choosing a preset shape, you leave the Retain style box checked, Paint Shop Pro draws the shape with the color and fill as displayed in the Tool Options Palette sample box. You can, however, choose your own stroke and fill for a preset shape.

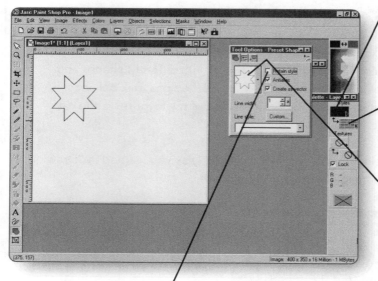

1. **Select** a **Stroke color**, **gradient**, or **pattern**. Remember that stroke style is the outline of the object, not the interior.

2. **Select** a **Fill color**, **gradient**, or **pattern**. The fill style is the interior of an object.

3. **Select** a **shape** from the Tool Options Palette. The selected shape appears in the sample box.

4. **Remove** the **check mark** √ in the **Retain style check box**. Removing the check mark tells Paint Shop Pro to use the colors and styles you selected in steps 1 and 2.

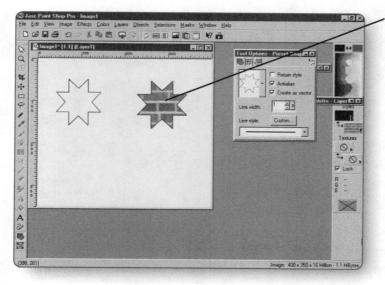

5. **Draw** the **object** as usual. The object appears on the image with the selected styles.

Adding Vector Lines

Use the Drawing tool to draw freehand lines, straight lines, Point to Point lines, and Bezier (pronounced bez'-zee-ay) curves. Bezier curves, created based on mathematical calculations, are beyond the scope of this book and are not covered.

Like the Shapes tool, when lines are drawn as vector objects, you'll be able to move and edit them without affecting the rest of the image objects.

Drawing Freehand

Use the Freehand Drawing tool just like you would a pencil to freely draw any shape you want. Be creative!

> **TIP**
>
> If you like to draw freehand, you may want to check into using an electronic, pressure-sensitive drawing tablet, which lets you draw with better precision. Paint Shop Pro supports most tablets on the market today.

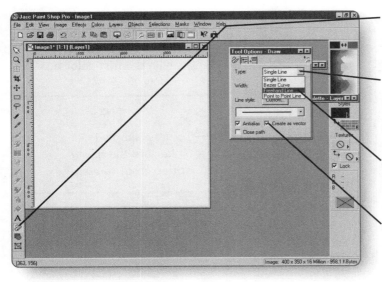

1. Click on the **Draw tool**. The mouse pointer displays a white cross with a pencil beside it.

2. From the Tool Options Palette, **click** on the **drop-down box** next to the Type: box. A list of line types appears.

3. Click on **Freehand Line**. Freehand Line appears in the Type: box.

4. If not already checked, **click** on **Create as vector**. A check mark appears in the box when the option is selected.

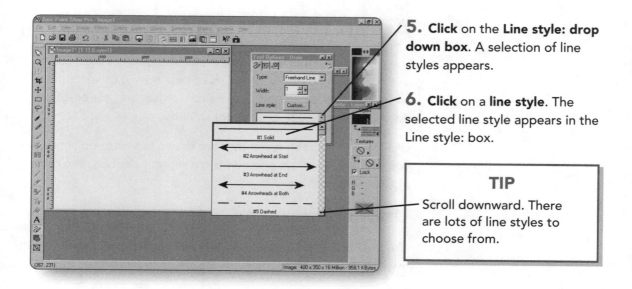

5. Click on the **Line style: drop down box**. A selection of line styles appears.

6. Click on a **line style**. The selected line style appears in the Line style: box.

TIP

Scroll downward. There are lots of line styles to choose from.

7. In the Width: box, **enter** a **line thickness value**. The higher the value, the heavier the line.

8. Select an **option** from the Stroke style box. This option cannot be null.

9. Select a **foreground stroke color**. The selected color appears in the first color box.

TIP

To draw simple lines, make sure the fill style option is set to null.

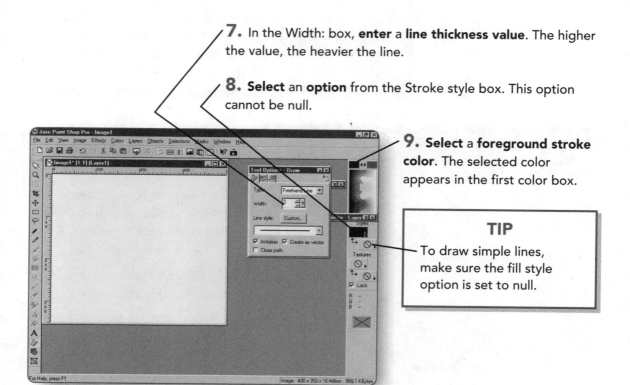

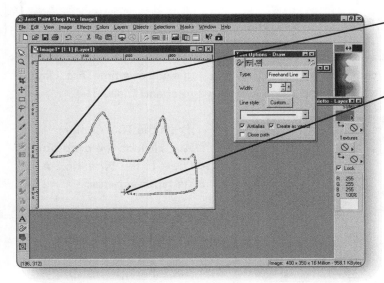

10. Position the **mouse pointer** on the image where you want the line to begin.

11. Click and **drag** the **mouse** along the path you want the line to take. Keeping the mouse button down, move up and down the image as desired. Paint Shop Pro draws an outline to show the width of the line.

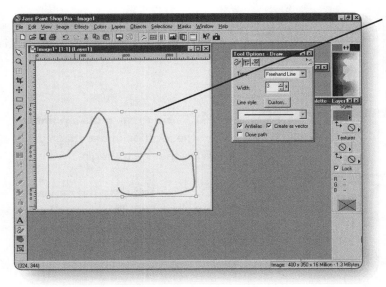

12. Release the **mouse button**. Paint Shop Pro draws the line based on the selected options. The line has selection handles surrounding it and the rotate bar in the center.

Drawing Single Lines

Drawing single lines is very similar to drawing freehand lines, except that you only draw one single line at a time, not a line with bends and corners as with a freehand line.

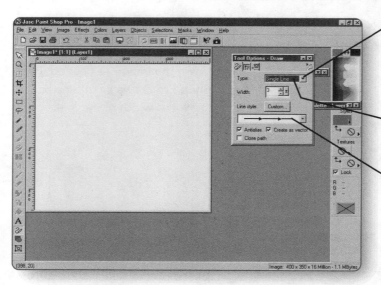

1. From the Tool Options Palette, **click** on the **drop-down box** next to the Type: box. A list of line types appears.

2. **Click** on **Single Line**. Single Line appears in the Type: box.

3. **Set** other **options** such as line style, thickness, and stroke.

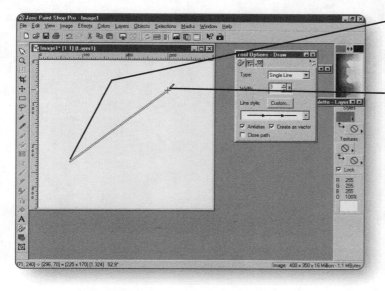

4. **Position** the **mouse pointer** at the location in the image you want the line to begin.

5. **Click** and **drag** the **mouse** to draw the line. The line can be horizontal, vertical, or at any angle.

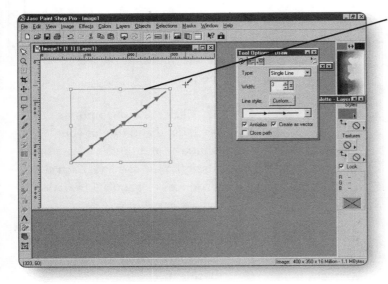

6. Release the **mouse button**. The single line appears on the image as a selected object.

Drawing Point to Point

Drawing a point-to-point line is like drawing a mixture of the freehand and single line styles. Each time you want to make a bend or turn, you create a node or a point of editing. In the next chapter, you'll learn how to edit nodes.

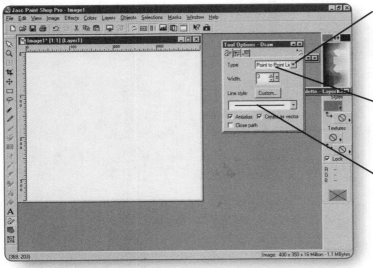

1. From the Tool Options Palette, **click** on the **drop-down box** next to the Type: box. A list of line types appears.

2. Click on **Point to Point Line**. Point to Point Line appears in the Type: box.

3. Set other **options** such as line style, thickness, and stroke.

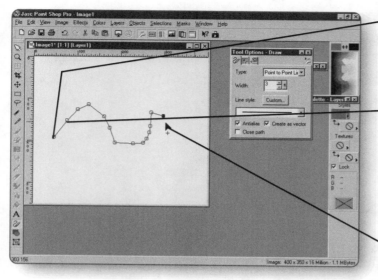

4. Position the **mouse pointer** at the location in the image where you want the line to begin.

5. Click the **mouse pointer** at each bend and turn of your image or at intervals across the straight part of a line. Each click produces a "handle," or node, on the line.

The mouse pointer resembles a black arrowhead with a plus sign beside it.

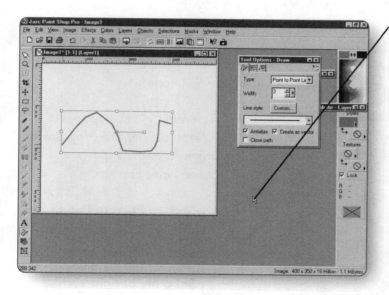

6. Click the mouse pointer anywhere **outside of** the **image** to complete the line. The completed line with color appears.

12

Editing Vectors

Because vector objects are independent elements, you can modify, move, reshape, or delete any of them without affecting the rest of the image. In this chapter, you'll learn how to:

- Select vector objects
- Move, resize, rotate, and flip vector objects
- Delete vector objects
- Edit vector nodes
- Arrange, align, and distribute space between objects
- Convert vector objects to raster images

Selecting Vector Objects

Before you can modify any vector object, the object(s) must be selected. Only objects on the active layer can be selected at any one time.

Selecting with the Object Selector

Paint Shop Pro provides a tool for working with vector objects called the Object Selector. The Object Selector is available only when the current active layer is a vector layer.

Selecting Individual Objects

Use the Object Selector to choose which objects you want selected.

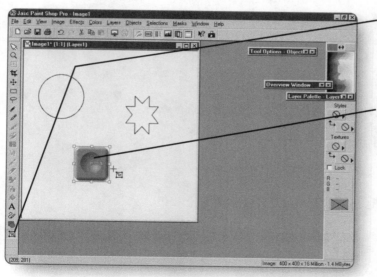

1. **Click** on the **Object Selector**. The mouse pointer turns into a white cross with a boxed arrowhead beside it.

2. **Click** on the **object**. Selection handles appear around the object.

If the object is filled in the center, you can click anywhere on the object to select it; however, if the object has no fill, you've got to smile, hold your mouth just right, and click on the outline of the image.

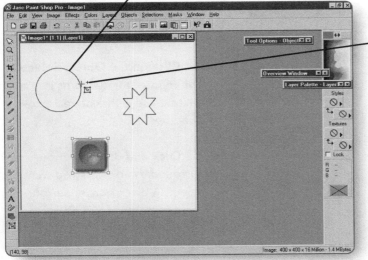

TIP

Hold down the Shift key and click to select additional objects (the mouse pointer displays a plus sign), or hold down the Ctrl key and click to deselect objects (the mouse pointer displays a minus sign).

To deselect all objects, choose Selections, Select None or press Ctrl+D.

Drawing around Objects

Another method of selecting objects with the Object Selector tool is to draw a boundary box around the objects you want to select. Paint Shop Pro selects all objects *completely* surrounded by the boundary box.

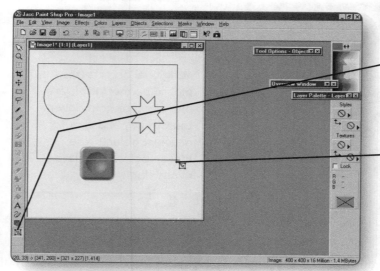

1. **Click** on the **Object Selector**. The mouse pointer turns into a white cross with a boxed arrow head beside it.

2. **Click** and **drag** the **mouse** to surround the objects you want to select. A black border surrounds the perimeter of the objects.

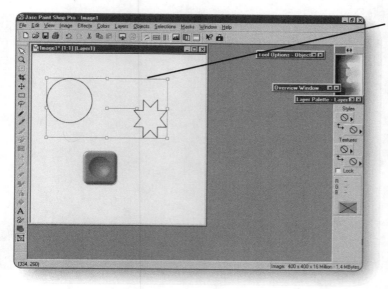

3. **Release** the **mouse button**. All objects completely surrounded appear with selection handles.

In this example, the button wasn't completely surrounded so it isn't included in the selection.

Selecting in the Layer Palette

An optional method to select objects is to select them from the Layer Palette.

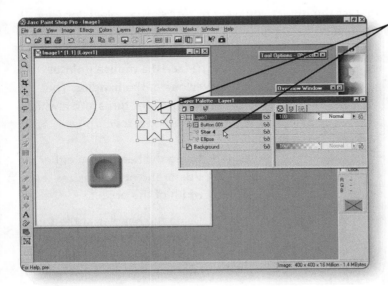

1. On the Layer Palette, **click** on the **object name**. The object becomes selected.

TIP

If you can't see the objects, click on the plus sign next to the layer name. The layer expands to display all objects.

2. If desired, **hold** down the **Shift key** and **click** on additional **layer objects**.

To deselect objects, choose Selections, Select None.

Resizing a Vector Object

Change the size of a vector object.

1. Select the **object** you want to resize. The object appears with selection handles.

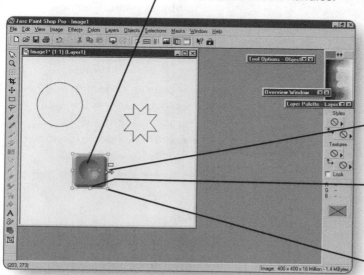

2. Place the **mouse pointer over** one of the **handles**. The mouse pointer turns into a white, two-headed arrow.

- Using the handles on either side of the object resizes the width of the object.

- Using the handles at the top or bottom of the object resizes the height of the object.

- Using one of the corner handles resizes both width and height at the same time.

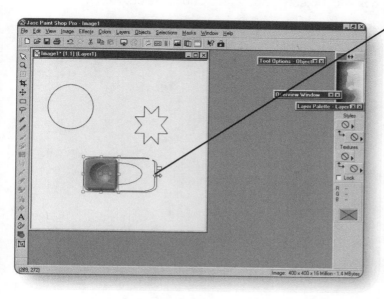

3. Click and **drag** the **handle**. An outline of the object indicates the new size.

4. Release the **mouse button**. The object resizes.

Deleting an Object

You can easily delete unwanted objects from your image.

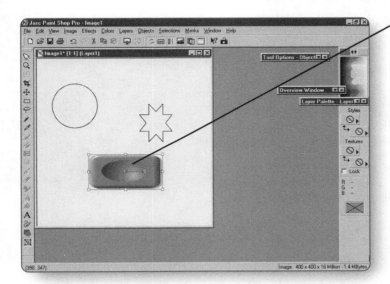

1. **Select** the **object** you want to delete. The object appears with selection handles.

2. **Press** the **Delete key**. The object disappears.

TIP

Don't forget! If you make a mistake and delete the wrong object, click on Edit, Undo.

Rotating a Vector Object

Freely rotate any vector object to any angle.

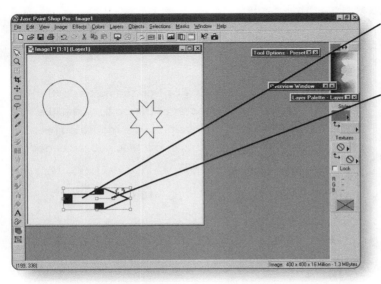

1. **Select** the **object** you want to rotate. The object appears with selection handles.

2. **Position** the **mouse pointer** over the **rotation handle** in the middle of the object. The mouse pointer turns into two curved arrows.

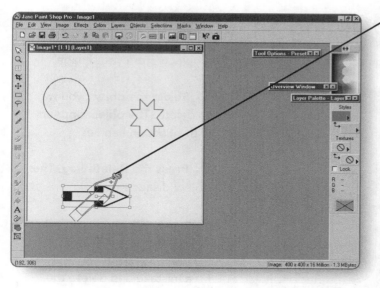

3. **Click** and **drag** the **rotation handle**. An outline of the image rotation appears.

4. **Release** the **mouse button**. The image moves to the new rotation.

Moving a Vector Object

If an object is not in the position you desire, move it easily using your mouse. Moving vector objects is a little different than moving raster objects. With raster objects you use the mover tool, but you don't use the mover tool with vector objects.

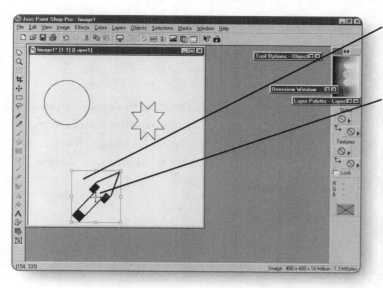

1. **Select** the **object** you want to move. The object appears with selection handles.

2. **Position** the mouse in the center of the object, over the move box. The mouse pointer turns into a black, four-headed arrow.

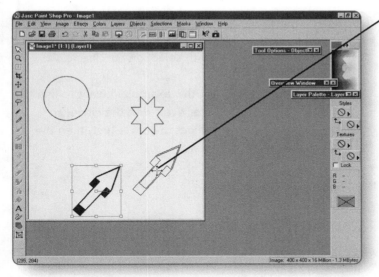

3. **Click** and **drag** the **object** to the new position. An outline of the object indicates the move.

4. **Release** the **mouse button**. The object moves to the new position.

Arranging Multiple Objects

Paint Shop Pro includes several very handy features for working with multiple objects. You'll find features to line up object edges, to create equal spaces between objects, to make objects equal size, and even to combine multiple objects into one.

The secret to working with most multiple object features is the order of selection. The object you select *first* is considered the "base" object—the one the others will adjust to. This applies to alignment, spacing, and resizing features.

Aligning Objects Together

Suppose you have two or more objects and you want them to be at the same vertical position on the image, or you want one (or more) of the objects to be centered in another. Well, you could use your mouse to move the objects, but it's very difficult to visually align them. Instead, let the alignment feature do the guesswork for you.

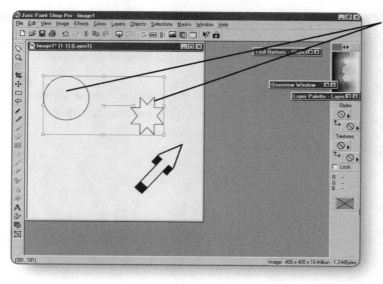

1. Select the **objects** you want to line up. The objects appear with selection handles.

In this example, I want to line the star even with the circle, so I select the circle first, then the star.

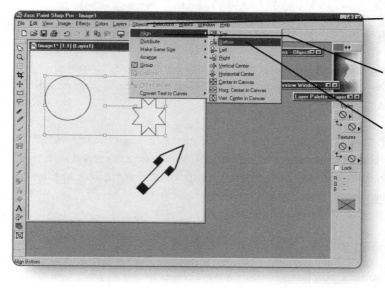

2. Click on **Objects**. The Objects appears.

3. Click on **Align**. The Align submenu appears.

4. Click on an **alignment** option. The objects realign together.

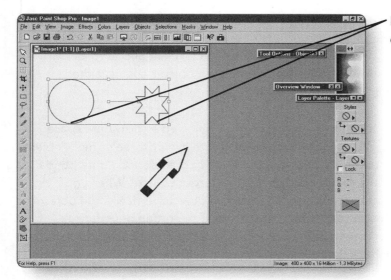

In this example, the bottom edges of the star and circle align.

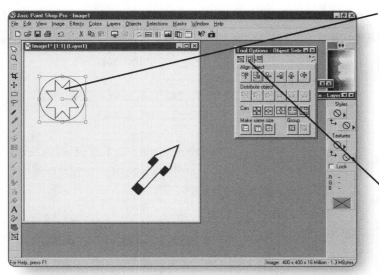

Some alignment choices may take two steps. In this example, to get the star in the center of the circle, the alignment is accomplished in two steps. First they were aligned Vertical Center, then Horizontal Center.

TIP

Optionally, make alignment choices from the Object Alignment tab on the Tool Options Palette.

Distributing Space between Objects

Any time you have multiple objects, Paint Shop Pro can distribute the space between the objects evenly, either horizontally or vertically.

At least three objects must be selected to distribute space evenly. If you choose to distribute evenly three or more objects horizontally, the objects closest to the left and right boundaries of the group become the two target objects. When you distribute evenly three or more objects vertically, the objects closest to the top and bottom of the group boundaries become the target objects. The distance between these target objects determines the spacing of the objects in between them.

1. **Select** the **objects** you want to distribute. The objects appear in a group surrounded by selection handles.

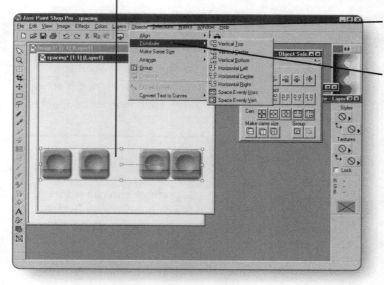

2. **Click** on **Objects**. The Objects menu appears.

3. **Click** on **Distribute**. The Distribute submenu appears.

There are a number of ways to distribute space evenly. Here are six of them:

- Distribute Vertical Top: spaces objects evenly between the top edges of the top and bottom targets.

- Distribute Vertical Center: spaces objects evenly between the centers of the top and bottom targets.

- Distribute Vertical Bottom: spaces objects evenly between the bottom edges of the top and bottom targets.

- Distribute Horizontal Left: spaces objects evenly between the left edges of the left and right targets.

- Distribute Horizontal Center: spaces objects evenly between the centers of the left and right targets.

- Distribute Horizontal Right: spaces objects evenly between the right edges of the left and right targets.

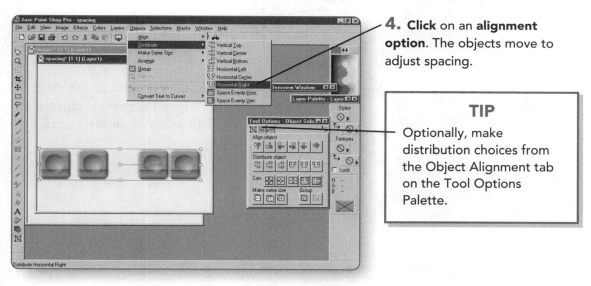

4. **Click** on an **alignment option**. The objects move to adjust spacing.

TIP

Optionally, make distribution choices from the Object Alignment tab on the Tool Options Palette.

Grouping Multiple Objects

Grouping multiple objects is like linking the objects together for easier manipulation. Grouped objects can be ungrouped at any time.

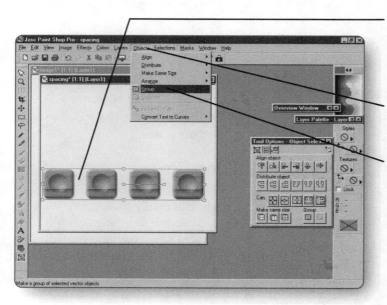

1. **Select** the **objects** you want to group together. Selection handles appear around the objects.

2. **Click** on **Objects**. The Objects menu appears.

3. **Click** on **Group**. Paint Shop Pro joins the multiple objects into a single selected object.

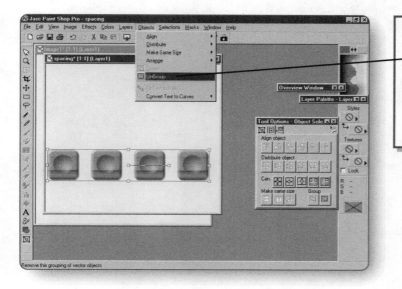

TIP

To ungroup an object back to the original multiple objects, select the object, then click on Objects, Ungroup.

Altering Vector Properties

Even after creating a vector object, you can change its line style, color, style, thickness, and other properties. You can even give the vector object a specific name.

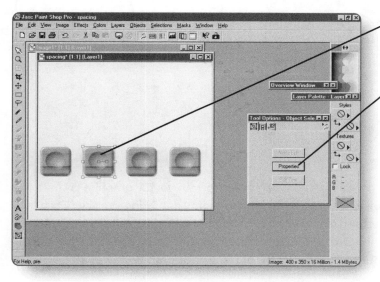

1. **Select** the **object** you want to modify. The object appears with selection handles.

2. On the Tool Options Palette, **click** on **Properties**. The Vector Properties dialog box opens.

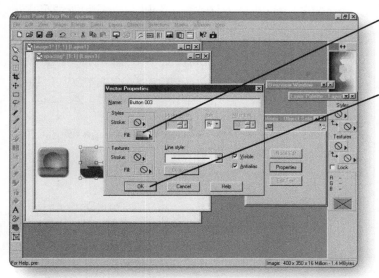

3. **Modify** any desired **options**. The changes reflect on the object as you make them.

4. **Click** on **OK**. The Vector Properties dialog box closes.

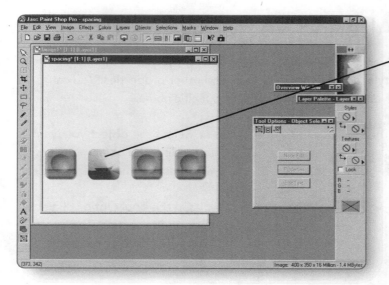

Editing Nodes

A handy feature when working with vector graphics is the ability to create new shapes from an existing graphic. Each vector graphic has a form of control points called *nodes* stored along the outline or path of the object. By adjusting the nodes, you change the shape of the vector graphic.

Control the overall shape of an object by using Paint Shop Pro's Node Editing feature. Not all vector preset shapes can be easily node edited. For example, the 3D arrows, buttons, and traffic signs cannot be edited without ungrouping them.

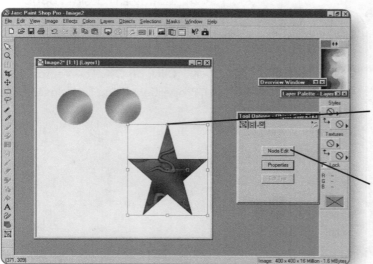

1. **Select** the **image** to edit. The image appears with selection handles.

2. From the Tool Options Palette, **click** on **Node Edit**. Nodes surround the image at and in between each corner of the object.

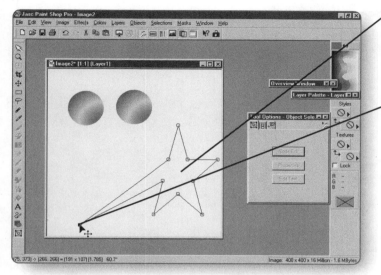

While in Node Edit mode, any fill colors, gradients, or patterns on the selected object temporarily disappear.

3. Click and **drag a node** to a different area. The node stretches as you drag the mouse, thereby reshaping the image.

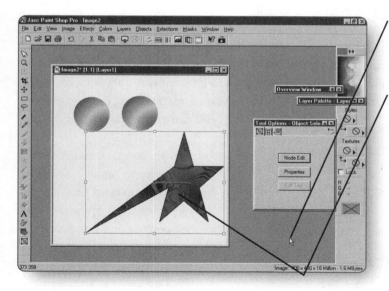

Click outside of the image to close Node Edit mode and return to vector object selection.

After the image is reshaped and you've left Node Edit mode, the color and fill are reapplied to the selected object.

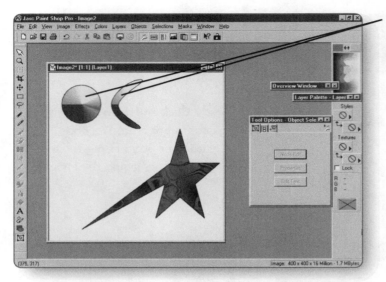

Node editing allows you to reshape objects in many imaginative ways.

Converting Vector Objects to Raster

The main drawback to vector objects is that you cannot apply effects and filters to vector images. But, don't give up hope! Paint Shop Pro includes a feature to convert vector layers with all its objects to raster objects on a raster layer. From there, you can apply effects.

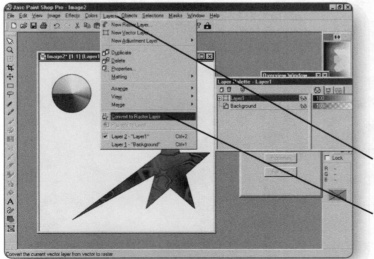

Another reason to convert a vector image to raster is file size. A raster file could be smaller than a vector file if the image has a lot of vectors and many areas of uniform color.

1. Click on **Layers**. The Layers menu appears.

2. Click on **Convert to Raster Layer**. The layer becomes a raster layer.

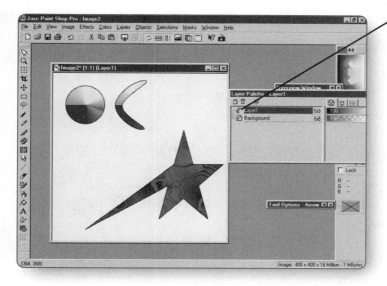

The Layer Palette reflects the change to a raster layer.

NOTE

If you plan on saving the image as a .GIF, a .JPEG, or any format other than .PSP, Paint Shop Pro automatically converts the image to a raster image.

Part III Review Questions

1. What type of information is stored in a vector object? See *"Constructing Vector Objects"* in Chapter 11.

2. Can vector objects and raster objects be mixed on the same layer? See *"Creating a Vector Layer"* in Chapter 11.

3. Which tools can you use to create a vector object? See *"Drawing Vector Shapes"* in Chapter 11.

4. When drawing a shape, what does the Retain style check box do? See *"Drawing Shapes with Style"* in Chapter 11.

5. What are the four types of lines you can draw with the Drawing tool? See *"Adding Vector Lines"* in Chapter 11.

6. Why can you move, modify, reshape, or delete vector objects without affecting the rest of the image? See *"Editing Vectors"* in Chapter 12.

7. What must you do to a vector object before you can modify it? See *"Selecting Vector Objects"* in Chapter 12.

8. Where do you place the mouse pointer when you want to resize a selected vector object? See *"Resizing a Vector Object"* in Chapter 12.

9. Should you use the Mover tool to move a vector object? See *"Moving a Vector Object"* in Chapter 12.

10. Can grouped objects be ungrouped? See *"Grouping Multiple Objects"* in Chapter 12.

PART IV

Working With Text

13

Generating Text

We've been told that a picture is worth a thousand words, and Paint Shop Pro has certainly proved that statement to be true over and over. But, sometimes you just have to spell it out. You can create text with Paint Shop Pro's text feature. In this chapter, you'll learn how to:

- Create text objects
- Work with the Text Entry dialog box
- Edit text
- Change text appearance
- Move or resize a text object

Selecting the Text Tool

Create raster or vector text with the Text tool.

1. **Click** on the **Text tool**. The mouse pointer resembles a cross with the letter A beside it.

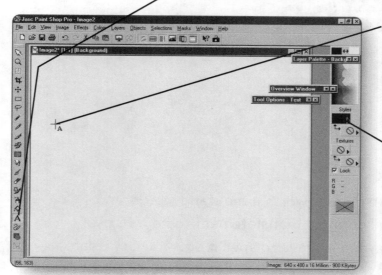

2. **Click** the **mouse pointer** on the image where you want the text to appear. The Text Entry dialog box appears.

> ### NOTE
> Both Style boxes cannot be set at Null to generate text. There must be a color, gradient, or pattern selection in at least one of the two boxes.

Understanding the Text Entry Dialog Box

The Text Entry dialog box is one of the busiest dialog boxes in Paint Shop Pro. Not only do you enter your text, but you select a font and size, style, alignment, kerning, and leading options as well as determining what method you want Paint Shop Pro to use when placing the text on your image.

Entering Text

Entering Paint Shop Pro text is different than using a word processor. The text doesn't wrap around to the next line. You need to tell Paint Shop Pro when you want the text to begin on a new line.

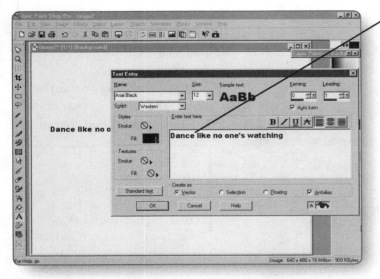

1. **Type** the **text** you want. The text appears in the Enter text here box.

2. **Press Enter** if you have more text to add under the first line. The insertion point drops to the next line.

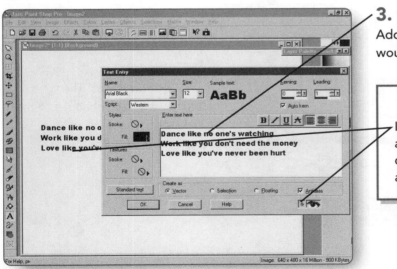

3. **Type** the **additional text**. Add as many lines of text as you would like.

TIP

If the text doesn't also appear on your image, click on the Auto Proof arrow.

Font

Choose from any font on your machine.

1. Click and **drag across** the **text** in the Enter text here box. The text appears highlighted.

TIP

If you don't want to change font for all the text, highlight only the text you want to change.

---

2. Click on the **Font drop-down list**. A selection of fonts appears.

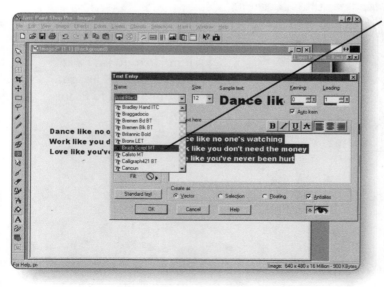

3. Click on a **font**. The highlighted text changes to the new font.

Font Size

Choose a font size. As a rule of measurement, when printing, a 72-point font is 1 inch tall; however, when viewing text on a computer screen, the sizes vary depending on the screen resolution.

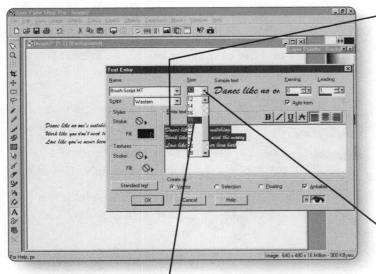

1. **Click** and **drag across** the **text** in the Enter text here box. The text appears highlighted.

TIP

If you don't want to change size for all the text, highlight only the text you want to change.

---

2. **Click** on the **Size: drop down list**. A selection of font sizes appears.

3. **Click** on a **size**. The highlighted text changes to the new size.

Font Attributes

Paint Shop Pro provides text enhancements such as bolding, underlining, italics, or strikethrough on any portion of your text.

1. Click and **drag across** the **text** you want to enhance. The text appears highlighted.

2. Click on one or more of the four available **options**. The text takes the selected attributes.

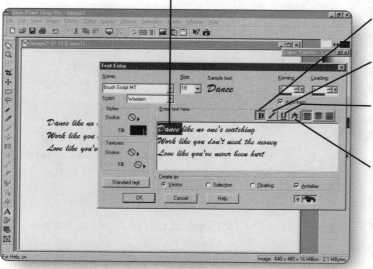

- **Bold**: makes the text characters darker and thicker.

- *Italics*: makes the text characters slightly slanted.

- <u>Underline</u>: provides a line under each character and space.

- ~~Strikethrough~~: provides a line through the middle of each character and space.

Text Alignment

Alignment determines how multiple lines of text line up with each other.

1. Click an **Alignment button**. The alignment option applies to the text object. Text alignment results appear on the image, but not in the Text Entry dialog box.

> **NOTE**
> Alignment settings affect the entire text object and cannot be changed for individual lines or words.

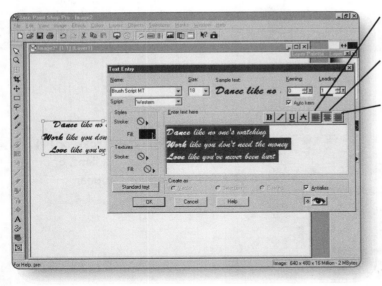

- Left: The left edges of each text line align together.

- Center: Each line centers to the one above it.

- Right: The right edges of each text line align together.

Style

In Chapter 4, "Understanding the Color Palette," you discovered the options available for choosing colors, gradients, patterns, and textures. When working with text objects, you have those same options available, except that the options apply to only the text, not the rest of the image. Since text styles apply to the entire text object, you don't have the option of applying one style to part of the text and another style to a different part of the text. To accomplish that, you need to create two separate text objects.

The stroke style is the color of the edge around the letters, while the fill style is the center or body of the letters.

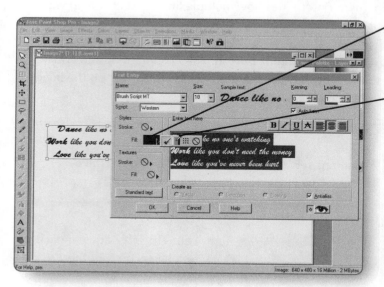

1. **Click** and **hold** the mouse button down on a **Style button**. The optional styles appear.

2. **Click** on the **color**, **gradient**, or **pattern button**. The current selection appears on the button.

TIP

You cannot choose Null for both the stroke and fill. Choosing Null for the fill creates outlined text.

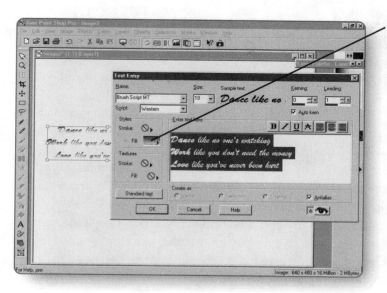

3. **Click** on the **Stroke** or **Fill button**. Color, gradient, or pattern options appear.

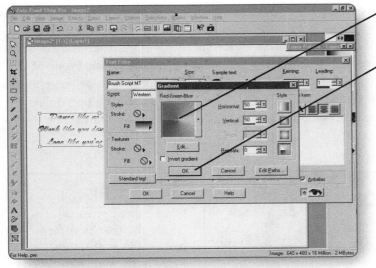

4. **Select** from the **options** as discussed in Chapter 4.

5. **Click** on **OK**. The Fill or Stroke button reflects your choices.

Kerning and Leading

Kerning refers to the spacing between letters while leading refers to the space between lines of text.

In most cases, I suggest you let Paint Shop Pro make the kerning decision by leaving Auto kern checked. However, if you have multiple lines of text, you may want to adjust the leading.

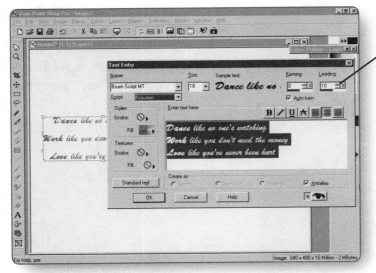

1. **Click** on a **leading** arrow. Click on the up arrow to increase the space between the text lines or the down arrow to decrease the spacing.

Text Type

Now comes the most important factor in the Text Entry dialog box—the text type. Paint Shop Pro provides three types of text objects: vector, floating, or selection. The type you choose determines what kind of editing you can do. The text object type cannot be changed once the text object appears on the image.

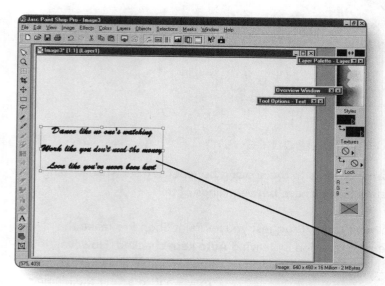

TIP

I find it most practical to create the text as vector text, until I'm absolutely sure I'm finished with the placement and appearance of the object. Then I convert the vector layer to a raster layer and apply effects.

● Vector: Creates the text as a vector object and adds a new vector layer, if necessary. Remember that vector objects are easily moved or edited, but effects cannot be added.

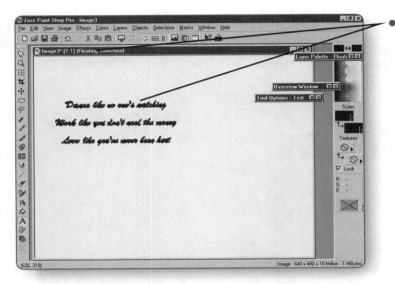

● Floating: Creates the text as a selection that floats above the current layer. The text is moveable and effects can be applied, but neither the text nor the style can be modified. After effects are applied, you can "defloat" the text, which places it on the next lowest raster layer. After the text is placed on the raster layer, it can no longer be easily moved.

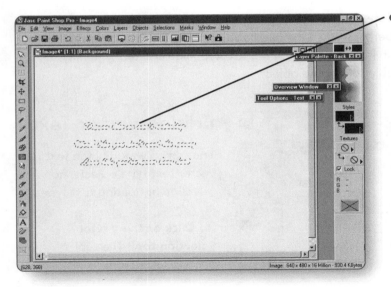

● Selection: Creates the text as an empty selection on the current layer. The text cannot be moved or edited, although you can apply a few effects to the text.

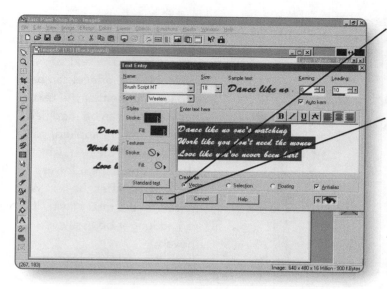

1. **Click** on an **option**. The option appears selected. The image does not reflect text type options.

2. **Click** on **OK**. The Text Entry dialog box closes.

Editing Text

Suppose that after you created your text, you see a problem—perhaps you misspelled a word, or you want a different font or style. Depending on the text type you created, you may be able to edit the object.

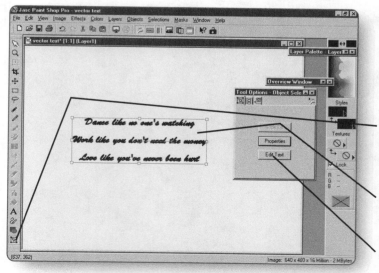

Editing Vector Text

You can only modify the text on vector text type objects, not selection or floating text types.

1. **Click** on the **Vector Selection tool**. The tool becomes selected.

2. **Click** on the **text object**. The object becomes selected.

3. On the Tool Options Palette, **click** on **Edit Text**. The Text Entry dialog box opens.

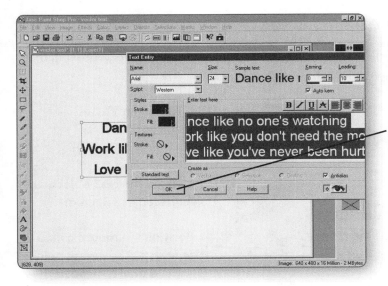

4. Edit the **text**, the **font**, **size**, **attributes**, **alignment**, **leading**, or **style**. The text in the preview box reflects the changes, as does the text on the screen.

5. Click on **OK**. The Text Entry dialog box closes.

Editing Floating and Selection Styles

Although you cannot easily edit the font size or the actual text on floating or selection type text, you can edit the style with the Paintbrush.

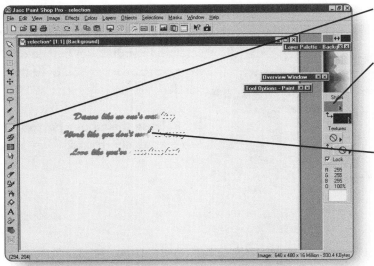

1. Click on the **Paintbrush tool**. The tool becomes selected.

2. Select a foreground **color**, **gradient**, or **pattern**. The selection appears in the foreground button.

3. Paint over the **text**. Because the text is selected, the paint will not go over the boundaries of the selection. (See...you really *can* color within the lines!)

Resizing a Text Object

Only vector type text can be resized. Resize vector text in the same manner you resize any vector object.

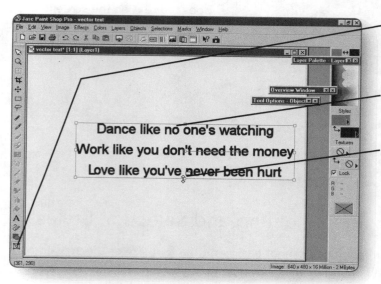

1. **Click** on the **Vector Selection tool**. The tool becomes selected.

2. **Click** on the **text object**. The object becomes selected.

3. **Position** the **mouse** over a resize handle. The mouse pointer turns into a double-headed arrow.

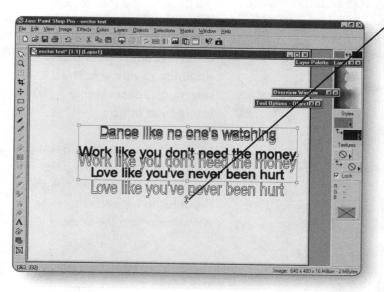

4. **Click** and **drag** any of the selection **handles**. An outline of the text appears as you drag the handle.

5. **Release** the **mouse button**. The text object resizes.

Moving Text

All three text types can be moved...but with totally different results.

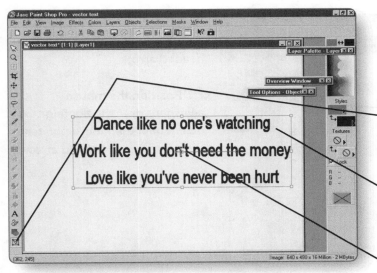

Moving Vector Text

Move vector text in the same manner as moving any vector object.

1. Click on the **Vector Selection tool**. The tool becomes selected.

2. Click on the **Vector text object**. The object becomes selected.

3. Position the **mouse** over the center move box. The mouse pointer turns into a four-headed arrow.

4. Click and **drag** the **text** to a new position. An outline of the text appears.

5. Release the **mouse button**. The text moves to the new position.

Moving Floating Text

Floating text is raster-style text but can be moved anywhere on the image as long as the text is still floating and not yet merged into a raster layer.

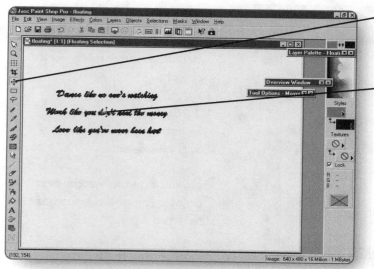

1. **Click** on the **Mover tool**. The mouse pointer resembles a four-headed arrow.

2. **Position** the **mouse** anywhere over the floating text object until the mouse pointer turns into a four-headed arrow.

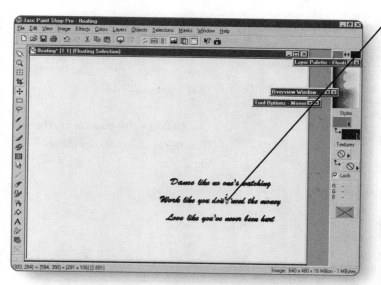

3. **Click** and **drag** the **text** to a new position. The text moves as you drag the mouse.

4. **Release** the **mouse button**. The text remains in the new position and remains selected.

TIP

To deselect floating text, (which also defloats the text), choose Selections, Select None or press Ctrl+D.

Moving Selection Text

Moving selection text is quite different from moving the other two types. When you move selection text, the fill color remains underneath the moved selection. In fact, moving selection text just a tiny bit can give the effect of 3D text.

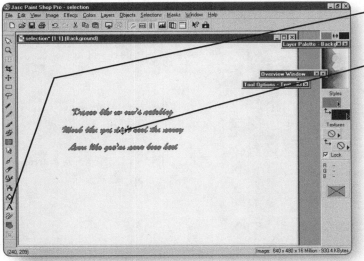

1. **Click** on the **Text tool**. The tool appears selected.

2. **Position** the **mouse pointer** over the text, making sure the mouse pointer is a four-headed arrow.

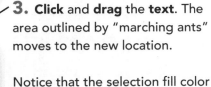

3. **Click** and **drag** the **text**. The area outlined by "marching ants" moves to the new location.

Notice that the selection fill color remains.

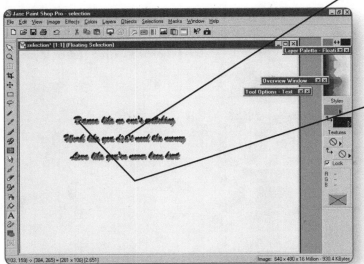

4. **Release** the **mouse button**. The selection moves to the new position.

TIP

To deselect the selection text, choose Selections, Select None or press Ctrl+D.

Defloating Text

Once you've placed the floating text where you want it, you'll need to defloat it to the next lowest raster layer.

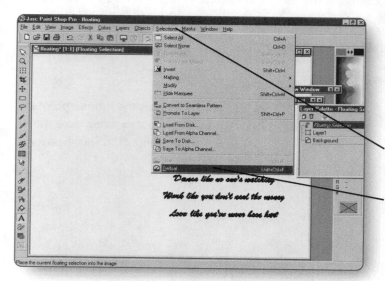

If you want special effects applied to the text only, apply the effect before you defloat it. Once you defloat the text, any effects applied will apply to the entire layer.

1. Click on **Selections**. The Selections menu appears.

2. Click on **Defloat**. A warning message appears.

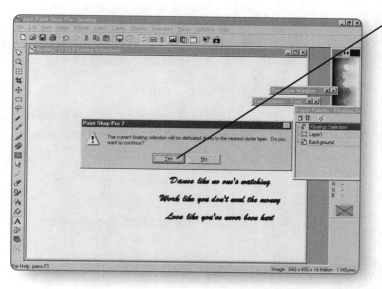

3. Click on **Yes**. The text no longer floats above the layers and merges with a raster layer.

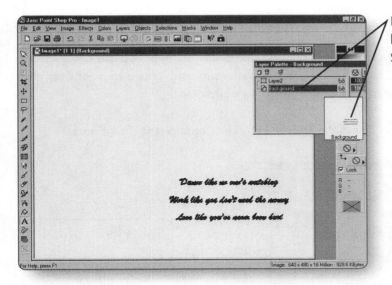

Notice that the Layer Palette no longer displays "Floating Selection."

Deleting Text Objects

The method to delete text objects depends on the type of object.

Deleting Vector Text

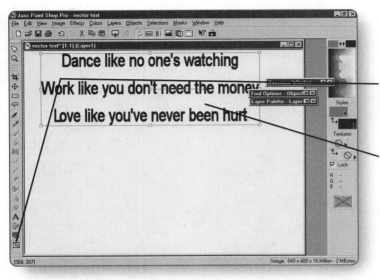

Delete vector text in the same manner as you would delete any vector object.

1. Click on the **Vector Selection tool**. The tool becomes selected.

2. Click on the **text object**. The object becomes selected.

3. Press the **Delete key**. Paint Shop Pro deletes the text.

Deleting Floating Text

As long as the floating text is still floating, you can easily delete it. If the floating text is defloated, you'll need to paint over the area with a desired background color.

1. **Press** the **Delete key**. The floating text disappears.

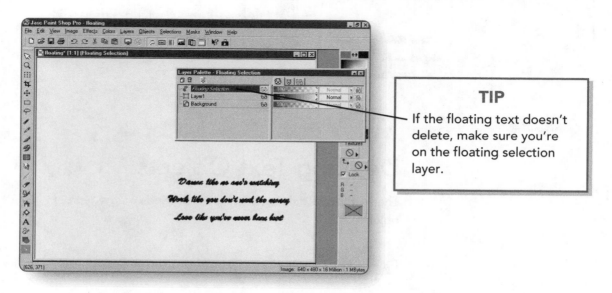

TIP

If the floating text doesn't delete, make sure you're on the floating selection layer.

Deleting Selection Text

Deleting selection text is a little different because it isn't really a text object; it's a selection.

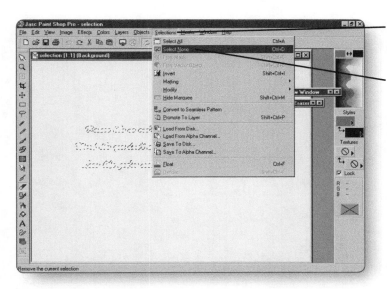

1. Click on **Selections**. The Selections menu appears.

2. Click on **Select None**. The area outlined with "marching ants" disappears.

This method works only if the selection text has not been painted or moved.

TIP

If the selection text has been painted or moved, deselect the text, then paint over the entire image with your desired background color.

14

Creating Text Effects

This chapter's a little different from the chapters you've seen so far. By following this book, you've learned how to work with objects, tubes, effects, and text. This chapter shows you how you can combine some of those Paint Shop Pro features to create some spectacular text effects. In this chapter, you'll learn how to:

- Add special effects to text
- Color individual letters
- Use picture tubes to fill text
- Combine special effects
- Create text around shapes

Adding Effects to Your Text

Adding special effects to text objects is a lot of fun—you're limited only by your imagination!

Using 3D Cutouts

Give your text a three-dimensional stenciled effect with the 3D Cutout effect.

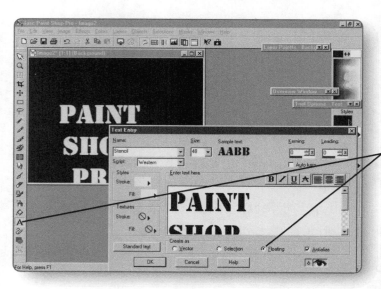

TIP

This effect is especially cool if used with a very dark or black background.

1. Using the Text tool, **create** some **text**. Make the text a "floating" type.

TIP

Make the text color (both stroke and fill) something bright, perhaps white or yellow, and use a large, bold font. In this example, I used a yellow Stencil 48 point font.

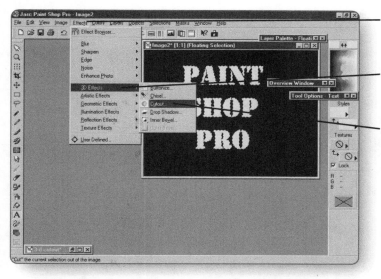

2. **Click** on **Effects**. The Effects menu appears.

3. **Click** on **3D Effects**. The 3D Effects menu appears.

4. **Click** on **Cutout**. The Cutout dialog box opens.

5. **Select** the following **options** from the Cutout dialog box:

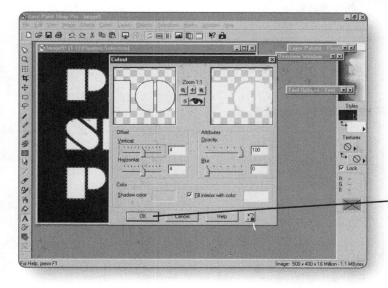

- Vertical offset = 4

- Horizontal offset = 4

- Opacity = 100

- Blur = 0

- Shadow color = Gray

- Interior Color = White

6. **Click** on **OK**. The Cutout dialog box closes and the text takes on a stencil effect.

TIP

Press Ctrl+D or choose Selections, Select None to deselect the text.

Filling Text with Tubes

Create text and fill it with any picture tube image. This works best with smaller picture tubes.

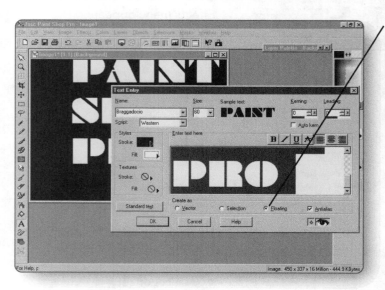

1. Using the Text tool, **create** some **text**. Use a large heavy font and make the text a "floating" type.

2. Click on the **Picture Tube tool**. The tool becomes selected.

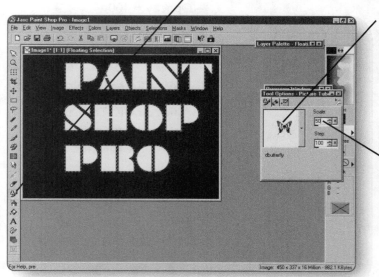

3. From the Tool Options Palette, **select** a **picture tube,** preferably a small one. In the example shown, I'm using a collection of small butterflies.

TIP

If the image you want to use is larger than you need, decrease the scale.

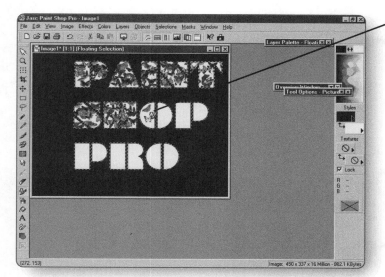

4. Using the Picture Tube tool, **paint over** the **text letters**. Because the text is selected, the tube images do not extend beyond the letters of text.

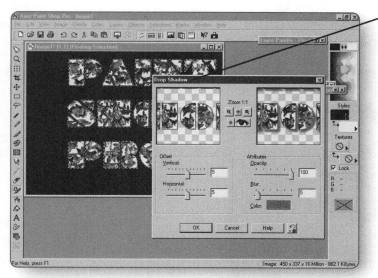

5. Optionally, **apply** an **effect**. Select your effects from the Effects Browser or the Effects menu.

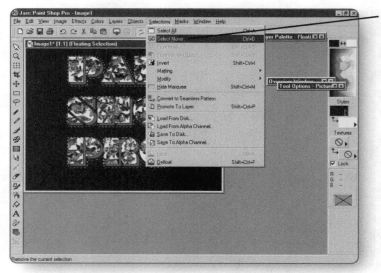

6. Deselect the **text** by choosing Selections, Select None or pressing Ctrl+D. The "marching ants" disappear.

Coloring Individual Letters

A colorful way to present your text is to individually color each letter of the text.

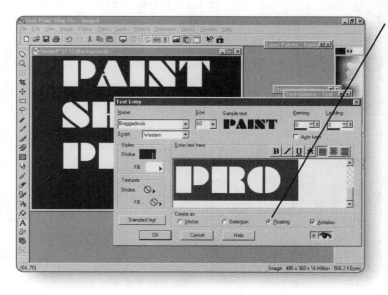

1. Using the Text tool, **create** some **text**. Make the text a "floating" type.

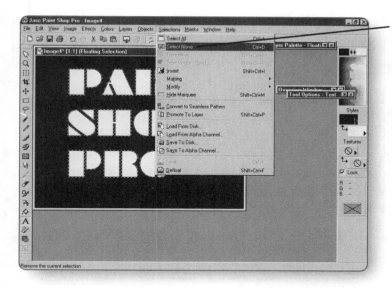

2. Deselect the **text** by choosing Selections, Select None.

Now we need to select each letter individually and apply a style to it.

3. Click on the **Magic Wand tool**. We'll use it to select the individual letters.

4. Click on the first **letter** you want to modify. The letter becomes selected.

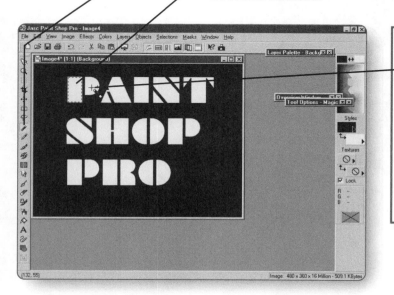

TIP

If you want to select additional letters, or in the example shown where the letter is actually made of multiple pieces, hold down the Shift key and click on the additional selections with the Magic Wand.

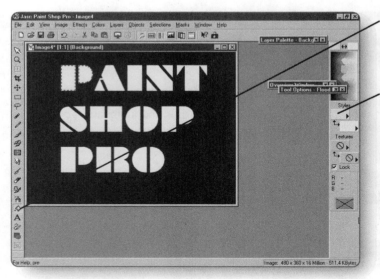

5. **Select** the **Flood Fill tool**. We'll use the flood fill to quickly fill each letter with color.

6. **Select** a **color** from the foreground style button. You could also choose patterns or gradients.

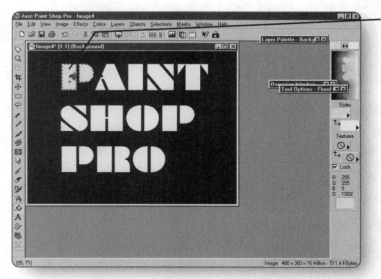

7. **Click** on the **selection** to flood fill the selected letter. The letter takes on the new color.

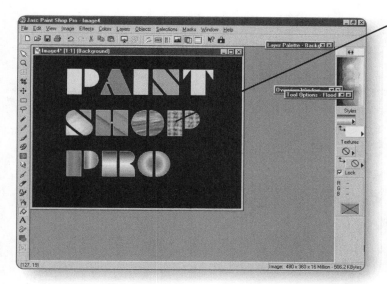

8. **Repeat steps 3 through 7** for each letter of your text.

Creating Reflection Magic

This is one of my favorites. You just have to try it to see the effect! Again, this looks best against a dark background.

1. Using the Text tool, **create** some **text** with the following guidelines.

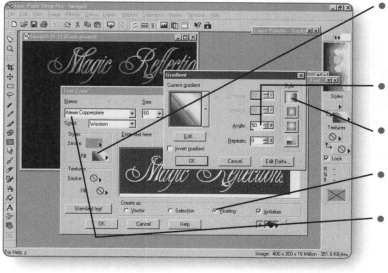

- Set the fill pattern to a gradient type. This is especially pretty with the gradient called Sunset.

- Set the gradient angle at 50 degrees.

- Set the gradient type to Linear.

- Make the text a "floating" type.

- Select a large script type font, such as Monotype Corsiva or Alexei Copperplate (shown here).

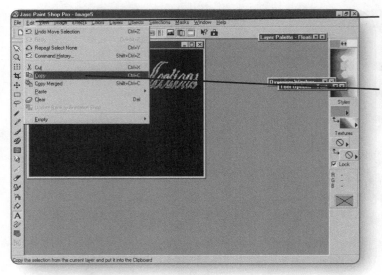

2. While the text is still floating and selected, **click** on **Edit**. The Edit menu appears.

3. Click on **Copy**. The text copies to the clipboard.

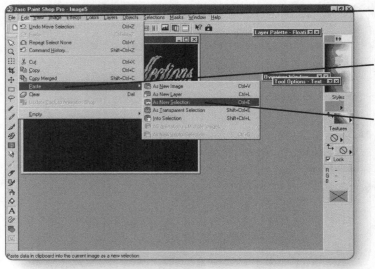

4. Click on **Edit**. The Edit menu appears.

5. Click on **Paste**. The Paste submenu appears.

6. Click on **As New Selection**. You now have two identical copies of the text. The new copy of the text is "stuck" to your mouse.

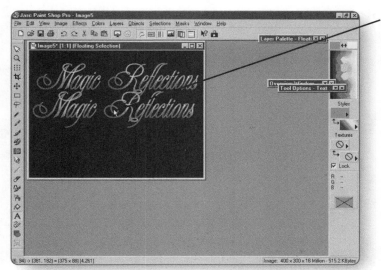

7. **Move** the **mouse** under the original text and **click**. The new text is laid down and is selected.

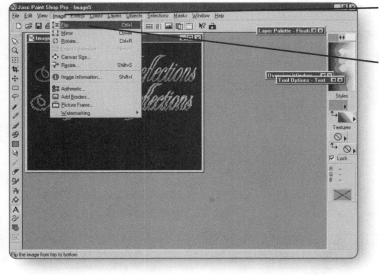

8. **Click** on **Image**. The image menu appears.

9. **Click** on **Flip**. The selected text flips upside down.

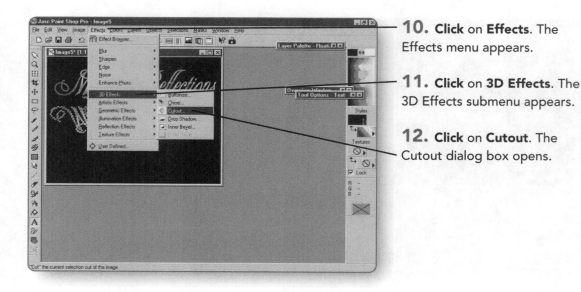

10. **Click** on **Effects**. The Effects menu appears.

11. **Click** on **3D Effects**. The 3D Effects submenu appears.

12. **Click** on **Cutout**. The Cutout dialog box opens.

13. **Select** the following **preferences** in the Cutout dialog box:

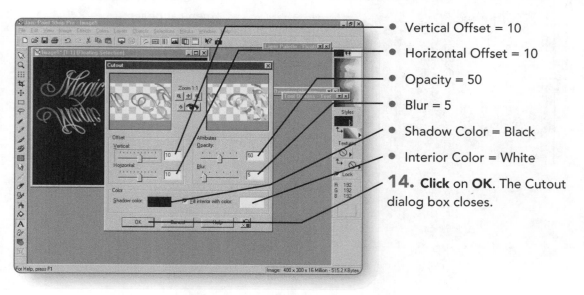

• Vertical Offset = 10

• Horizontal Offset = 10

• Opacity = 50

• Blur = 5

• Shadow Color = Black

• Interior Color = White

14. **Click** on **OK**. The Cutout dialog box closes.

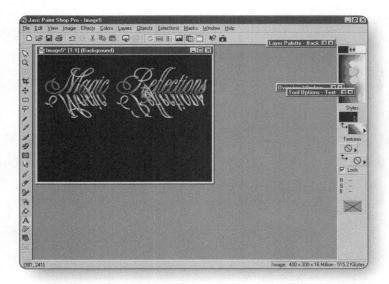

TIP

If necessary, move the selected text closer to the original text.

15. Press Ctrl+D to **deselect** the **text**. The image takes on the appearance of a reflection.

Combining Effects to Create Cool Text Objects

Be creative! Experiment with combining multiple special effects together to see what happens. For example, create a glow-in-the-dark effect by combining the drop shadow and the glowing edges effects. Your text will look like it came right out of the X Files!

1. Create a new document with a black or very dark background.

2. Using the Text tool, **create** some **floating text**, making sure the text fill color is also very dark.

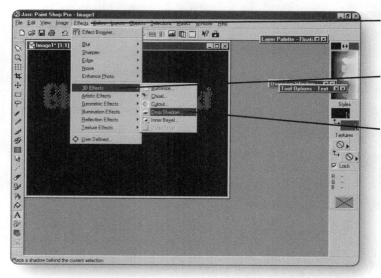

3. **Click** on **Effects**. The Effects menu appears.

4. **Click** on **3D Effects**. The 3D Effects submenu appears.

5. **Click** on **Drop Shadow**. The Drop Shadow dialog box appears.

6. **Change** the following drop shadow **settings**:

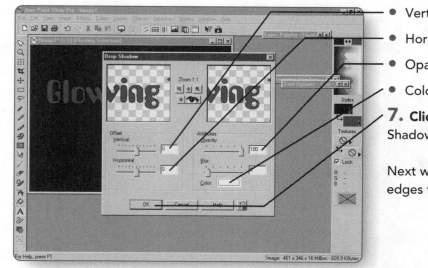

- Vertical Offset = 0
- Horizontal Offset = 0
- Opacity = 100
- Color = White

7. **Click** on **OK**. The Drop Shadow dialog box closes.

Next we'll apply some glowing edges to the text.

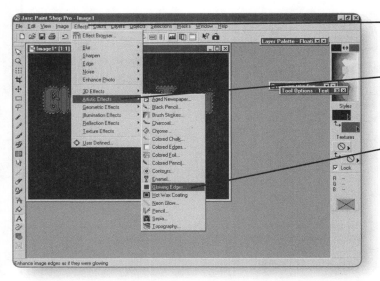

8. Click on **Effects**. The Effects menu appears.

9. Click on **Artistic Effects**. The Artistic Effects submenu appears.

10. Click on **Glowing Edges**. The Glowing Edges dialog box opens.

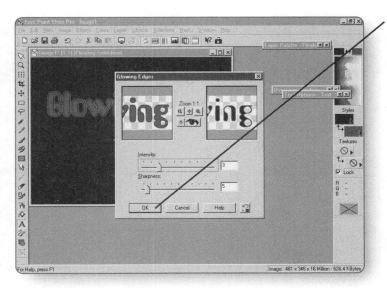

11. Click on **OK**. The Glowing Edges dialog box closes.

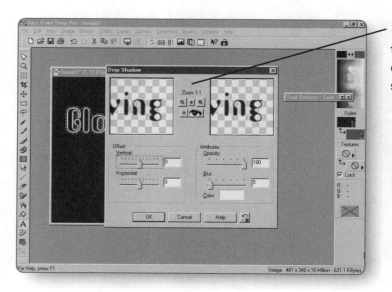

12. Repeat steps 3 through 7 to apply the 3D drop shadow effect a second time. Use the same settings as in step 6.

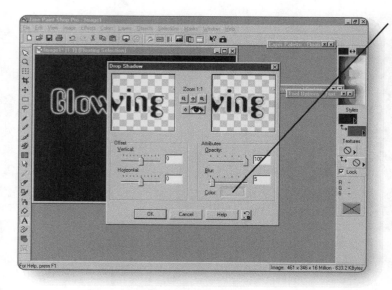

13. Repeat steps 3 through 7 a third time, but this time, select a bright glowing color for the shadow color. For example, the neon green gives a really eerie glow!

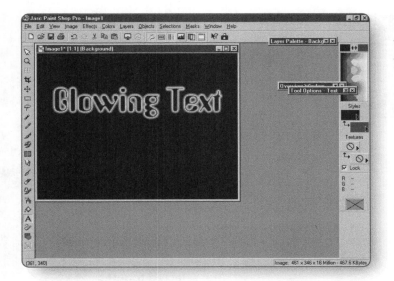

14. **Press Ctrl+D** to deselect the text. Now all that's missing is the mysterious music.

Converting Text to Curves

Suppose you want to place your text in sort of a helter-skelter pattern. You could create one letter at a time, place it, then move on to the next one. But...Paint Shop Pro has a Convert Text to Curves feature that does all that work for you!

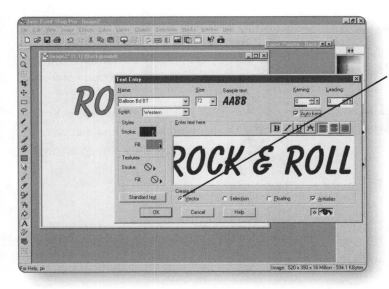

1. **Create** a **new image** with any color background you want.

2. Using the Text tool, **create** some **vector text**. Using vector text enables us to break the text into individual characters.

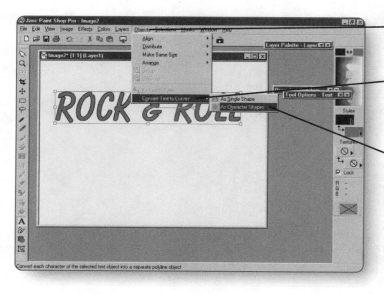

3. **Click** on **Objects**. The Objects menu appears.

4. **Click** on **Convert Text to Curves**. The Convert Text to Curves submenu appears.

5. **Click** on **As Character Shapes**. Paint Shop Pro converts each letter of the text into separate vector objects.

It doesn't look like anything happened because all objects are selected together as a group.

6. **Press Ctrl+D** (or click on Selections, Select None). The letters are deselected.

7. **Click** on the **Vector Selection tool**. The tool becomes selected.

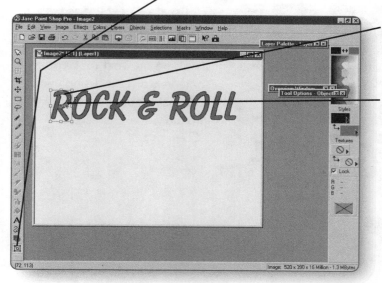

8. **Click** on the **first letter** of your text. The individual letter appears with selection handles.

9. **Position** the **mouse** over the rotation handle. The mouse pointer has two curved arrows.

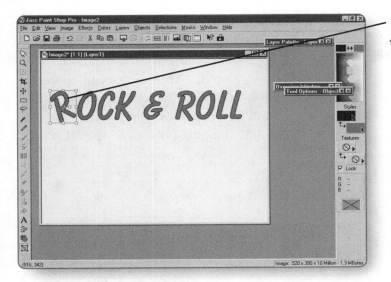

10. **Rotate** or **move** the **letter** to a new position.

11. **Repeat steps 8 through 10** for each letter of the text.

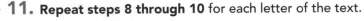

Once the letters are sufficiently jumbled, you'll need to place them on a raster layer so you can apply an effect.

12. **Click** on **Selections**. The Selections menu appears.

13. **Click** on **Select All**. All letters of the text are selected together.

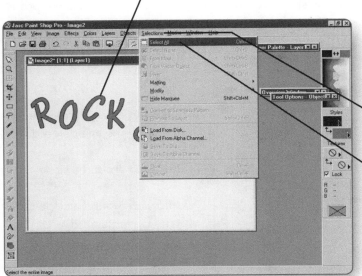

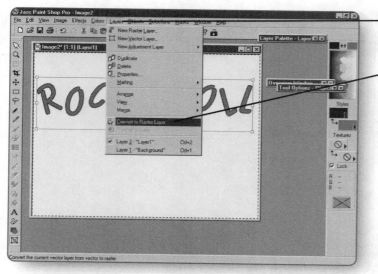

14. **Click** on **Layers**. The Layers menu appears.

15. **Click** on **Convert to Raster Layer**. The text converts to raster text and you can now apply any desired special effect.

Wrapping Text around Shapes

Text doesn't have to flow on a straight path. You can wrap it around circles, make it wave along a line, or generally have it take on any shape you want. Paint Shop Pro calls this feature Creating Text on a Path.

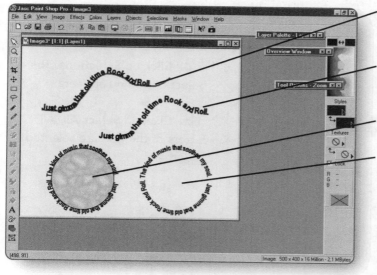

Text flowing along a freehand line

Text flowing along a freehand line but with the line deleted

Text flowing around a circle

Text flowing around a circle but with the circle deleted

The first thing you'll need is a path or shape for the text to follow. The path can be a line, a circle, a star, or almost any vector object.

NOTE

The 3D vector shapes, such as the 3D arrows, buttons, or traffic signs, are actually made up of multiple objects. Therefore, you cannot use them to create text on a path unless you ungroup the object first.

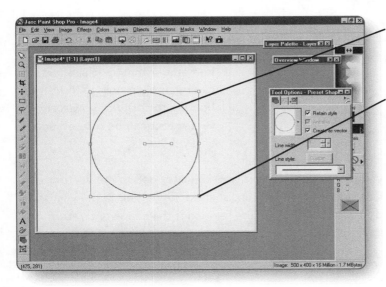

1. Draw a vector **shape**. Use either the preset shapes or the line tools to draw the shape.

2. If not already selected, use the Vector Selection tool to **select** the vector **object**. Selection handles appear around the object.

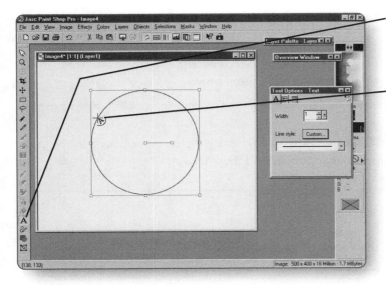

3. Click on the **Text tool**. The mouse pointer resembles a cross with the letter A under it.

4. Position the **mouse** over the vector shape until the mouse pointer has a half circle under the pointer. This indicates the text you create should wrap around the vector object.

5. Click the **mouse**. The Text Entry dialog box opens.

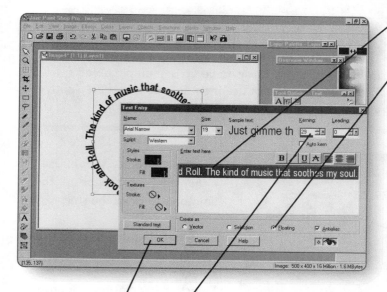

6. Enter some **text**, also selecting a style and font.

7. Select a **text type**. Floating text gets placed on a separate layer, later to be defloated to a raster layer, while vector text remains on the same layer as the vector object.

Remember that special effects can be applied only to the floating raster text; however, vector text can be rotated and easily moved.

If you create floating text, you can later delete the vector image and the text remains shaped. If you delete the vector shape with vector text, the text loses the shape and returns to a straight line.

TIP

Depending on the font and size you've selected as well as the shape you're wrapping around, you may have to experiment with the kerning. Make sure you can see the object and text and adjust the kerning until the letters flow the smoothest. Also, keeping the shape and font simple creates better text flow.

---

8. Click on **OK**. The Text Entry dialog box closes and the text appears wrapped around the image.

TIP

If you created floating text, you can, at any time, select the vector shape and delete it.

Part IV Review Questions

1. What type of text can you create with the Text tool? See *"Selecting the Text Tool"* in Chapter 13.

2. When creating text, can both style boxes be set at Null? See *"Selecting the Text Tool"* in Chapter 13.

3. Does Paint Shop Pro automatically wrap text around to the next line? See *"Entering Text"* in Chapter 13.

4. What is the stroke style? See *"Style"* in Chapter 13.

5. What is kerning? See *"Kerning and Leading"* in Chapter 13.

6. Can the object text type be changed once the text object appears on the image? See *"Text Type"* in Chapter 13.

7. In which type of text object can you actually modify the text? See *"Editing Vector Text"* in Chapter 13.

8. Can Paint Shop Pro's effects be added to text objects? See *"Adding Effects to Your Text"* in Chapter 14.

9. What happens to your text when you choose *"As Character Shapes"* from Convert Text to Curves? See *"Converting Text to Curves"* in Chapter 14.

10. What does Paint Shop Pro call the ability to wrap text around a shape? See *"Wrapping Text around Shapes"* in Chapter 14.

PART V

Creating Web Graphics

15

Designing Web Page Components

Today's Web pages must look good and yet still convey your message accurately. The competition for "hits" on a Web site is fierce. Paint Shop Pro can help you create backgrounds and patterns designed to catch the eye of the surfer. Pages that contain similar topics should have a similar look and feel.

Although you can create your backgrounds and graphics in Paint Shop Pro, it doesn't do the HTML code for you. You'll need to either create the HTML text yourself or use one of the many Web page creation applications such as FrontPage or Dreamweaver. In this chapter, you'll learn how to:

- Create a Web page background
- Resize an image
- Preview in a Web browser
- Save in Web graphic formats

Creating a Simple Web Background

Use Paint Shop Pro to create exciting backgrounds for use on your Web pages. While there are a number of different ways to create Web page backgrounds, here's one of the easier methods.

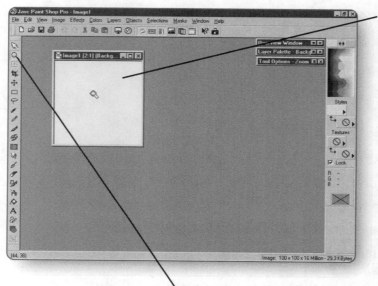

1. **Create** a **new image** approximately 100 pixels wide by about 100 pixels high. The blank image appears in the Paint Shop Pro Window.

TIP

Don't make the image too big or it will take too long to load in the Web page. When the background is small, the browser tiles (repeats) the image to cover the entire page.

2. If desired, **click** on the **Zoom tool**, then **click** on the **image** to enlarge the view.

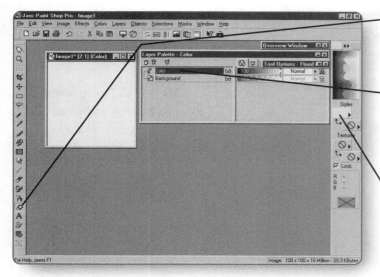

3. Click on the **Flood Fill tool**. The mouse pointer takes the shape of a paint bucket.

4. Add a new **raster layer**, naming the layer "Color." To review adding raster layers, see Chapter 7, "Developing Layers."

5. Click on the **Foreground styles box** and **select a color** or style for your Web page background. To review selecting foreground colors and styles, see Chapter 4, "Understanding the Color Palette."

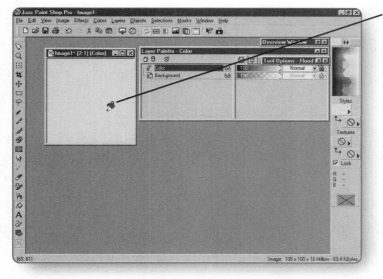

6. Click in the **image**. (Make sure the "Color" layer is the active layer.) The image fills with the selected color.

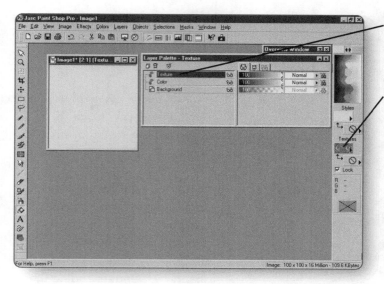

7. **Add** another **new raster layer**, naming the layer "Texture."

8. **Click** on the **Foreground Textures button** and **select** a **texture**. To review selecting textures, see Chapter 4.

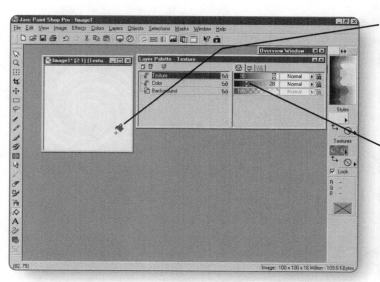

9. **Click** in the **image**. (Make sure the "Texture" layer is the active layer.) The image fills with the selected texture.

TIP

If you don't see the texture, you may need to adjust the layer opacity for the Color and Texture layers.

Understanding Web Graphic Formats

Up to this point, you've been saving all your images in the standard Paint Shop Pro format, which applies a .PSP extension to files. Unfortunately, the .PSP format is not supported on the Web. The two most widely used graphic formats supported by today's Web browsers are the GIF (Graphics Interchange Format) and the JPEG (Joint Photographic Experts Group) formats.

NOTE

A new kid is moving into the Internet graphics block— PNG (Portable Network Graphics) format. Paint Shop Pro can save images as PNG formats, but, unfortunately, many older Web browsers don't support the PNG format at all and the newer versions only partially support PNG.

ALWAYS save your image in the standard Paint Shop Pro format before you begin saving it as other formats. If you've saved the only copy of your new background or logo as a GIF image, then decide you want to save it as a JPEG (or vice versa), you'll lose quite a bit of valuable graphic data should you ever need to edit the image.

Saving Images in Paint Shop Pro Format

Saving an image in Paint Shop Pro format retains support for layers, selections, and other features that the other formats don't support. Image compression does not occur when saving an image in Paint Shop Pro format.

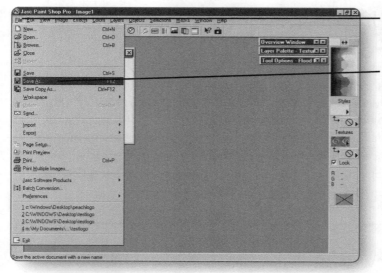

1. **Click** on the **File menu**. The File menu appears.

2. **Click** on **Save As**. The Save As dialog box opens.

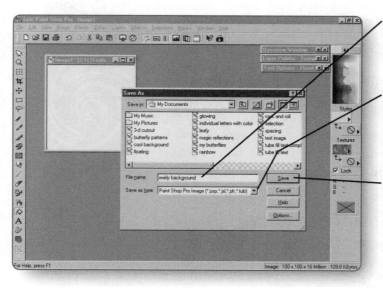

3. **Type** a **name** for the image. The file name appears in the File name: text box.

4. **Click** on the **Save as type: arrow** and **select Paint Shop Pro Image**. The file type appears in the Save as type: box.

5. **Click** on **Save**. The image saves as a Paint Shop Pro image.

Saving Images as Transparent GIF

Save any image with transparent areas in it in an Optimized GIF format. GIF images also work well with cartoons, drawings, and images with high contrast and similar colors; however, GIF only supports up to 256 colors, so it's not the best choice for high-color photographs.

NOTE

While you can just save your file as a .GIF without optimization, an uncompressed file size may be too large to work well on a Web page.

---

1. **Click** on **File**. The File menu appears.

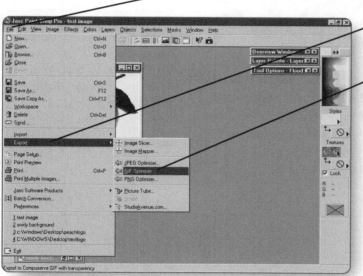

2. **Click** on **Export**. The Export submenu appears.

3. **Click** on **GIF Optimizer**. The GIF Optimizer dialog box opens.

GIF Transparency

The first screen of the GIF Optimizer dialog box relates to how you want Paint Shop Pro to handle transparency.

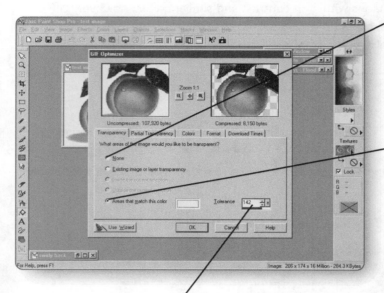

1a. Click on **None** if you have no transparent areas in the image. Paint Shop Pro doesn't block any area of the image.

OR

1b. Click on **Areas that match this color** if you need a particular color on the image blocked out. Areas matching the color box appear transparent.

2. Optionally, **adjust** the **Tolerance scale** from 1–200. The tolerance factor indicates how closely colors must match the color in the box before they are selected.

TIP

Click on the color box to select a color to block. In the example shown, Paint Shop Pro blocks out all white areas in the image.

NOTE

The higher the tolerance, the wider the range of color matching that will occur. For example, at a low tolerance of the color red, images containing light red may not be included; however, if the tolerance were increased to say, 150, not only light red would be included, but perhaps pink or magenta.

GIF Format

Next, you need to select a format option for use when displaying the image.

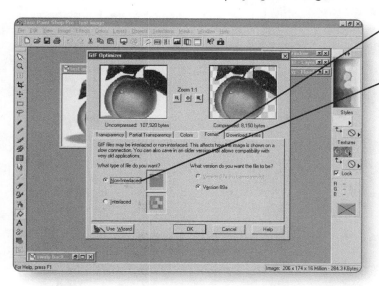

1. **Click** on the **Format tab**. The Format tab comes to the front.

2. **Click** on a **format option**. Two options are available:

- **Non-Interlaced**. The image downloads one line at a time, starting from the top.

- **Interlaced**. The image is displayed in several passes with greater detail added each time. (This option works better for larger images.)

GIF Download Times

View the approximate download times for your image using your current settings and various modem speeds.

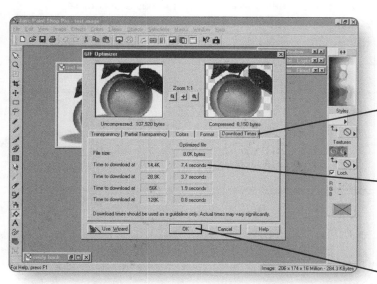

1. **Click** on the **Download Times tab**. The Download Times tab comes to the front.

2. **View** the **download times** for various modem speeds. The values change with the options you previously selected.

3. **Click** on **OK**. The Save As dialog box opens.

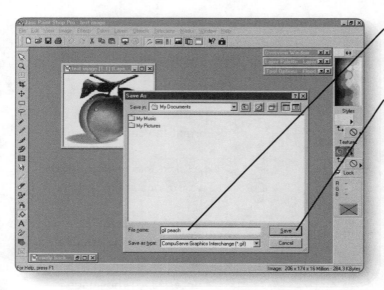

4. **Type** a **name** for the image. The file name appears in the File name: text box.

5. **Click** on **Save**. Paint Shop Pro saves the image in a .GIF format.

Saving Images as Compressed JPEG

JPEG images can often be smaller in file size than GIFs, which translates to faster loading time for the Web surfer. While JPEG images can support higher file colors and frequently produce better quality in an image such as a photograph, JPEGs do not support any transparent areas and are not the best format to use for line art, cartoons, and other high-contrast images.

NOTE

While you can just save your file as a .JPEG without using Optimization, an uncompressed file size may be too large to work well on a Web page.

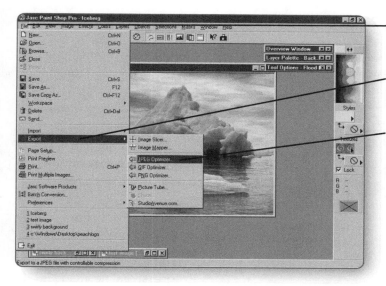

1. **Click** on **File**. The File menu appears.

2. **Click** on **Export**. The Export submenu appears.

3. **Click** on **JPEG Optimizer**. The JPEG Optimizer dialog box opens.

JPEG Compression

When saving images as JPEG, you'll need to determine a compression factor between 1 and 99. The larger the factor, the more compression, which results in smaller file size but lower quality.

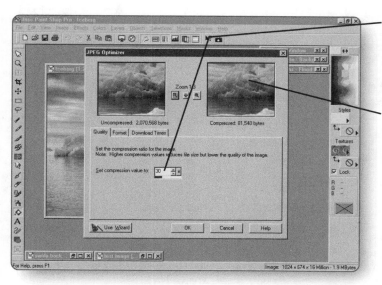

1. **Click** on the **Set compression value to: up/down arrows**. The compression value displays in the text box.

View the before and after compression images along with uncompressed and compressed file sizes.

JPEG Format

Next, you need to select a format option for use when displaying the image.

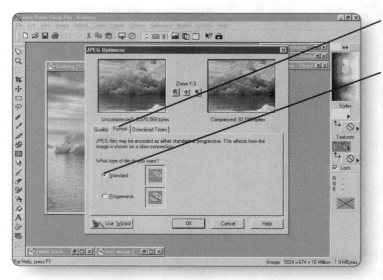

1. Click on the **Format tab**. The Format tab comes to the front.

2. Click on a **format option**. Two options are available:

- **Standard**. The image downloads one line at a time, starting from the top.

- **Progressive**. The image is displayed in several passes with greater detail added each time. (This option works better for larger images.)

JPEG Download Times

View the approximate download times for your image using your current settings and various modem speeds.

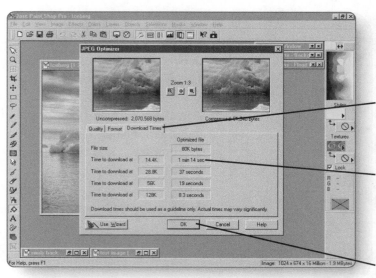

1. Click on the **Download Times tab**. The Download Times tab comes to the front.

2. View the **download times** for various modem speeds. The values change with the compression factor you selected.

3. Click on **OK**. The Save As dialog box opens.

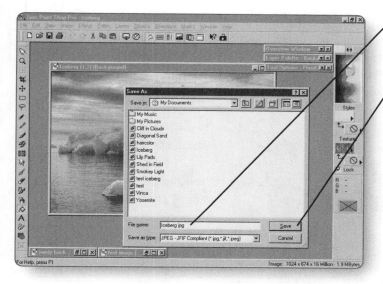

4. **Type** a **name** for the image. The file name appears in the File name: text box.

5. **Click** on **Save**. Paint Shop Pro saves the image in a .JPEG format.

Saving Images as PNG

The newer PNG format is the best of both GIF and JPEG worlds, but remember that most Web browsers in use today don't yet fully support PNG format.

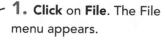

1. **Click** on **File**. The File menu appears.

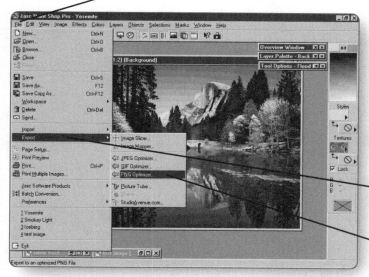

NOTE

While you can just save your file as a .PNG without using Optimization, an uncompressed file size may be too large to work well on a Web page.

2. **Click** on **Export**. The Export submenu appears.

3. **Click** on **PNG Optimizer**. The PNG Optimizer dialog box opens.

PNG Colors

The PNG format works similarly to a combination GIF and JPEG. The PNG format supports higher-color image types plus transparency.

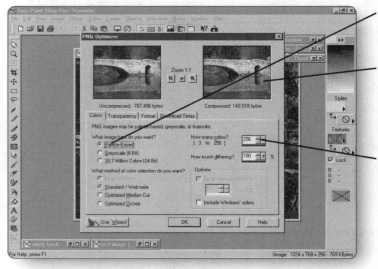

1. Select an **image type**. The option appears selected.

View the before and after images along with uncompressed and compressed file sizes.

If you select Palette-Based, you'll need to specify a maximum number of colors.

PNG Transparency

The transparency screen of the PNG Optimizer dialog box relates to how you want Paint Shop Pro to handle transparency.

1. **Click** on the **Transparency tab**. The Transparency tab comes to the front.

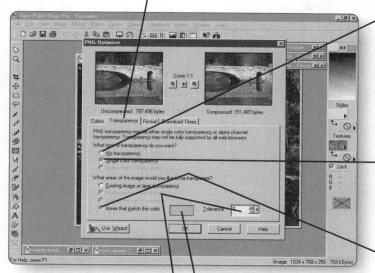

2a. **Click** on **No transparency** if you have no transparent areas in the image. Paint Shop Pro doesn't block any area of the image.

OR

2b. **Click** on **Single color transparency** if you need a particular color on the image blocked out.

3. **Click** on **Areas that match this color.** Areas matching the color box appear transparent.

TIP

Click on the color box to select a color to block.

4. Optionally, **adjust** the **Tolerance scale** from 1–200. The tolerance factor indicates how closely colors must match the color in the box before they are selected.

PNG Format

Next, you need to select a format option for use when displaying the image. PNG format options are identical to GIF options.

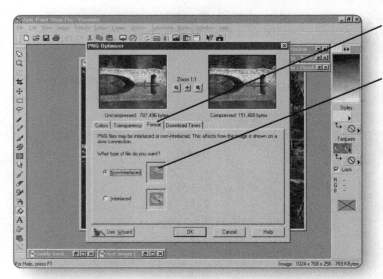

1. Click on the **Format tab**. The Format tab comes to the front.

2. Click on a **format option**. Two options are available:

- **Non-Interlaced**. The image downloads one line at a time, starting from the top.

- **Interlaced**. The image is displayed in several passes with greater detail added each time. (This option works better for larger images.)

PNG Download Times

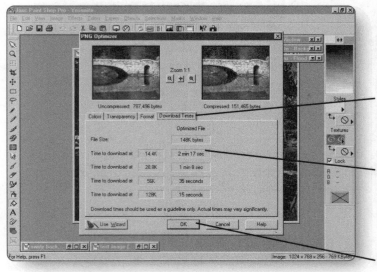

View the approximate download times for your image using your current settings and various modem speeds.

1. Click on the **Download Times tab**. The Download Times tab comes to the front.

2. View the **download times** for various modem speeds. The values change with the compression factor you selected.

3. Click on **OK**. The Save As dialog box opens.

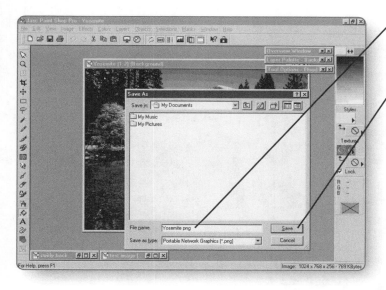

4. Type a **name** for the image. The file name appears in the File name: text box.

5. Click on **Save**. Paint Shop Pro saves the image in a .PNG format.

Modifying Image Size

When you first created an image, Paint Shop Pro prompted you for the image size; however, you can resize any image. Be aware that resizing may distort or affect the clarity of the image.

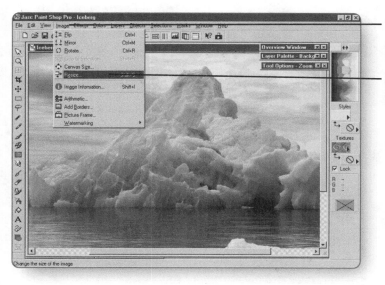

1. Click on **Image**. The Image menu appears.

2. Click on **Resize**. The Resize dialog box opens.

3. **Select** a resize **method**. You have three methods to resize your image:

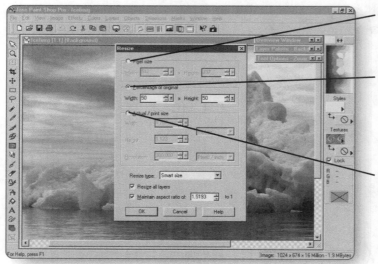

- Modify pixel size, where you select a new size by choosing a new measurement in pixels.

- Change the percentage of original, where you select a new size based on a percentage increase or decrease from the original.

- Select an Actual/Print Size, where you select a new size by changing the resolution or the dimensions.

4. If necessary, **select Smart size** from the Resize type: list. Paint Shop Pro is a pretty smart program. It knows what to do.

5. If not already checked, **check** the **Maintain aspect ratio of: box** to keep from distorting your image.

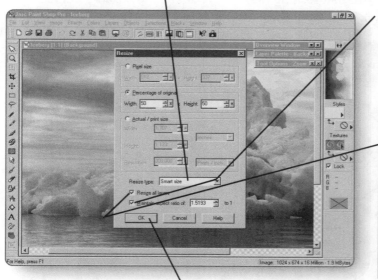

TIP

If you only want to resize a particular layer, make sure the layer is active before entering the Resize dialog box and remove the check mark from the Resize All Layers box. Only the current layer resizes.

6. **Click** on **OK**. The Resize dialog box closes.

The image resizes.

Previewing in a Web Browser

Two popular browsers are Internet Explorer and Netscape; however, a number of different Web browsers are on the market today. When working with Web graphics, you should view the graphic in a variety of different browsers, as each one supports different features. If possible, even view your images in different versions of different browsers.

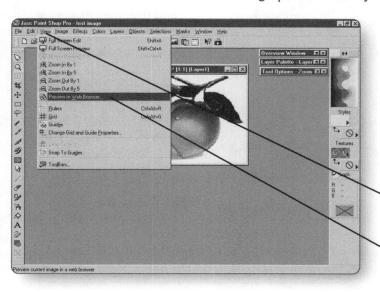

Paint Shop Pro allows you to preview an image in a variety of formats on each browser you have installed on your computer.

1. Click on **View**. The View menu appears.

2. Click on **Preview in Web Browser**. The Preview in Web Browser dialog box opens.

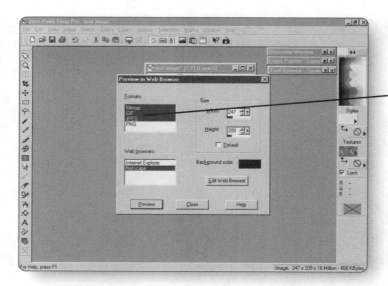

Paint Shop Pro supports four types of Web graphics: Bitmap, GIF, JPEG, and PNG.

3. Click on the **Formats** in which you'd like to preview your image. I suggest selecting multiple formats to compare your image.

TIP

Click a second time on a format to deselect it.

Paint Shop Pro lists the Web browsers installed on your computer.

TIP

If you have other Web browsers available that are not listed, click on the Edit Web Browser button to add the location of your Browser.

4. Click on the **Web browser** in which you want to view your image. Again, I suggest you view the image in a variety of Web browsers. The more the better...

5. Click on the **background color box** and **select** a background **color** for the Web page.

6. Click on **Preview**. If you selected the GIF, JPEG, or PNG format, the optimizer window for the appropriate graphic type appears.

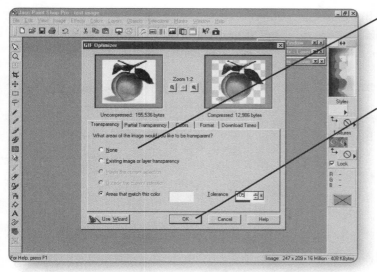

7. Enter options for the graphics types. Refer to "Understanding Web Graphic Formats" earlier in this chapter.

8. Click on **OK**. The Web browser you specified opens.

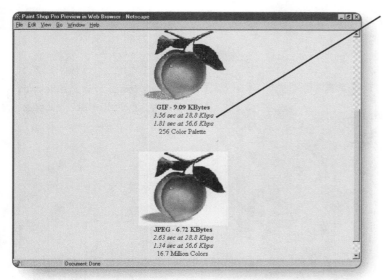

The Web browser previews your image in each format you selected along with display size and approximate loading time.

In this example, even though we selected a BMP image type, this browser does not support BMP image types. A white box appears indicating the browser cannot display the image.

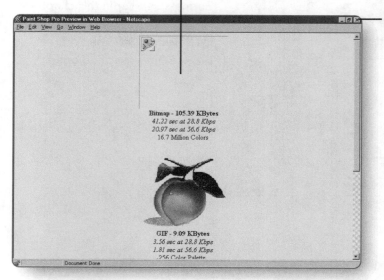

9. Click the **Close box** ⊠. The Web Browser Window closes.

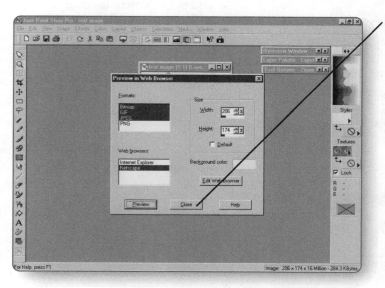

10. Click Close. The Preview in Web Browser dialog box closes.

16

Discovering Animation Shop

When we were children, most of us created our own cartoon flip books. We took a tablet of paper and on each page drew an image, with each page being slightly different than the previous one. Then, when the pages were quickly flipped, the image looked like it was moving, thus creating an animation.

Paint Shop Pro includes an application that uses those same principles to create digital animations. You create a series of sequential images, and optionally apply a transition effect. In this chapter, you'll learn how to:

- Start Animation Shop
- Discover the Animation Shop Window
- Open and view an animation

Starting Animation Shop

Animation Shop is a stand-alone application, but can be accessed from your Windows Start button or through the Paint Shop Pro program.

Starting from the Desktop

When you installed Paint Shop Pro, an additional icon was created to launch Animation Shop.

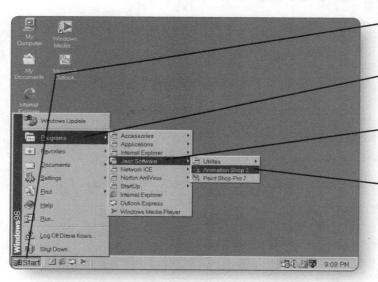

1. **Click** on **Start**. The Start menu appears.

2. **Click** on **Programs**. The Programs submenu appears.

3. **Click** on **Jasc Software**. The Jasc Software submenu appears.

4. **Click** on **Animation Shop 3**. The Animation Shop application begins.

Starting from Paint Shop Pro

Although you can launch Animation Shop from the Windows Start menu, most users prefer to launch it from Paint Shop Pro.

1. **Click** on **File**. The File menu appears.

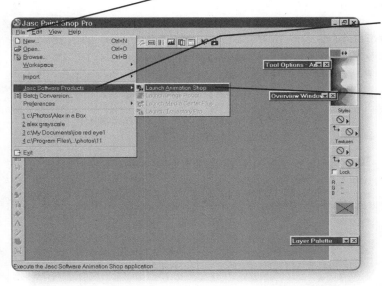

2. **Click** on **Jasc Software Products**. The Jasc Software Products submenu appears.

3. **Click** on **Launch Animation Shop**. The Animation Shop application begins.

Peeking at the Animation Shop Window

The Animation Shop Window includes many of the same tools as Paint Shop Pro, but also includes several tools specific to working with animations.

- Toolbar: contains frequently used menu commands, many of which are the same as Paint Shop Pro (such as Open, Save, Cut, and Copy) while others are specific to Animation Shop (such as Animation Wizard and Delete Frame).

- VCR Controls: contains movement buttons such as Pause, Rewind, or Fast Forward, used while viewing animations.

- Style Bar: contains the options for the currently selected tool from the Tool Palette.

- Tool Palette: contains tools used to modify frames.

- Color Palette: contains the selection of available colors.

- Status Bar: displays information about the current animation and indicates the progress as the animations run in the Animation Shop Window.

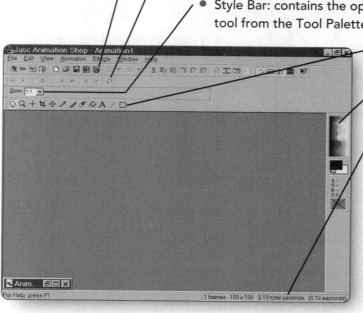

Opening an Animation

Animation Shop supports several animation and video file formats such as GIF, FLC, FLI, MNG, and AVI. To get you started with animations, Paint Shop Pro includes several animations for you to explore.

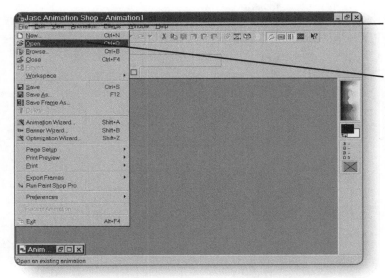

1. Click on **File**. The File menu appears.

2. Click on **Open**. The Open dialog box opens.

To view the sample animations, you'll need to locate the Anims folder supplied by Paint Shop Pro.

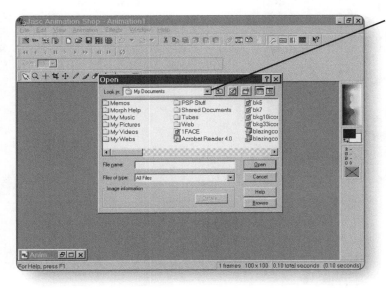

3. Click on the **Look in: down arrow**. A folder list appears.

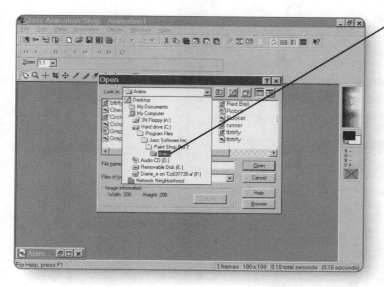

4. Locate and **click on** the **Anims folder**, located under the Paint Shop Pro 7 folder. (Usually located under Program Files, Jasc Software, Paint Shop Pro 7, Anims.) A list of animations appears.

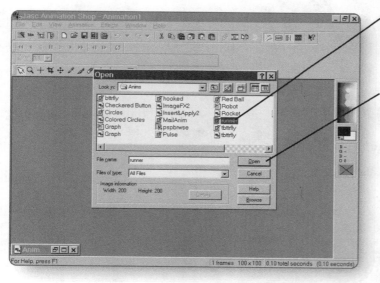

5. Click on an **animation file name**. The animation name becomes highlighted.

6. Click on **Open**. The animation opens in Animation Shop.

Examining an Animation

Animations are made of a series of frames, each of which indicates a step in the image movement.

Each frame has two numbers under it. The first number, F:, indicates the frame number while the D: number indicates the delay before the next frame displays. The value is measured in 1/100th of a second.

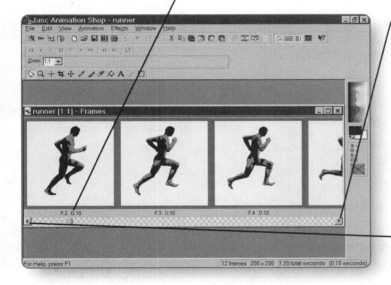

1. **Click** on the **right scroll arrow**. Each click displays the next frame of the animation.

TIP

Click fast enough and you'll see the animation movement.

2. **Click** the **left scroll arrow** and see the animation run backward.

Viewing an Animation

View the currently selected animation repeatedly in a separate window.

1. **Click** on the **View menu**. The View menu appears.

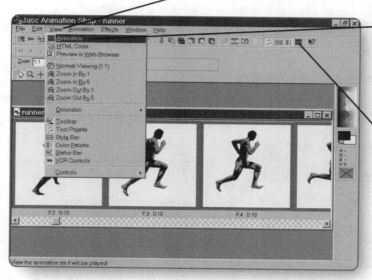

2. **Click** on **Animation**. The animation opens in a separate Play window and begins playing repeatedly.

TIP

Optionally, click on the Animation button.

3. **Click** on the **Fast Forward button**. The animation plays at twice the normal speed.

4. **Click** on the **Slow Forward button**. The animation plays at half the normal speed.

Pausing an Animation

Temporarily stop the animation.

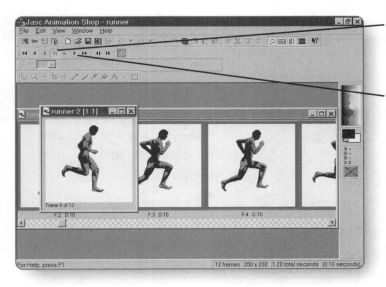

1. **Click** on the **Pause button**. The animation stops in the current frame.

2. **Click** on the **Play button**. The animation resumes.

Running Backward

Review the animation in reverse at normal speed or double speed.

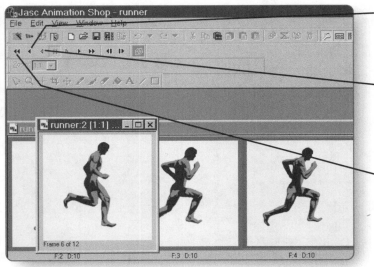

1. **Click** on the **Reverse button**. The animation plays at normal speed, but in reverse motion.

2. **Click** on the **Slow Reverse button**. The animation plays backward at half the normal speed.

3. **Click** on the **Rewind button**. The animation plays backward at twice the normal speed.

Looking Frame by Frame

Review the animation one frame at a time, either forward or backward.

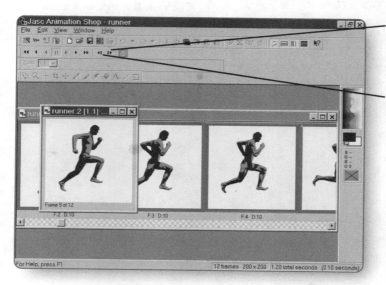

1. **Click** on the **Advance One Frame button**. The animation advances one frame.

2. **Click** on the **Retreat One Frame button**. The animation reverses one frame.

Closing Animation View

When you've finished viewing the animation, close the Animation Play Window.

1. **Click** on the **Close button**. The Play Window closes.

Closing Animation Shop

If you launched Animation Shop from within Paint Shop Pro, when you close Animation Shop, the Paint Shop Pro Window reappears.

If you launched Animation Shop from the Windows Desktop, the Windows Desktop reappears.

1. Click on the **Close button**. The Animation Shop application closes.

NOTE

Animation Shop prompts you to save the current animation if any unsaved changes exist.

17

Creating an Animation

Now that you've seen how animations work, you'll soon discover how easy they are to create using Animation Shop. The animations created with Animation Shop can be used on a Web site, or used in presentations. In this chapter, you'll learn how to:

- Use the Animation Wizard
- Save and edit an animation
- Add animation transitions and effects
- Print an animation

Launching the Animation Wizard

Use the Animation Wizard to quickly assemble an animation. The Animation Wizard walks you through a step-by-step information-collecting process before building your animation.

1. Click on the **Animation Wizard button**. The Animation Wizard launches, prompting you for specifics about the animation you want to create.

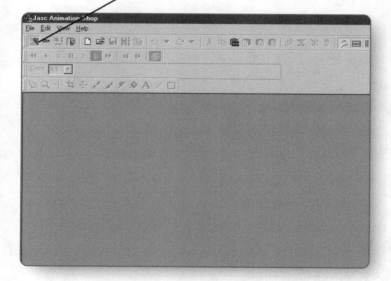

TIP

Optionally, click on Animation Wizard from the File menu.

Specifying Dimensions

The first page of the Wizard prompts you for the animation frame size. Two options appear:

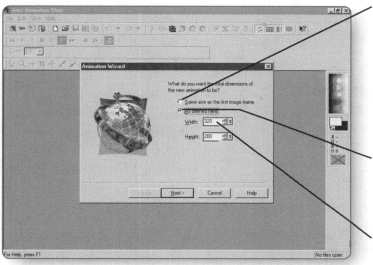

- Same size as the first image frame: Choose this if you want all animation frames the same size as the first image you select. You actually select images in a later step. (I recommend you use this method.)

- As defined here: Choose this if you want to customize the exact dimensions of the animation frames.

If you activate the second option, you specify the frame height and width in pixels.

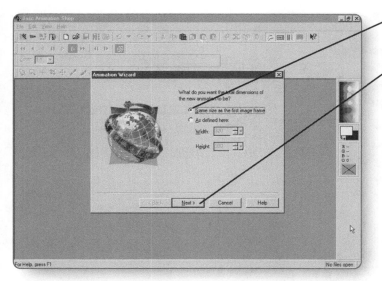

1. **Click** on an **option**. The option appears selected.

2. **Click** on **Next**. The canvas color page appears.

Choosing a Background Color

The background color page prompts you to set a transparent or an opaque (solid) canvas color. If you select the transparent option, any images behind the animation show through the canvas.

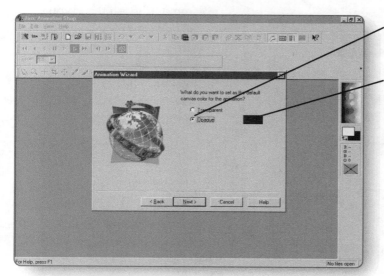

1. **Click** on an **option**. The option appears selected.

2. Optionally, if you selected Opaque, **click** on the **color box**. The Color dialog box appears. This is the same color box you use in Paint Shop Pro.

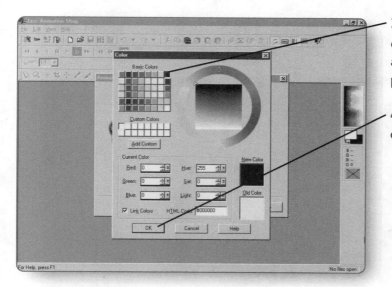

3. **Click** on a **color** for your canvas. The selected color appears in the New Color preview box.

4. **Click** on **OK**. The Color dialog box closes.

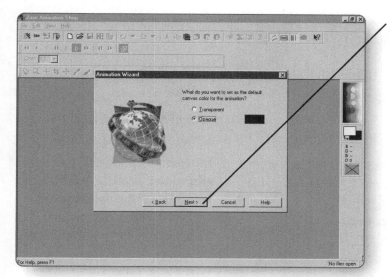

5. Click on **Next**. The Frames Positioning screen appears.

Placing Images

The Frames Positioning screen prompts you to choose how you want to place your images in their frames. In the first screen, you elected either to make all images be the size of the first image (which you still have not selected...that's two screens away) or to have the frames a specified size. The current screen wants to know what to do with images that don't exactly fit the specified frame size.

The top option contends with images too small or not shaped exactly for the frames:

- Upper-left corner of the frame: Aligns all images in the upper-left corner of their respective frames.

- Centered in the frame: Aligns all images centered in the frames regardless of the image size.

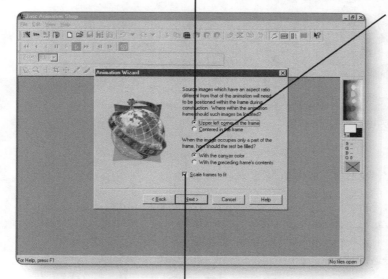

The middle option also manages images too small for the frames. What should Animation Shop do with the frame space not occupied by the image:

- With the canvas color: Fills the empty area with the canvas color specified in the second Animation Wizard screen.

- With the preceding frame's contents: Fills the empty area with the contents of the previous frame.

The final option on this Positioning screen handles what PSP should do with an image that's too large for the frame: scale frames to fit the image. If you don't select this option, parts of an image may not be visible in the frame.

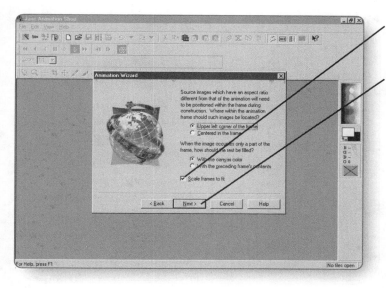

1. **Click** on any desired **options**. The options are selected.

2. **Click** on **Next**. The animation timing screen appears.

Determining Timing

The timing screen queries whether you want the animation to play repeatedly or a specified number of times.

1a. **Click** the **option** to repeat the animation indefinitely and the animation plays continuously until you manually stop the animation.

OR

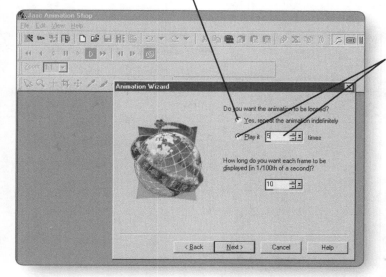

1b. **Click** the **option** to play the animation a specified number of times. Click the up/down arrow to specify the number.

NOTE

Although most popular Web browsers support the loop feature, some older browser versions may not contain the ability to repeat an animation.

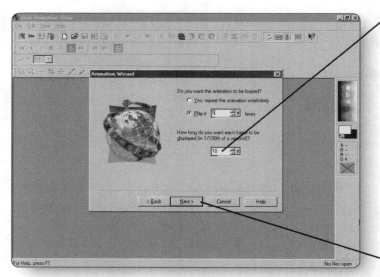

2. Set the **display time** for each frame. Measured in 1/100th of a second, all frames in the animation set to the same display time.

> ### NOTE
> You can later edit the animation to apply an individual display time to each frame.

3. Click on **Next**. The Animation Wizard's fifth page appears, prompting you to choose which images you want to use in your animation.

Selecting Images

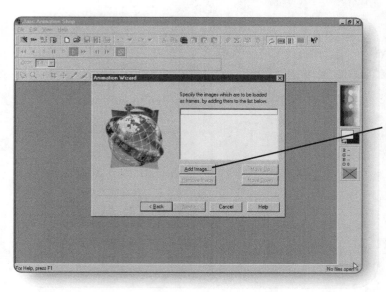

Without sounding too obvious, each animation must begin with at least one image. The maximum number of images is unlimited.

1. Click on **Add Image**. The Open dialog box opens.

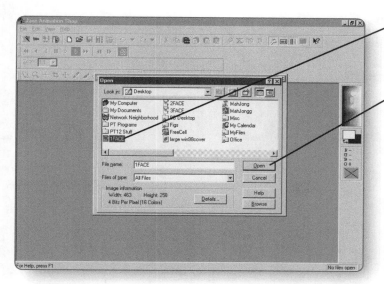

2. Locate and **click** on the first **image** you want to add. The file name is highlighted.

3. Click on **Open**. The file name gets added to the Animation Wizard file name box.

TIP

To select multiple images at once, hold the Ctrl key while clicking on file names.

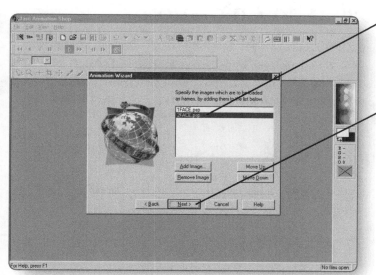

4. Repeat steps 1 through 3 for each image you want to add. A list of file names appears in the Animation Wizard file name box.

5. Click on **Next**. The sixth and final page of the Animation Wizard appears.

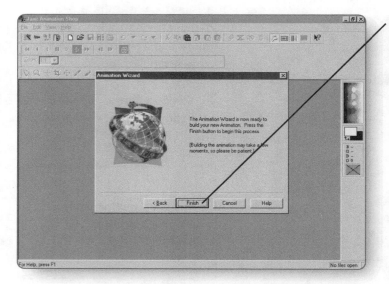

6. Click on **Finish**. The Animation Wizard builds the animation and displays it in the Animation Shop Window.

Saving an Animation

Animation Shop provides a number of different file formats in which to save your animation. Choose from GIF, MNG, AVI, FLC, FLI, and ANI formats. Remember that most Web browsers support only GIF formats. FLI format requires that images be 320 x 200 pixels in size.

Naming an Animation

First, you'll specify a file name, type, and location for your animation.

1. Click on the **Save button**. If this is the first time you save the animation, the Save As dialog box opens.

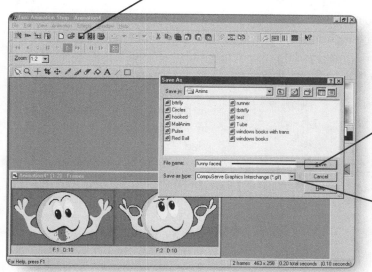

2. Type an **animation name**. The name appears in the File name: text box.

3. Click on the **Save as type: down arrow**. A list of file types appears.

4. Click on a **file type**. The option appears in the Save as type: box.

5. Click on **Save**. Depending on the file type you selected, one of several things can happen:

- GIF, FLC, and FLI formats open the Animation Quality Versus Output Size dialog box.

- AVI format opens the Export Type dialog box. From there you'll be prompted for Export Type, Color Depth, Compression, and Display Rate.

- MNG and ANI formats save immediately with no additional options.

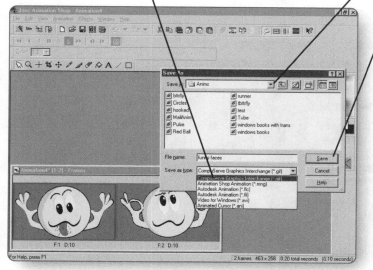

Optimizing Image Quality

If you elect to save your animation as a GIF, FLC, or FLI format, you'll be prompted to optimize the image quality. The better the image quality, the larger the file size. Large file sizes can be slow when loading, which often discourages the Web surfer. Animation Shop allows you to choose to preserve image quality and consequently save a larger file, or sacrifice some image quality for a smaller file size.

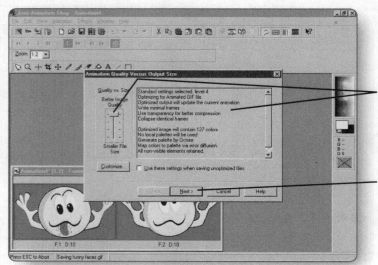

1. Slide the **Quality versus Size handle.** The window to the right of the slider will display details specific to the slider setting.

2. Click on **Next.** The Optimization Progress Window appears.

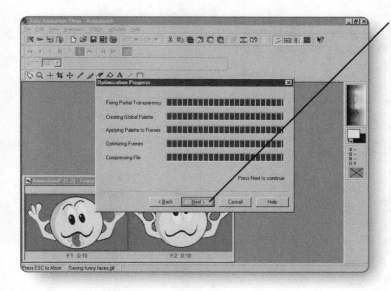

3. Click on **Next.** The Optimization Preview Window appears.

From here you can preview the animation as originally created and with the settings you selected.

4. Click on **Next**. The Optimization Results Window appears.

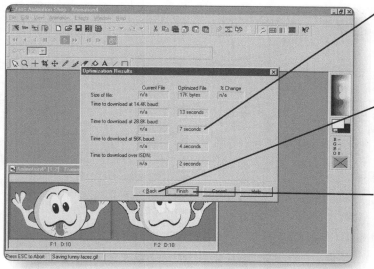

You can view the approximate load times and file sizes.

TIP

Click on Back twice to return to the modify settings screen.

5. Click on **Finish**. Animation Shop saves the animation and the file name appears at the top of the Animation Shop Window.

Editing Animations

After creating the animation, you can add or delete frames, modify frame timings, or change the frame order. Additionally, Animation Shop does not automatically update transitions with changes made to images. If you modify an image used in a transition, you need to delete the frame using that image, and insert a new frame containing the modified image. You'll learn about transitions later in this chapter.

Adding Frames

Insert a new frame with an image or with a blank that uses just the canvas color.

1. Click on **Animation**. The Animation menu appears.

2. Click on **Insert Frames**. The Insert Frames submenu appears.

3. Click on **From File**. The Insert Frames from File dialog box opens.

TIP

Optionally, click on Empty to insert a specified number of blank frames.

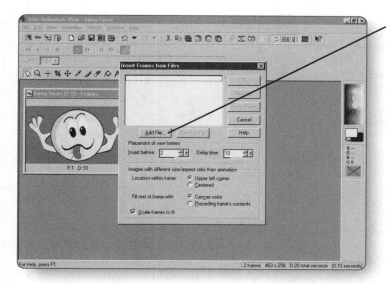

4. Click on **Add File**. The Open dialog box opens.

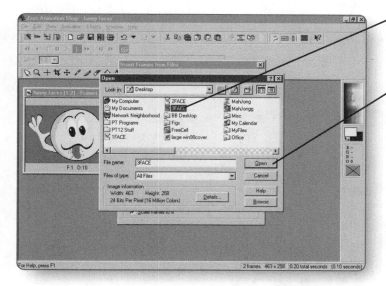

5. Click on the **file name** you want to add. The file name is highlighted.

6. Click on **Open**. The file name appears in the list.

7. **Select** the **frame placement order**. Animation Shop places the new images before the specified frame.

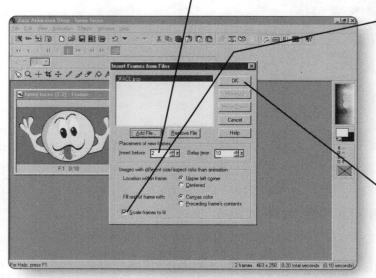

8. **Select** any **sizing options** for the specified frame. The options are the same options that appeared when you ran the Animation Wizard.

9. **Repeat steps 4 through 8** for any additional frames.

10. **Click** on **OK**. Animation Shop inserts the new frames into the current animation.

Removing Frames

If you decide you no longer want a particular frame as part of the animation, you can easily delete it.

TIP
Make sure you have the Arrow tool selected before selecting a frame.

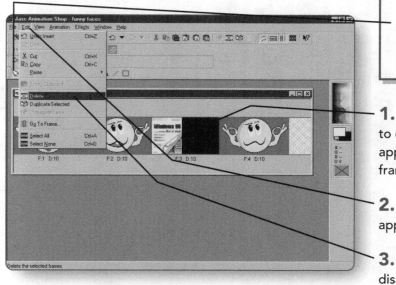

1. **Click** on the **Frame** you want to delete. A colored border appears around the selected frame.

2. **Click** on **Edit**. The Edit menu appears.

3. **Click** on **Delete**. The frame disappears from the animation.

Modifying Frame Timing

When you originally created the animation, the Animation Wizard prompted you for a timing. Measured in 1/100th of a second, all frames in the animation are set to the same display time. You can however, apply a specific timing for individual frames.

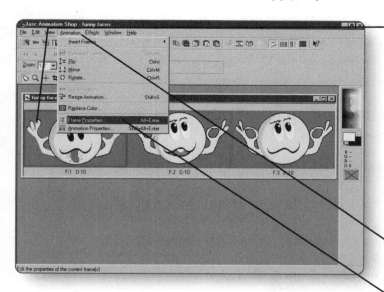

1. Click on the **frame** for which you want to modify timing. A colored border appears around the selected frame.

> **TIP**
>
> To modify multiple frames at the same time, hold down the Ctrl key and click on additional frames.

2. Click on **Animation**. The Animation menu appears.

3. Click on **Frame Properties**. The Frame Properties dialog box opens.

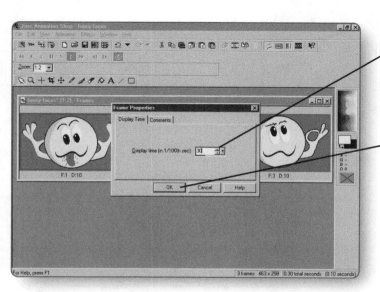

4. Click the **up/down arrow** to increase or decrease the display time. The display time appears in 1/100th of a second.

5. Click on **OK**. The new display time appears under the image.

Changing Frame Order

Change the frame sequence by using the cut and paste features.

TIP

Make sure you have the Arrow tool selected before selecting a frame.

1. **Click** on the **frame** you want to move. A colored border appears around the selected frame.

2. **Click** on the **Cut button**. The selected image disappears and copies to the Windows clipboard.

TIP

Optionally, click on Cut from the Edit menu.

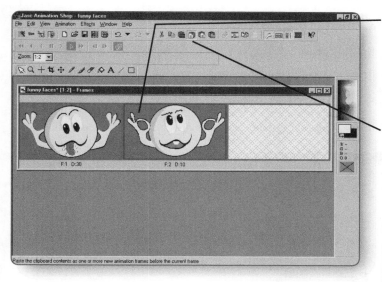

3. Click on the **image** where you want Animation Shop to place the moved image. A colored border appears around the selected frame.

4. Click on the **Paste Before Current button**. Animation Shop inserts the cut image in front of the selected image.

TIP

Optionally, click on the Edit menu and select Paste, then Before Current Frame.

Adding Transitions and Effects

Animation Shop provides a variety of transitions and special effects you can apply to animations. Effects are movements applied to a single frame, while transitions are effects that insert additional frames between a specific frame (the source frame) and the frame next to it to smooth the movement between images.

TIP

To help you view and understand transitions, open and run a sample animation, located in the Anims folder, named **TRANSNFX2**. The animation begins with a series of images, then demonstrates different Animation Shop transition effects.

Adding Transitions

Adding transitions inserts additional frames after a selected frame.

1. Click on the **source frame** where you want to add a transition. A colored border appears around the selected frame.

2. Click on **Effects**. The Effects menu appears.

3. Click on **Insert Image Transition**. The Insert Image Transition dialog box opens.

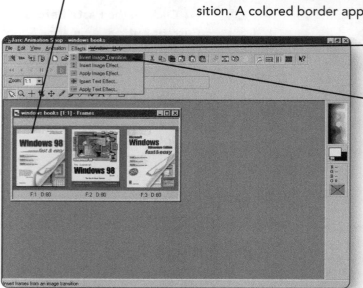

4. Click on the **Effect: down arrow**. A list of transitional effects appears.

5. Click on an **effect**. The transition window demonstrates the effect.

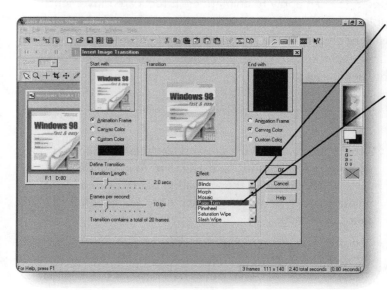

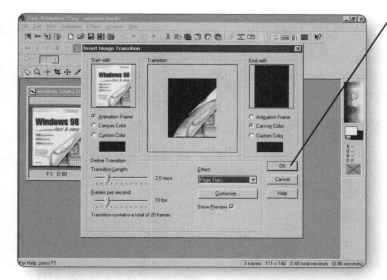

6. **Click** on **OK**. The Insert Image Transition dialog box closes.

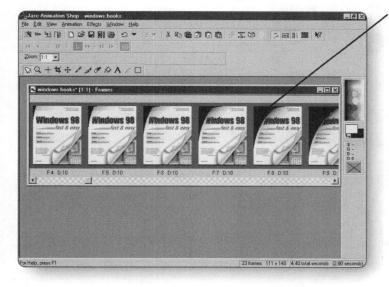

Animation Shop adds additional frames to the animation.

Adding Effects

Create an animation from a single image by using effects. Animation Shop provides a different selection of image effects from transitional effects.

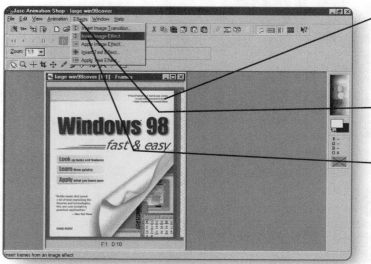

1. Open an **image** to which you want to add an effect. The image appears in an Animation Shop Window.

2. Click on **Effects**. The Effects menu appears.

3. Click on **Insert Image Effect**. The Insert Image Effect dialog box opens.

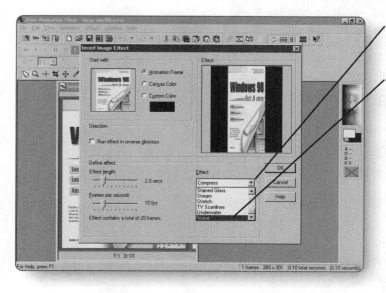

4. Click on the **Effect: down arrow**. A list of effects appears.

5. Click on an **effect**. The Effect window demonstrates the effect.

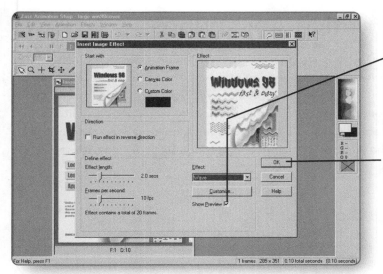

TIP

Make sure a check mark appears in the Show Preview box to see the animation effect.

6. **Click** on **OK**. The Insert Image Effect dialog box closes.

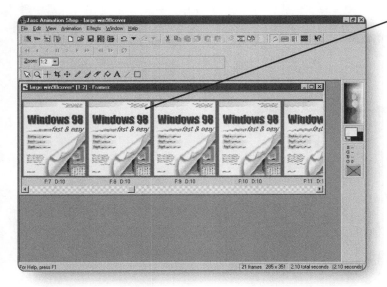

Animation Shop adds additional frames to the animation.

Printing Animations

Animations are primarily for viewing on a computer; after all, you can't see something move on a piece of paper. However, you might want to print a copy of your animation to keep in your records. The format for printed animations is multiple frame thumbnails on each page. Animation Shop determines the number of thumbnails per page by your Page Setup options.

Using Page Setup

Within the Page Setup dialog box, you define the margins, orientation, paper size, and paper source you want when printing your animation.

1. **Click** on **File**. The File menu appears.

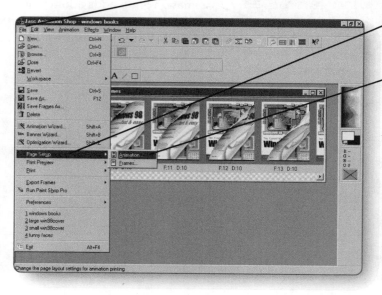

2. **Click** on **Page Setup**. The Page Setup submenu appears.

3. **Click** on **Animation**. The Page Setup dialog box opens.

4. Click on an **orientation**. The preview box displays a sample animation with your current selections.

5. Click on the **Size down arrow** and **select** a paper **size**. Only paper sizes supported by your printer are listed.

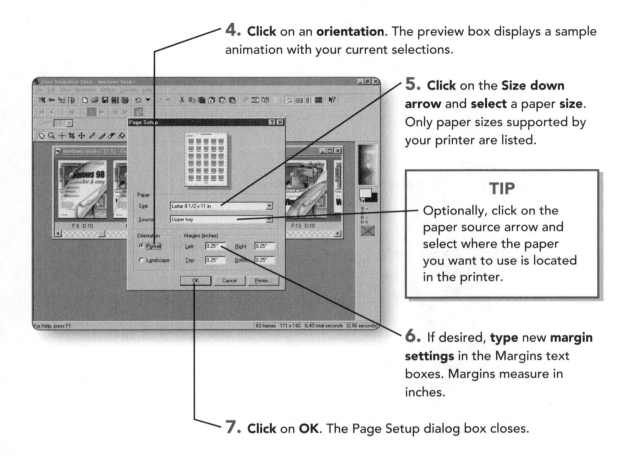

TIP

Optionally, click on the paper source arrow and select where the paper you want to use is located in the printer.

6. If desired, **type** new **margin settings** in the Margins text boxes. Margins measure in inches.

7. Click on **OK**. The Page Setup dialog box closes.

Previewing

If you want to print an animation, you should preview it first.
Previewing allows you to make sure the animation looks right
before you print it, thereby preventing any unwelcome
surprises that sometimes occur during printing.

1. Click on **File**. The File menu appears.

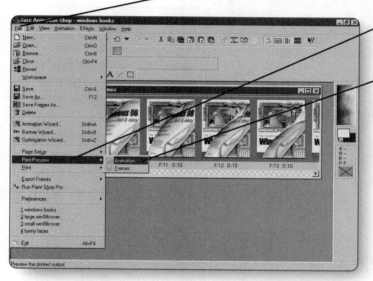

2. Click on **Print Preview**. The
Print Preview submenu appears.

3. Click on **Animation**. A Print
Preview window appears,
displaying the animation
as it would print using any
specifications you determined
during Page Setup.

A page header prints, indicating the animation file name and location.

A legend prints, indicating the frame number and display time.

A page footer prints, indicting the page number.

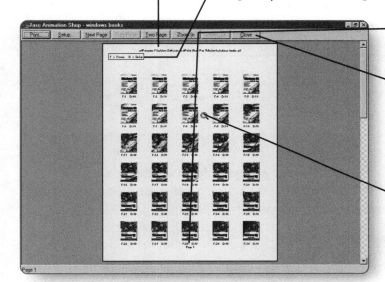

5. Click on **Close**. The Print Preview Window closes and you return to the Animation Shop Window.

TIP

Click on the image to magnify the page.

Printing

The fastest method for printing is using the Animation Shop toolbar.

1. **Click** on the **Print button**. The Print dialog box opens.

> ### TIP
> Optionally, click on the File menu and select Print, then Animation.

2. If desired, **Click** the **Name: down arrow** to select a different printer. Unless you select otherwise, Animation Shop prints to your Windows default printer.

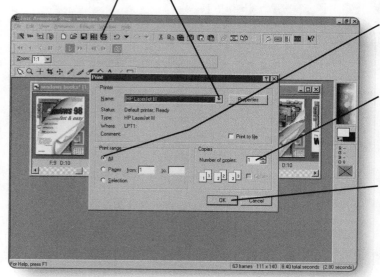

3. **Make** a **selection** from the print range to print the entire animation or only a portion of it.

4. **Click** on the **Number of copies: up/down arrow** to specify the number of copies you want to print.

5. **Click** on **OK**. The animation prints to the designated printer.

18

Building Animated Banners

Text banners are those animations you often see on Web pages, usually at the top, that have text moving around. Text banners are simply animations with text instead of images. In this chapter, you'll learn how to:

- Start the Banner Wizard
- Add banner text
- Add a banner transition

Starting the Banner Wizard

A series of wizard pages will appear, assisting you in creating an animated text banner.

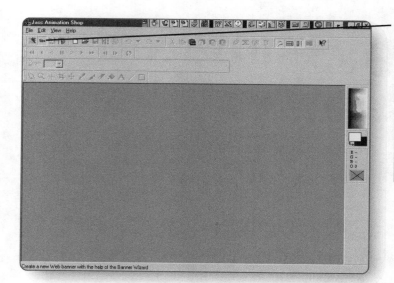

1. **Click** on the **Banner Wizard button**. The first page of the Banner Wizard appears.

TIP

Optionally, click on Banner Wizard from the File menu.

Choosing a Background

The first page of the Banner Wizard prompts you to set the background for the banner. You can fill the banner background with no color (transparent), with an opaque color, or with an image.

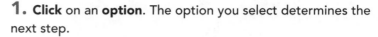

1. Click on an **option**. The option you select determines the next step.

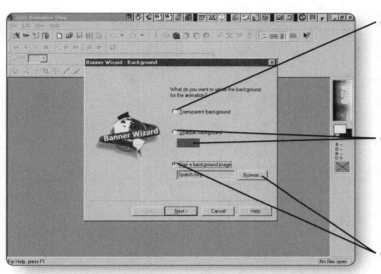

- Click on the Transparent background option to have a transparent banner background. No further background options are needed.

- Click on the Opaque background option to have an opaque banner background, then click inside the color box to pick a background color from the Color dialog box.

- Click on the Use a background image option to have an image for your banner background, then click the Browse button to select a background image to use for the banner.

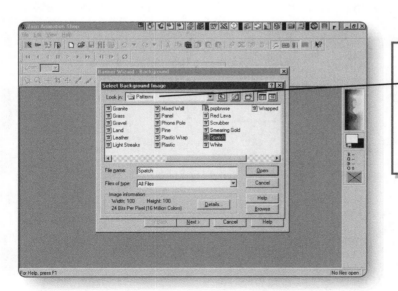

TIP

For a nice effect, select a file from the Paint Shop Pro Patterns or Textures to use as a background image.

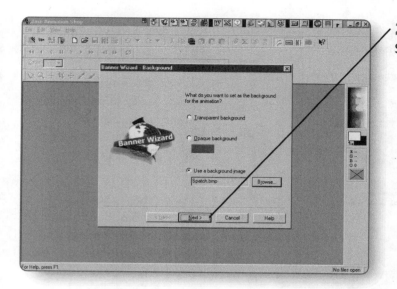

2. Click on **Next**. The Banner Size page appears.

Determining Banner Size

The second page of the Banner Wizard prompts you for the size of the banner. Animation Shop supplies six common sizes; you can also specify your own size.

This figure illustrates the six different common banner sizes.

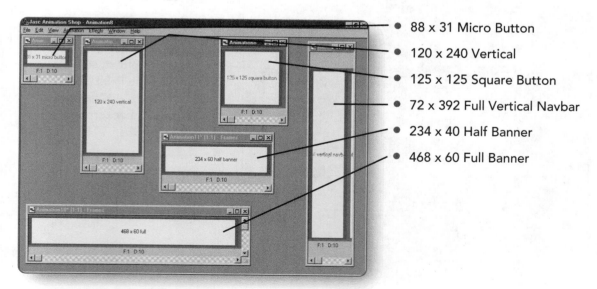

- 88 x 31 Micro Button
- 120 x 240 Vertical
- 125 x 125 Square Button
- 72 x 392 Full Vertical Navbar
- 234 x 40 Half Banner
- 468 x 60 Full Banner

1. Click on an **option**. The option you select determines the next step.

- Click the arrow next to Use a standard banner size to display and select from one of the six standard choices.

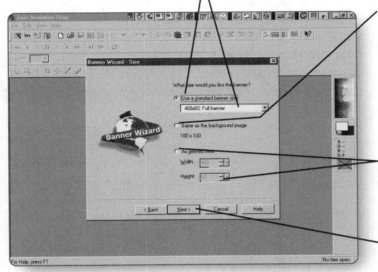

- Click on the Same as the background image option to set the banner size to match the background image size. If you did not select the "Use a background image" option in the background page, this option is unavailable.

- Click on the As defined here: option to enter custom banner size values in the Width: and Height: boxes.

2. Click on **Next**. The Timing screen appears.

Timing the Banner

Because a banner is really a standard animation, you'll see some of the same options you selected when creating other types of animations. One of those options concerns the timing. The Timing screen queries whether you want the animation to play repeatedly or a specified number of times.

1. **Enter** the **display time** for each frame of the banner. Measured in 1/10th of a second, all frames in the banner set to the same display time. The value appears in the How long would you like the animation to last box.

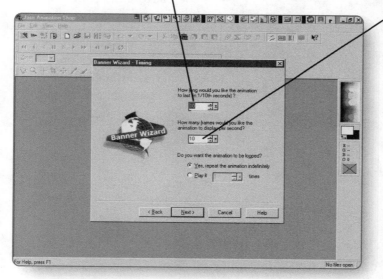

2. **Enter** the number of animation **frames per second** to display. The value appears in the How many frames would you like the animation to display per second box.

> ### NOTE
> Remember that the larger the physical size and quantity of frames, the larger the animation file size. That translates to slower loading times for your readers.

Next, you determine whether you want the banner to repeat indefinitely or for a specified number of times.

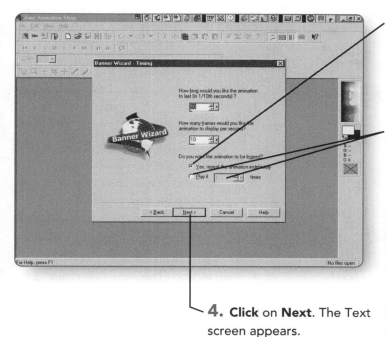

3a. Click the **option** to repeat the animation indefinitely. The option appears selected.

OR

3b. Click the **option** to play the animation a specified number of times. **Click** the **up/down arrow** to specify the number.

4. Click on **Next**. The Text screen appears.

NOTE

Although most popular Web browsers support the loop feature, some older browser versions may not contain the ability to repeat an animation.

Entering Banner Text

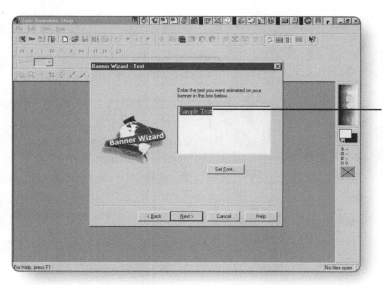

Now you must specify the text you want to appear in the banner, as well as the font and appearance options.

1. If not already highlighted, **drag** the **mouse across** the existing sample **text**. The text appears highlighted.

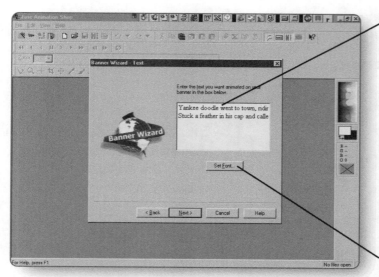

2. Type the **text** you want in your banner. The new text appears in the text preview box.

TIP

Press the Enter key to begin a new line. Keep the banner text very simple and don't type more than the banner length allows.

3. Click on the **Set Font button**. The Add Text dialog box opens.

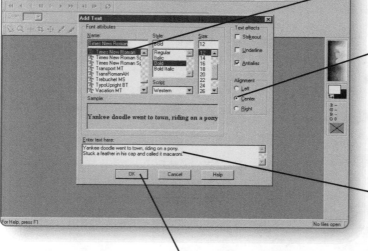

4. Select text attributes such as font, style, and size. The text appears in the Sample box.

5. If your text is multiple lines in length, **select** an **alignment option**. Alignment options determine how multiple lines in the banner align with each other.

TIP

Optionally, you can edit or modify your text by typing in the Enter text here: text box.

6. Click on **OK**. The Add Text dialog box closes.

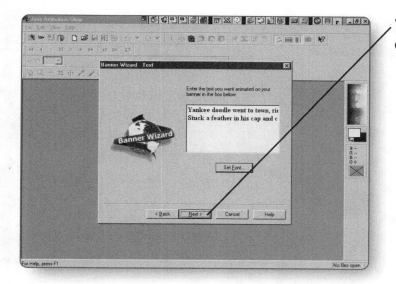

7. Click on **Next**. The Text Color screen appears.

Choosing Text Color

Earlier, you selected a background option for the text banner. Now you must select a text color. Generally speaking, if your background is dark or busy, you should select a lighter colored text.

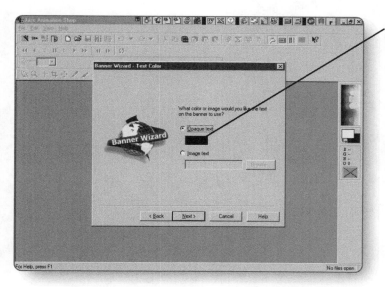

1. Click on the **color box**. The Color dialog box opens.

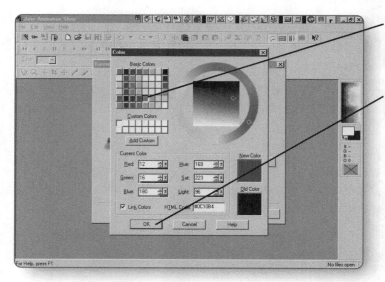

2. **Click** on a **color**. The selected color appears in the New Color box

3. **Click** on **OK**. The Color dialog box closes.

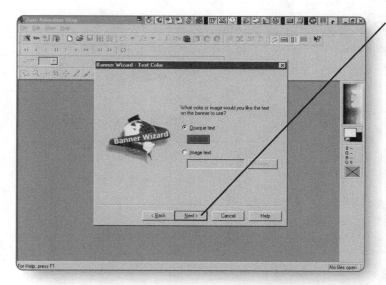

4. **Click** on **Next**. The Transition screen appears.

Picking a Transition

Now you need to assign a transition to your banner. Animation Shop includes seven different varieties of transition effects.

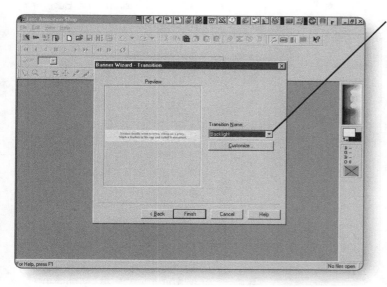

1. Click on the **Transition Name: drop down box**. A list of transitions appears.

- Backlight: Gives the appearance of rays of light shining though the text from the back.

- Bouncing: Moves the text across each frame, bouncing in a different direction each time the text reaches a frame edge.

- Drop Shadow: Gives the appearance of a light source moving across the text, casting a shadow. (Similar to Highlight.)

- Flag: Distorts the text as if it were a flag flying in the wind.

- Highlight: Gives the appearance of a light source moving across the text. (Similar to Drop Shadow, but no shadow effect.)

- Marquee: Slides the text across the frame.

- Wheel: Places the text in a circular pattern and rotates it around the circle.

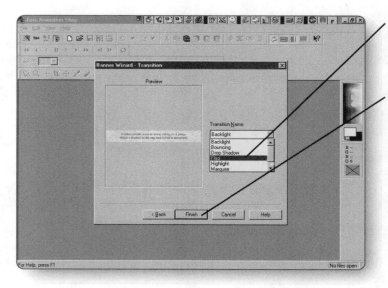

2. Click on a **transition**. The Preview Window displays your banner with the text effect.

3. Click on **Finish**. The Banner Wizard closes.

Your animation appears in a new Animation Shop Window.

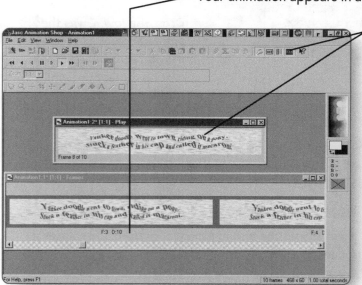

View the animation by clicking on the View Animation button.

TIP

The content of banner frames cannot be edited except by use of the tools on the Tool Palette. If you need to edit the text, font, or color, it's best to restart the Banner Wizard and start over.

Part V Review Questions

1. Does Paint Shop Pro create HTML code for your Web page? See *"Designing Web Page Components"* in Chapter 15.

2. What does a Web browser do to small background images to cover the entire page? See *"Creating a Simple Web Background"* in Chapter 15.

3. In what format should you save an image before you save it as GIF, JPEG, or other formats? See *"Understanding Web Graphic Formats"* in Chapter 15.

4. How many colors can GIF images support? See *"Saving Images as Transparent GIF"* in Chapter 15.

5. What application does Paint Shop Pro include that creates digital animations? See *"Discovering Animation Shop"* in Chapter 16.

6. What are animations made of? See *"Examining an Animation"* in Chapter 16.

7. What Animation Shop feature helps you quickly assemble an animation? See *"Launching the Animation Wizard"* in Chapter 17.

8. How many images must each animation include? See *"Selecting Images"* in Chapter 17

9. What is the difference between an animation effect and an animation transition? See *"Adding Transitions and Effects"* in Chapter 17.

10. What are text banners? See *"Building Animated Banners"* in Chapter 18.

PART VI

Special Photo Projects

19

Using Paint Shop Pro with Your Digital Camera

If you have a digital camera, there's a good chance you can download your images directly into Paint Shop Pro. If your camera is not one supported by Paint Shop Pro, you simply use the software provided by the camera manufacturer. Paint Shop Pro will still be able to edit the images you took with your camera. In this chapter, you'll learn how to:

- Install digital camera support
- Configure a digital camera
- Download images from a digital camera into Paint Shop Pro

Installing Digital Camera Support

With the exception of the Kodak DC120 and DC2xx model cameras, which are supported internally, Paint Shop Pro doesn't automatically install support for digital cameras. You must install it manually.

A separate installation program for camera support is included with the CD-ROM version of Paint Shop Pro. If you purchased the electronic download version of Paint Shop Pro, you'll need to download the free camera installation program from the Jasc Web site at www.jasc.com.

NOTE

If you downloaded the file electronically, locate the file digicam5.msi and double-click to begin installation. Proceed to step 6 below.

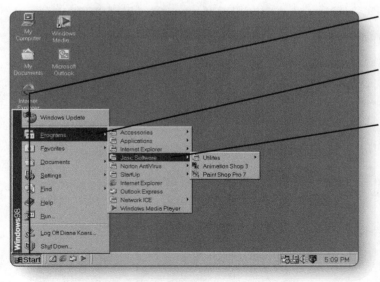

1. **Click** on **Start**. The Start menu appears.

2. **Click** on **Programs**. The Programs submenu appears.

3. **Click** on **Jasc Software**. The Jasc Software submenu appears.

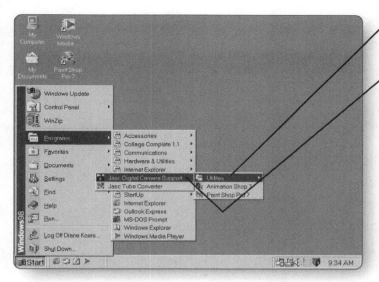

4. Click on **Utilities**. The Utilities submenu appears.

5. Click on **Jasc Digital Camera Support**. The camera installation program begins.

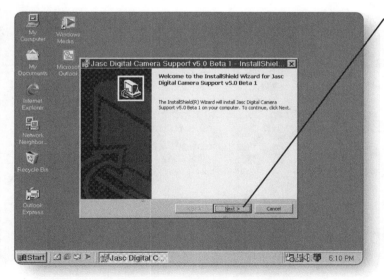

6. Click on **Next**. The Windows Certification screen appears.

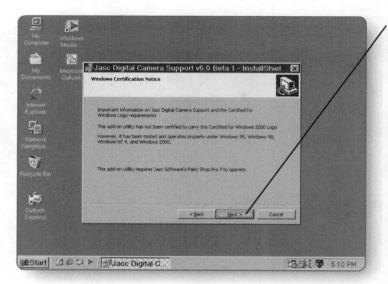

7. **Click** on **Next**. The Custom Setup screen appears.

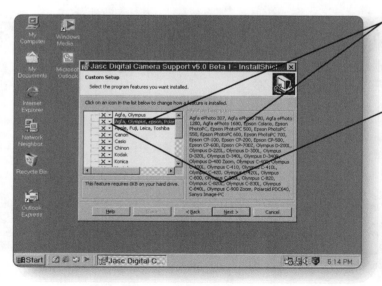

8. **Click** on the **brand** camera you use. A list of supported models appears on the right as you click on each selection.

9. **Click** on the **down arrow** next to the brand. A list of options appears.

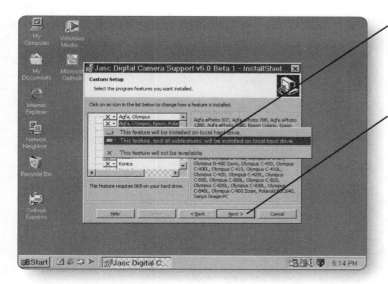

10. **Click** on **This feature, and all subfeatures**, will be installed on local hard drive. The option appears on the screen.

11. **Click** on **Next**. The Ready to Install the Program screen appears.

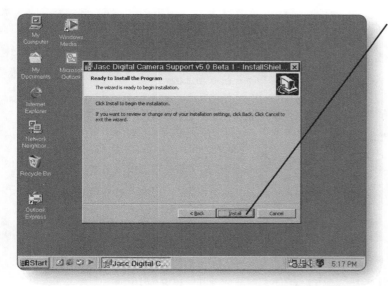

12. **Click** on **Install**. The installation process begins.

The installation process should only take a couple of minutes and displays a message when complete.

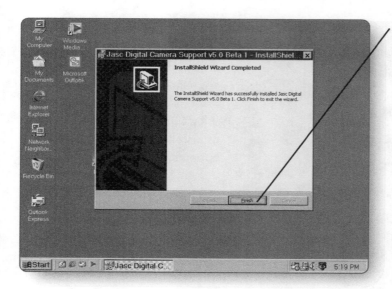

13. Click on **Finish**. The camera installation window closes.

Configuring Your Camera

Paint Shop Pro needs to know where your camera is connected to your computer and what transmission speed to use.

1. Click on **File**. The File menu appears.

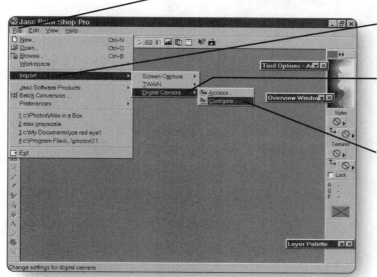

2. Click on **Import**. The Import submenu appears.

3. Click on **Digital Camera**. The Digital Camera submenu appears.

4. Click on **Configure**. The Digital Camera Configuration dialog box opens.

5. Select your camera **model**. The camera model appears in the Camera type: box.

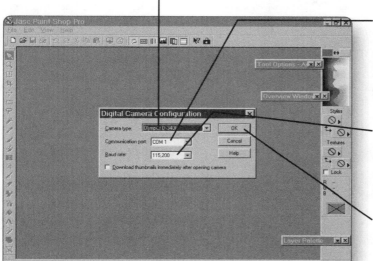

6. Select a communications **port**. The communications port tells Paint Shop Pro how your camera is physically hooked to your computer.

7. Select a communications **speed**. Refer to your camera documentation for this information.

8. Click on **OK**. The Digital Camera Configuration dialog box closes.

Downloading Images

Paint Shop Pro provides you the options of downloading the images and saving them directly to a file or opening them in Paint Shop Pro.

Make sure your camera is connected and turned on before proceeding. Refer to your camera documentation for instructions.

1. Click on **File**. The File menu appears.

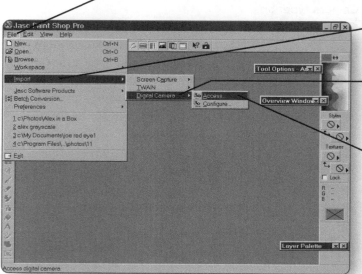

2. Click on **Import**. The Import submenu appears.

3. Click on **Digital Camera**. The Digital Camera submenu appears.

4. Click on **Access**. The Digital Camera dialog box opens.

Paint Shop Pro provides the ability to preview, open, or save all the images at the same time or review them one at a time.

5. Click on **Get Previews**. The images download from your camera.

Be patient. Depending on the number and resolution of the images, as well as the speed of your computer, this process could take several minutes.

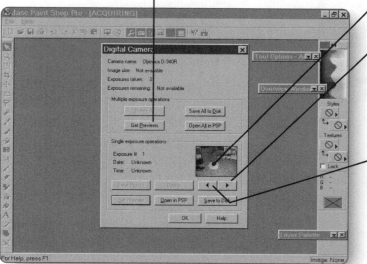

The first image displays in the thumbnail window.

6. Click on the **Next arrow**. The next image displays in the thumbnail window.

TIP

Click on the Back arrow to view the previous image.

To work with the images immediately, you can open them in Paint Shop Pro as untitled images.

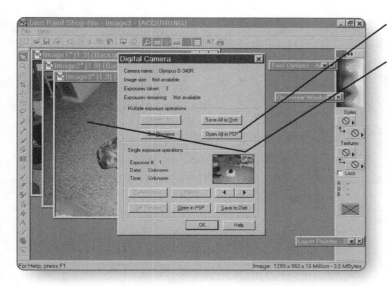

7. **Click** on **Open All in PSP**.

The images open in Paint Shop Pro.

You can also save the images directly to your disk drive, where you can open them and edit them at a later time.

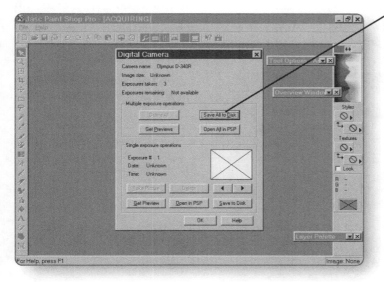

8. **Click** on **Save All to Disk**. The Save digital camera file(s) dialog box opens.

TIP

Optionally, select a different location from the Save in: list box.

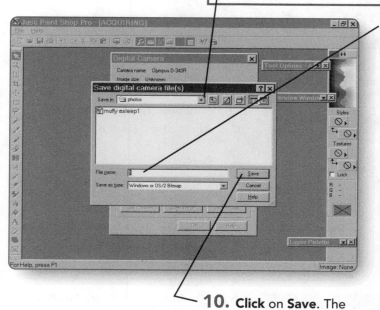

9. Enter a **file name** in the File name: text box. All the downloaded images begin with the file name followed by a sequential number. For example, if you enter "birthday party" in the file name, the images save as "birthday party1," "birthday party2," "birthday party3," and so forth.

TIP

Enter the current date as the file name to store your images by download date.

10. Click on **Save**. The images save to your disk drive.

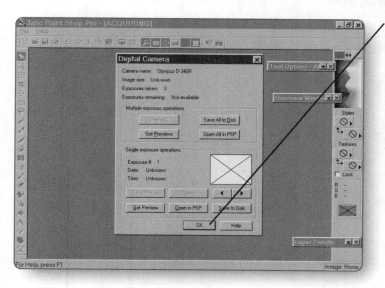

11. Click on **OK**. The Digital Camera dialog box closes.

TIP

Don't forget to turn off your camera!

20

Removing Red-eye from Photos

New to Paint Shop Pro 7 is the Red-eye Removal feature. Red-eye is the effect, caused by flash, that frequently occurs in photographs of humans and animals. You can also use this feature to enhance or change a person's or animal's eye color. In this chapter, you'll learn how to:

- Select a red-eye removal method
- Make red-eye automatic adjustments
- Adjust red-eye options
- Adjust red-eye manually

Opening the Red-eye Removal Dialog Box

The Red-eye Removal option does not work on an image containing a selection. Deselect any selections by pressing Ctrl+D to make the Red-eye Removal option available.

> **NOTE**
> If your image is not 24-bit color, the Red-eye Removal option is unavailable. You'll need to convert your image by clicking on Colors, Increase Color Depth, 16 million colors.

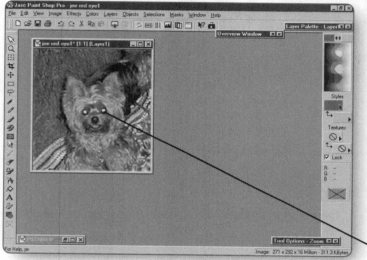

1. Open an **image** with red-eye. Red-eye doesn't have to be red; it can also be a white effect.

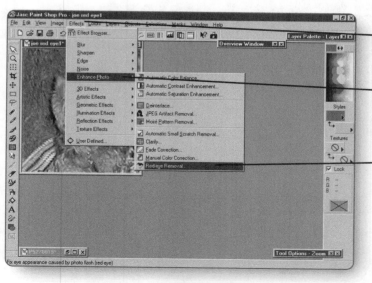

2. Click on **Effects**. The Effects menu appears.

3. Click on **Enhance Photo**. The Enhance Photo submenu appears.

4. Click on **Red-eye Removal**. The Red-eye Removal dialog box opens.

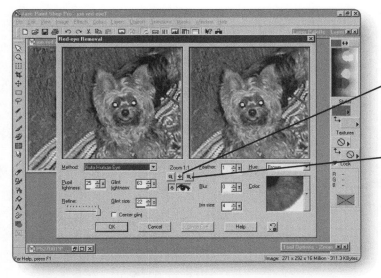

The "before" preview displays on the left and the "after" preview displays on the right.

5. If necessary, **click** on the **placement box** to relocate the preview area to the eyes.

6. If necessary, **click** on the **Zoom in button** to get a good view of the eye. The preview boxes display the enlarged images.

Selecting a Red-eye Removal Method

Paint Shop Pro provides several methods for making red-eye corrections:

- Auto Human Eye: Automatically selects the correction area and makes the appropriate corrections to a human eye.

- Auto Animal Eye: Automatically selects the correction area and makes the appropriate corrections to an animal eye.

- Freehand Pupil Outline: Lets you manually select the correction area using a Freehand selection tool. Use this method for difficult situations, such as a partially obscured eye.

- Point-to-Point Pupil Outline: Lets you manually select the correction area using a Point-to-Point selection tool. Use this method for difficult situations, such as a partially obscured eye.

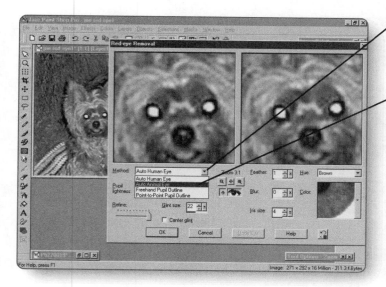

1. **Click** on the **Method: down arrow**. A list of methods appears.

2. **Click** on a **method**. The fastest and easiest methods are the automatic selections. For the purposes of this book, we are using the automatic selections process.

Next, you'll need to decide on an eye hue and color. Eye hue is not available when working with an animal eye.

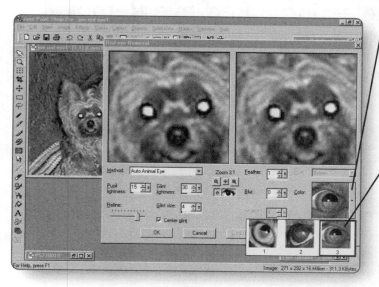

3. **Click** on the **Color: down arrow**. A selection of eye colors and types appears. When working with animal eyes, selection #1 is for a cat, while selections #2 and #3 are for dogs.

4. **Click** on an **eye type/color**. The selection appears in the Color: box.

You're now ready to define the eye area.

Using Automatic Selections

By using the automatic selections, you select the eye area and let Paint Shop Pro do the rest of the work.

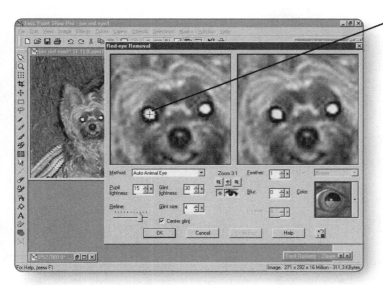

1. In the left preview box, **click** anywhere **inside** the red-eye area of one of the **eyes**. A selection control box appears around the eye.

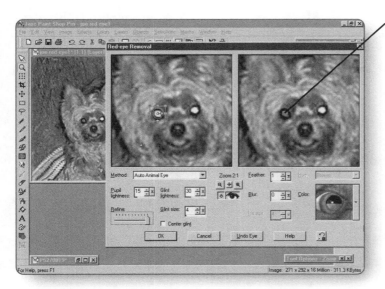

The correction appears in the "after" preview box on the right.

NOTE

Because the default settings can automatically correct a wide range of red-eye effects, you may only need to click the eye. However, in the next section you'll see how to customize the selection area and red-eye options.

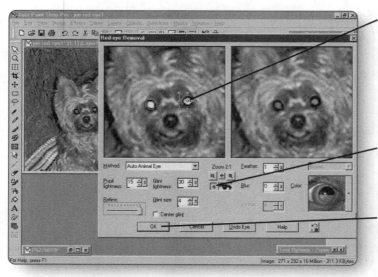

2. In the left preview box, **click** anywhere **inside** the red-eye area of the **other eye**. A selection control box appears around the eye and the right preview box displays the change.

To see the immediate effect on your image, click the proof or auto proof button.

3. Click on **OK**. The Red-eye Removal dialog box closes.

Adjusting Red-eye Options

Even though the Red-eye Removal feature can automatically correct a wide range of red-eye effects, sometimes you'll need to adjust the settings yourself.

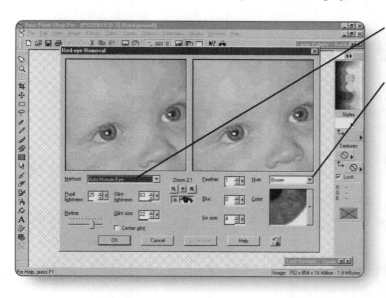

1. Click on a **method**. This image needs Auto Human Eye.

2. Click on the **Hue: down arrow**. A list of eye color selections appears.

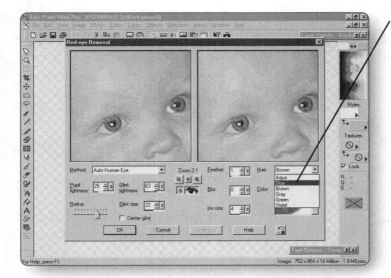

3. Click on a **color**. The option is selected.

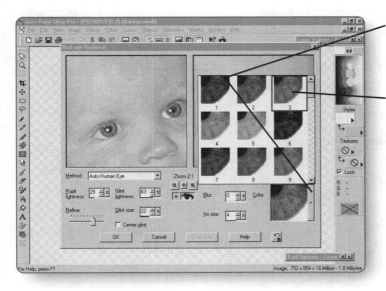

4. Click on the **Color: down arrow**. Thumbnails of the color variations appear.

5. Click on a **color**. The selection appears in the Color: box.

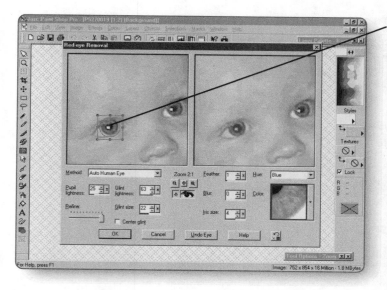

6. In the left preview box, **click** anywhere **inside the "red" area** of one of the **eyes**. A selection control box appears around the eye and the current settings apply to the eye.

Adjusting the Selection Area

In this example, the automatic selection process selected an area too large for the baby's eyes, so the selection area needs to be resized.

1. **Position** the **mouse** over any control handle. The mouse turns into a double-headed arrow.

2. **Click** and **drag** any of the **control handles**. The selection area resizes and the settings apply to the new size.

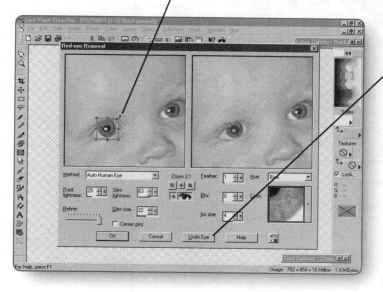

TIP

Click the Undo Eye button to remove a selection and start over.

Move the selection box if it is in the wrong position.

3. Position the **mouse** over the selection box, but not over a control handle. The mouse resembles a four-headed arrow.

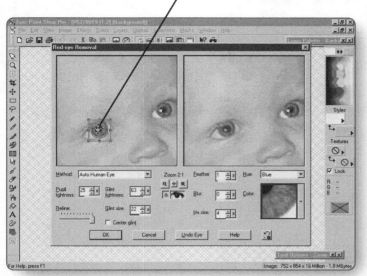

4. Drag the **selection box** to the new **location**, then **release** the **mouse button**. The selection area moves and the settings apply to the new location.

> ### TIP
> When the Auto Animal Eye method is used, a center rotation handle appears, allowing you to drag the handle to rotate the selection, or reshape the selection to an ellipse by pulling on its edges.

Adjusting Settings

There are settings for the iris area around the pupil, the pupil lightness and glint, feathering the selection, and blurring the area.

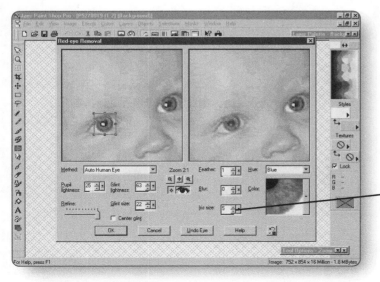

Modifying Iris Size

If you are correcting a human eye (animal eyes sometimes don't have an iris), look at the corrected eye in the right preview box and determine whether you need to modify the iris area around the pupil.

1. Click the **up/down arrow** on the Iris size: box. A larger number increases the size of the iris and decreases the pupil size.

Adjusting the Pupil

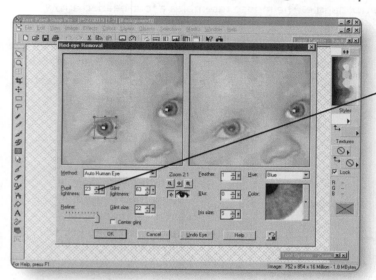

Determine whether the pupil should be lighter or darker, and, if necessary, adjust the settings.

1. **Click** the **up/down arrow** on the Pupil lightness: box. A lower value darkens the pupil while a higher value lightens it.

Modifying Glint

A glint in the eye adds a natural, lively look to the eye while absence of a glint makes the eye dull.

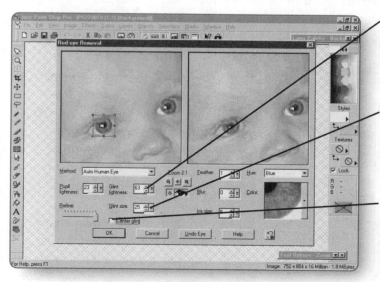

1. **Click** the **up/down arrow** on the Glint lightness: box. A larger number lightens the glint while lower values darken the glint.

2. **Click** the **up/down arrow** on the Glint size: box. A larger number increases the size of the glint.

3. Optionally, **click** on the **Center glint check box** to move the glint to the center of the pupil.

Refining the Eye Settings

Look at the eye in the left preview box. If part of the eye is obscured in the original image, adjust the corrected eye to look the same. For example, if the eyelid is covering part of the eye in the original, you should make it look that way in the corrected eye. Use the Refine, Blur, and Feather settings to make refinements.

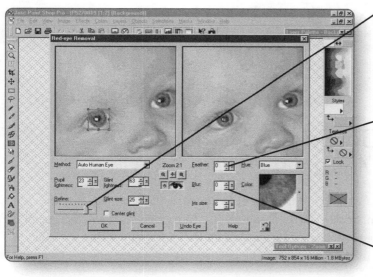

1. **Click** and **drag** the **Refine slider** to the left one notch at a time until the visible area of the corrected eye looks similar to the eye in the original image.

2. Optionally, **click** the **up/down arrow** on the Feather: box. Smaller values make the edges more pronounced, while larger values make them less pronounced.

3. **Click** the **up/down arrow** on the Blur: box. A larger number increases the blending of the surrounding pixels. Use this function when the photo has a grainy appearance.

TIP

As you correct the next eye, the controls retain their settings from the first correction, making it much easier to correct the second eye. When you select the next eye, the previously corrected eye still has a circle around it. You can click this circle to go back and make further corrections to the eye.

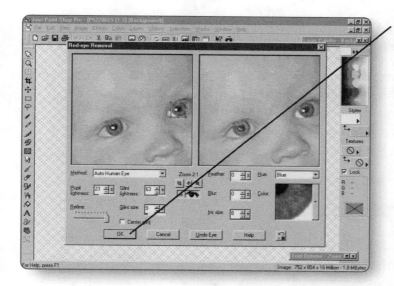

4. Click on **OK**. The Red-eye Removal dialog box closes.

Getting Rid of Red-eye Manually

If, after trying the red-eye reduction function, you are still unhappy with the image, you can try adjusting the eye, pixel by pixel. It's very tedious, but sometimes you need to use this method.

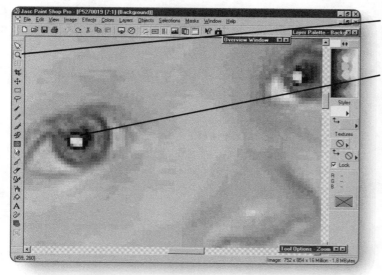

1. Click on the **Zoom tool**. The Zoom tool is selected.

2. Click to **zoom in** on the **eye area** of the image until you can see the individual pixels.

You need to determine the surrounding color choices to get a good match.

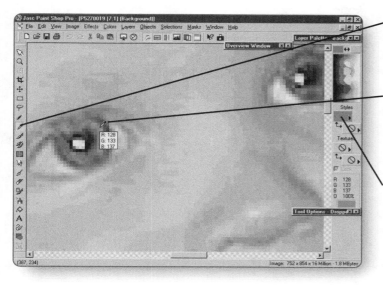

3. Click on the **Dropper tool**. The mouse pointer turns into an eyedropper shape.

4. Position the **mouse pointer** over a pixel color you want to duplicate. The color settings appear under the mouse pointer.

5. Click the mouse **pointer**. The foreground color box picks up the color you clicked.

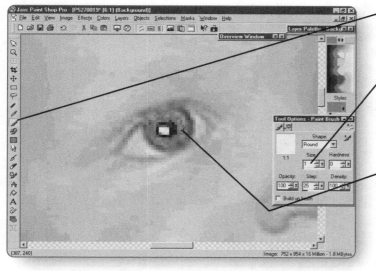

6. Click on the **Paint Brush tool**. The Paint Brush tool is selected.

7. From the Tool Options palette, **set** the **brush Size** to 1. This allows you to change the image one pixel at a time.

8. Click on an eye **pixel**. The pixel changes to the new color.

9. Repeat steps 3 through 8 for each color variation and pixel of the eye area.

TIP

Use different color shade variations. Using all brown or all blue, for example, leaves the eye looking hardened and unrealistic.

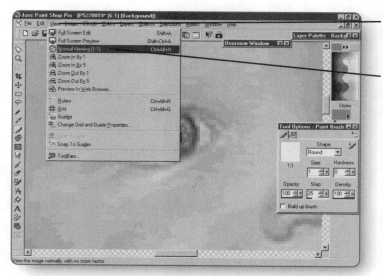

10. **Click** on **View**. The View menu appears.

11. **Click** on **Normal Viewing**. The image resizes to normal.

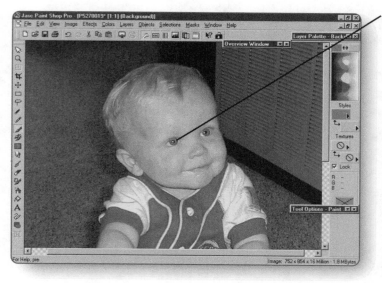

See the results of the editing.

21

Working with the Picture Frame Wizard

Paint Shop Pro contains a variety of picture frames ranging from wood to metal, stone, and other decorative surfaces. Additional frames are available through the Internet. In this chapter, you'll learn how to:

- Start the Picture Frame Wizard
- Position the frame on an image
- Add additional picture frames

Starting the Picture Frame Wizard

The Picture Frame Wizard takes all the work out of adding a frame to your image.

1. Open an **image** on which you want a picture frame.

2. Click on **Image**. The Image menu appears.

3. Click on **Picture Frame**. The Picture Frame Wizard launches.

TIP

If your image is not 24-bit or greyscale, the Picture Frame Wizard option is unavailable. You'll need to convert your image by clicking on Colors, Increase Color Depth, 16 million colors OR Colors, Grey Scale.

4. **Click** on the **frame list down arrow**. A listing of available picture frames appears.

5. **Click** on a **picture frame**. A sample appears in the preview window.

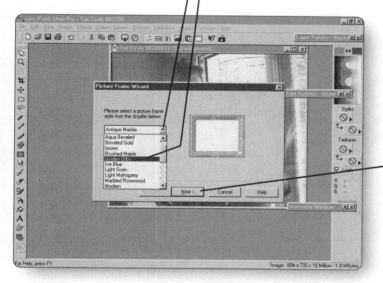

6. **Click** on **Next**. The next page of the wizard appears.

Depending on the shape of the frame you selected, you may be prompted to select a color to fill the transparent areas outside of the frame. Odd-shaped frames usually have a transparent area.

If the frame doesn't have a transparent area, the color selection page doesn't appear. Skip steps 7 through 9.

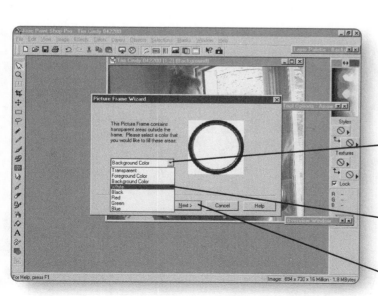

7. **Click** on the **color down arrow**. A list of color selections appears.

8. **Click** on a **color**. The option is selected.

9. **Click** on **Next**. The frame placement page appears.

10. Select a **frame position**. The option is selected.

If you select "Frame inside of the image," Paint Shop Pro resizes the frame to fit within the edges of the image. Part of the image is covered by the picture frame, and the dimensions of the image are not altered.

If you select "Frame outside of the image," Paint Shop Pro increases the canvas size to accommodate the frame. The original image is not covered, and the dimensions of the image are increased by the size of the frame.

11. Click on **Finish**. Paint Shop Pro applies the frame to your specifications.

The picture frame surrounds the image and appears on its own layer entitled Picture Frame.

Saving Images as Picture Frames

Whether you've downloaded from the Internet an image to use as a frame or whether you've created it yourself, you need to tell Paint Shop Pro that you plan to use the image as a frame.

The image must meet two criteria for a frame:

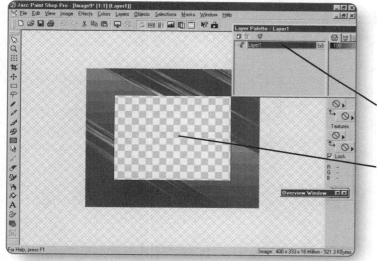

- The image must have only one layer and the layer must be a raster layer.

- All areas of the image canvas other than the frame must be transparent.

1. Click on **File**. The File menu appears.

2. Click on **Save As**. The Save As dialog box appears.

3. **Locate** the **folder** in which you want to store the frame. The folder name appears in the Save In: box.

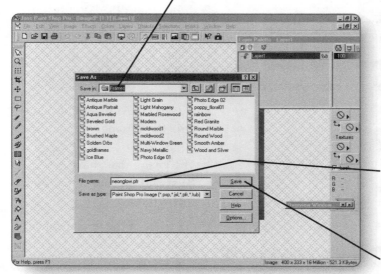

TIP

Make sure the folder you store your frames in is listed under File, Preferences, File Locations, Frames.

4. **Type** a **name** for the frame and **type .pfr** after the file name. The .pfr indicates a Paint Shop Pro frame.

5. **Click** on **Save**. The image saves as a Paint Shop Pro frame.

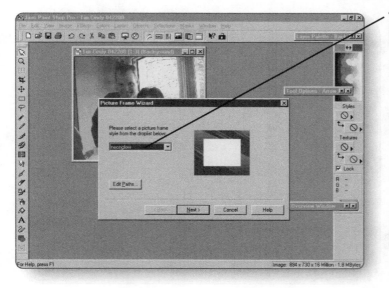

The saved frame appears in the Picture Frame Wizard box.

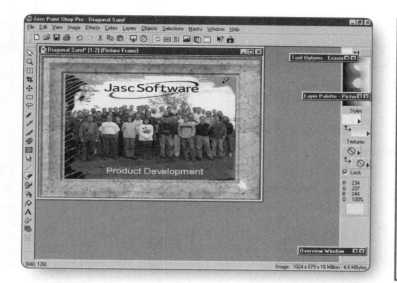

TIP

Want to see a surprise picture of the Jasc development team? Using the Picture Frame Wizard, apply the Antique Marble frame to an image. Click on the Eraser tool, right-click on the frame layer, and drag over the picture area (not the frame) to erase it. There you have it, the Jasc development team.

Part VI Review Questions

1. Does Paint Shop Pro automatically install support for digital cameras? See *"Installing Digital Camera Support"* in Chapter 19.

2. What type of information must you supply Paint Shop Pro about your camera? See *"Configuring Your Camera"* in Chapter 19.

3. Can you open an image in Paint Shop Pro directly from a digital camera? See *"Downloading Images"* in Chapter 19.

4. What is red-eye? See *"Removing Red-eye from Photos"* in Chapter 20.

5. Can you use the red-eye removal effect if your image has a selection? See *"Opening the Red-eye Removal Dialog Box"* in Chapter 20.

6. What are the four methods provided by Paint Shop Pro for making red-eye corrections? See *"Selecting a Red-eye Removal Method"* in Chapter 20.

7. Which red-eye removal method also includes a center rotation handle to rotate your selection? See *"Adjusting the Selection Area"* in Chapter 20.

8. What type of color must an image have to apply the Picture Frame Wizard? See *"Starting the Picture Frame Wizard"* in Chapter 21.

9. When saving an image as a picture frame, how many and what type of layers must the image have? See *"Saving Images as Picture Frames"* in Chapter 21.

10. What does .pfr mean when saving a frame? See *"Saving Images as Picture Frames"* in Chapter 21.

PART VII

Appendixes

Installing Paint Shop Pro 7

Installing Jasc Paint Shop Pro 7 is a painless process. In this chapter, you'll learn how to:

- Determine hardware requirements
- Install Paint Shop Pro 7
- Uninstall Paint Shop Pro 7

Discovering System Requirements

Paint Shop Pro 7 has specific requirements to run properly. The following table lists both the minimum and the recommended specifications:

Component	Minimum	Recommended
Processor	Pentium or >	P500 or >
Operating System	Win 95 or >	Win 95 or >
RAM Memory	32MB	128MB
Disk Space	70MB	70MB
CD Drive	4X or >	4X or >
Monitor	800 × 600 dpi	1024 × 768 dpi

Installing Paint Shop Pro 7

Paint Shop Pro 7 comes on a single CD. The Paint Shop Pro installation disk includes the Paint Shop Pro program and Animation Shop.

TIP

Before installing Paint Shop Pro 7, be sure to temporarily disable any antivirus programs running on your system.

---

1. **Place** the **Installation CD** into your CD-ROM drive. The setup program automatically begins.

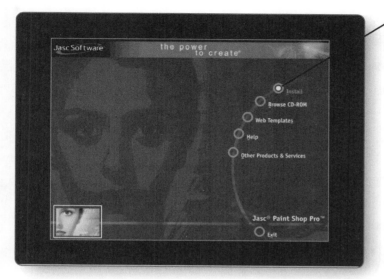

2. Click on **Install**. The Installer Wizard launches.

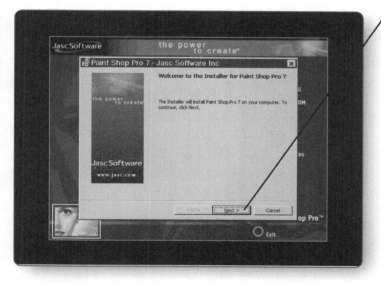

3. Click on **Next**. The License Agreement appears.

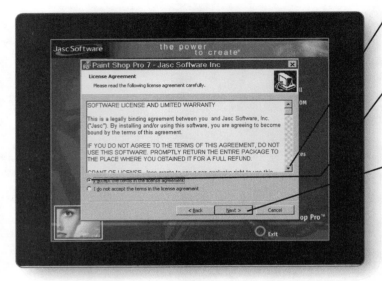

4. **Click** on the **down scroll arrow** to read the agreement in its entirety.

5. **Click** on **I accept the terms in the license agreement**. The option becomes selected.

6. **Click** on **Next**. The Setup Type screen appears.

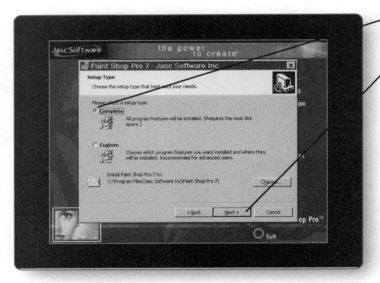

7. **Click** on **Complete**. The option appears selected.

8. **Click** on **Next**. The Ready to Install screen appears.

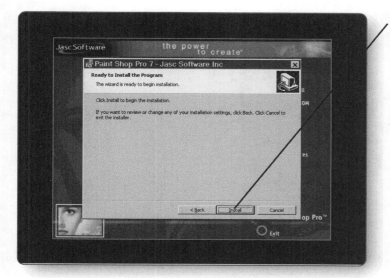

9. **Click** on **Install**. The installation process begins.

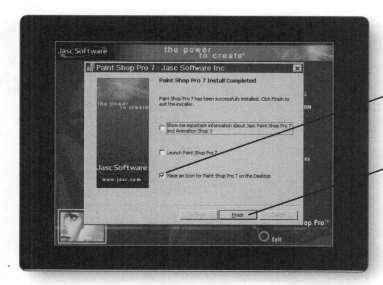

When the installation is complete, an options screen appears.

10. **Click** on any desired **options**. The options display a check mark.

11. **Click** on **Finish**. The Jasc Software opening screen reappears.

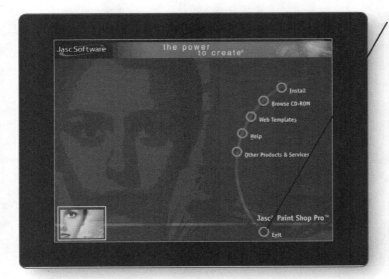

12. **Click** on **Exit**. The Jasc Software opening screen closes.

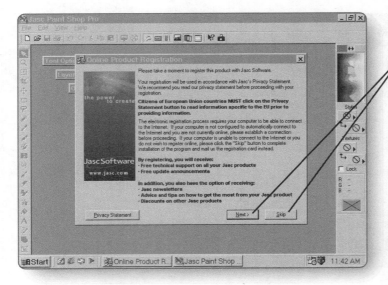

TIP

The first time you use your software, you'll be prompted to register it. If you have an Internet connection, you can register your product online by following the screens, or click on Skip to skip the online registration and mail your registration card to Jasc Software.

Uninstalling Paint Shop Pro 7

If you no longer want Paint Shop Pro on your system, you can easily uninstall it through the Windows Control Panel.

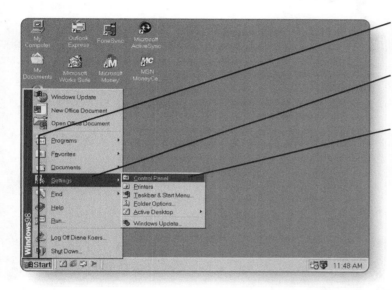

1. **Click** on **Start**. The Start menu appears.

2. **Click** on **Settings**. The Settings submenu appears.

3. **Click** on **Control Panel**. The Control Panel window opens.

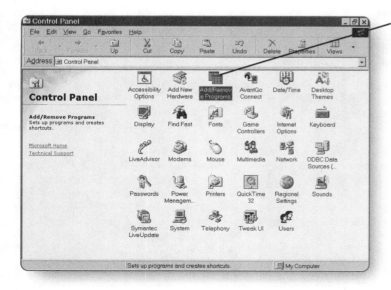

4. **Click** on **Add/Remove Programs**. The Add/Remove Programs dialog box opens.

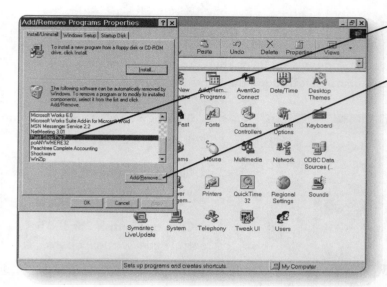

5. **Click** on **Paint Shop Pro 7**. The option appears highlighted.

6. **Click** on **Add/Remove**. The Paint Shop Pro Installer Wizard appears.

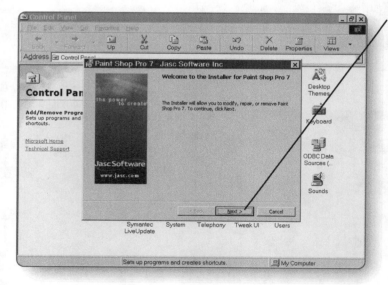

7. **Click** on **Next**. The Program Maintenance screen appears.

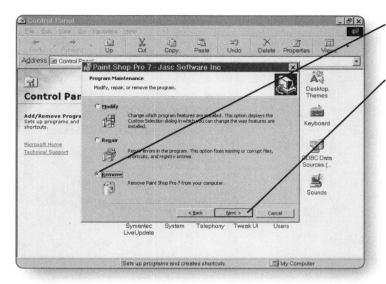

8. **Click** on **Remove**. The option appears selected.

9. **Click** on **Next**. The Remove the Program screen appears.

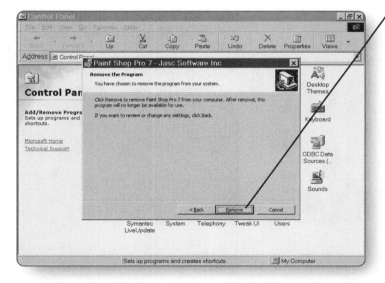

10. **Click** on **Remove**. The uninstall process begins.

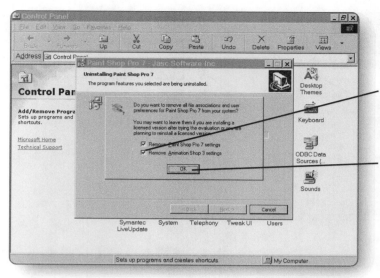

Customized preferences and file associations can be left or removed.

11. Click on any **option** you DON'T want to remove. The option becomes deselected.

12. Click on **OK**. The options dialog box closes and the uninstall process continues.

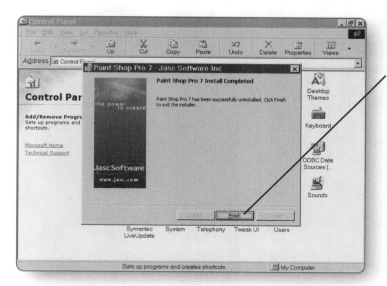

Paint Shop Pro prompts you when the uninstall is complete.

13. Click on **Finish**. The Paint Shop Pro Installer Wizard closes.

The Add/Remove programs dialog box reappears.

14. **Click** on **OK**. The Add/Remove Programs dialog box closes.

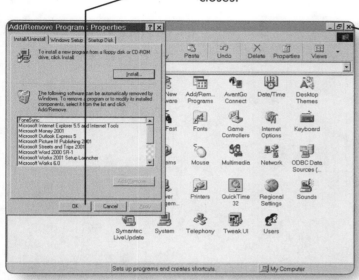

15. **Click** on the **Close box** . The Control Panel window closes.

B
Exploring Useful Web Sites

The World Wide Web has hundreds and maybe thousands of sites dedicated to using Paint Shop Pro. If you have Internet access, take some time to check out some of the links I've listed below. Some are general Paint Shop Pro help information while others are step-by-step tutorials on special tasks you can accomplish with Paint Shop Pro. Still others are links to lots of free or mostly free things you can download to use with your Paint Shop Pro—things like picture tubes, masks, filters, and frames.

I apologize in advance if any listed site closes or modifies its content. While at the time of publication these links were active and accurate, remember that Web sites change frequently. Also, always make sure your antivirus software is up to date *before you download anything from the Internet*. You cannot be too safe!

One other note. Many of these sites refer to prior versions of Paint Shop Pro, but you'll find you can use most of the information they offer with Paint Shop Pro 7 as well.

New User Sites

These links are geared toward new users of Paint Shop Pro, meaning they keep it simple for all of us newbies to Paint Shop Pro. Some even offer online classes to help you learn the software.

http://www.comm-unique.com.au/html/pspu.html

http://www.lvsonline.com

http://www.psptoybox.com

http://www.putertutor.net/paint/newuser.htm

http://www.xanthic.net/Tutorials16-bottom-main.htm

General Tutorial Sites

These sites list general step-by-step tutorials to assist you with specific tasks. Most have links to other tutorials and items including free graphic downloads.

http://www.geocities.com/SiliconValley/Heights/5226/index2.html

http://www.brovik.com/

http://www.compusmart.ab.ca/lastwords

http://www.comm-unique.com.au/html/pspu.html

http://www.rorony.net/windchimestutorial.html

http://www.geocities.com/SiliconValley/Heights/5226/index2.html

http://home.gallatinriver.net/~morris/PSPTutorials/PSPMain.htm

http://home.gallatinriver.net/~morris/SiteMap.htm

http://home.gallatinriver.net/morris/PSPTutorials/inside-outside/inside-out.htm

http://htmlhelp.rootsweb.com/imagehelp/psp7/index.html

http://mardiweb.com/web/

http://mars.ark.com/~gschorno/gfo/index.html

http://members.aol.com/campratty/eyes2.html

http://members.aol.com/campratty/tutorials.html

http://members.madasafish.com/~blue_daffodil/

http://members.nbci.com/lezzard/

http://moonlight-designs.com/tutorials/

http://msnhomepages.talkcity.com/CerfSt/psp_tubes/rhonniestutpage.htm

http://newdawn.gzinc.com/

http://psptips.com

http://ronstoons.com/

http://theglassegg.homestead.com/

http://www.arizonakate.homestead.com/tutorial1.html

http://www.artbygeegee.com/index.htm

http://www.autumnweb.com/Roxys/Tubes/

http://www.boopsie.net

http://www.c-gate.net/~msmith/psp.html

http://www.comm-unique.com.au/html/pspu.html

http://www.crosswinds.net/~angeal/

http://www.crosswinds.net/~bluegenie2

http://www.crosswinds.net/~deziner/index.html

http://www.crosswinds.net/~joflo/psp/index.htm

http://www.crosswinds.net/~joflo/psp/tutorials.htm

http://www.crosswinds.net/~kampes/index.htm

http://www.crosswinds.net/~psptips/

http://www.cutups.org/

http://www.cybertrails.com/~mreppe73/psplink.htm

http://www.dizteq.com

http://www.egroups.com/group/PSP7Newbies

http://www.flashpowdergraphics.com

http://www.fortunecity.com/westwood/alaia/354/

http://www.fortunecity.com/westwood/idea/909/index.html

http://www.fortunecity.com/westwood/line/209/index.html

http://www.frontiernet.net/~willshak/index.html

http://www.frontiernet.net/~willshak/mouseover.htm

http://www.geocities.com/groovyflashback/tutindex.html

http://www.geocities.com/Heartland/Cabin/6995/RaindropImages.htm

http://www.geocities.com/Heartland/Plains/9871/PSPlinks.html

http://www.geocities.com/jdmc83/Tutorials2.htm

http://www.geocities.com/mcjd83/Tutorials.html

http://www.jasc.com/tutorials/tsites.asp

http://www.kiwidream.f2s.com/

http://www.neocognition.com

http://www.onstagegraphics.com/

http://www.pspiz.com/

http://www.pspro1.bizland.com/

http://www.psptoybox.com

http://www.putertutor.net/

http://www.redrival.com/sholsan/index.html

http://www.rorony.net/windchimestutorial.html

http://www.state-of-entropy.com/

http://www.thecastle.com/

Masks and Mask Help

Chapter 9, "Forming Masks," showed you how to design and use masks to hide portions of an image. Here are a few more, free for you to download.

http://members.nbci.com/Ronald_Vick/mask1.htm

http://www.crosswinds.net/~deziner/masks.html

http://www.geocities.com/haylers/stripemasktutorial.html

http://www.geocities.com/Heartland/Plains/9316/masktut.html

http://www.putertutor.net/paint/masks2.htm

Web Page Help Sites

Since Paint Shop Pro is frequently used to design Web graphics, I thought we might include a few links where you can obtain additional help in creating Web pages.

http://hotwired.lycos.com/webmonkey/?tw=659

http://www.mountevansdesigns.com/

http://hotwired.lycos.com/webmonkey/?tw=659

http://htmlhelp.rootsweb.com/imagehelp/psp7/index.html

http://web.mit.edu/afs/athena/user/w/s/wsmart/WEB/tutorial/HTMLtutor.html

http://www.comm-unique.com.au/html/pspu.html

http://www.ezboard.com/

http://www.ihs.gov/misc/links_gateway/sub_categories.cfm?sub_cat_id=0502

http://www.killersites.com/

http://www.lvsonline.com

http://www.nobledesktop.com/guide.html

http://www.putertutor.net/

http://www.visionsnet.com/web/index.html

Picture Frames

Enhance your pictures with additional free downloadable frames. See Chapter 21, "Working with the Picture Frame Wizard."

http://www.thekoala.com/pspframes.htm

http://www.rsvlonline.net/ramco/frames_page_3.htm

http://www.geocities.com/jdmc83/AirBrush.htm

http://newdawn.gzinc.com/tutorials/frameadd6.html

http://www.geocities.com/Heartland/Bluffs/7089/PSP6FrameTutorial.htm

http://www.gloriouscreations.com/gcgraphics/pspframes/index.html

http://westwood.fortunecity.com/vivienne/150/psp6-frames.htm

http://www.pspiz.com/tutorials/PSP6/PicFrames/framer.html

http://www.crosswinds.net/~kampes/frames/framestut.htm

http://www.geocities.com/Heartland/Plains/6524/frames.html

http://loriweb.pair.com/psp6frame1.html

http://loriweb.pair.com/psp6frame3.html

http://www.mardiweb.com/web/psp6/frames/frames.htm

http://www.artbygeegee.com/squareframes.htm

http://www.designsbydonna.com/frame/frame.html

http://millerfg.home.mindspring.com/wpf2.htm

http://home.freeuk.net/brooksbank/frames.html

Picture Tubes

Tubes, tubes, tubes. They are everywhere! Download lots and lots of free tubes. Refer to Chapter 8, "Designing with Picture Tubes."

http://tearosecreations.com/gbt/tubes.html

http://www.fantasyrealm.com/

http://www.geocities.com/graphicsbytracy/tubesbytracy.html

http://www.geocities.com/yankee_lynn_2000/

http://www.kiwidream.f2s.com/

http://www.pspbook.com/IndexedLinks/TubeLinks.html

http://www.rsvlonline.net/ramco/teris_tubes.htm

Free Effects Filters & Filter Help

In Chapter 10, "Adding Effects, Filters, and Deformations," you learned how to apply effects to create dynamic special effects for your images. Here are links to other Paint Shop Pro users who have created their own effects and want to share them, or the knowledge of how to create them, with you. Best of all, these filters are free!

http://www.plugin-filters.com/

http://hem.passagen.se/grafoman/plugtool/plugs.html

http://pico.i-us.com/

http://www.comm-unique.com.au/html/pspu.html

http://www.dizteq.com

http://www.filtermeister.com/unplugged/index.html

http://www.geocities.com/Heartland/Plains/9871/downloads.html

http://www.mediaco.com/nvr/filters.html

http://www.netins.net/showcase/wolf359/plugins.htm

Commercial Filter Sites

More filters. Although these filters aren't necessarily free, most of these sites include trial downloads, so you can "try before you buy."

http://www.alienskin.com/

http://www.comm-unique.com.au/html/pspu.html

http://www.extensis.com/

http://www.flamingpear.com/blade.html

http://www.plugin-filters.com/

Customized Brushes

Although the subject of customized brushes was not covered in this book, as you get more and more comfortable with Paint Shop Pro, take some time to check out these sites, which offer free customized brushes.

http://www.geocities.com/~arravis_zen/psp_brush1.htm

http://www.geocities.com/Athens/Delphi/6422/brush1.html

http://www.nikkisgallery.com/brushes/brush12.htm

http://www.pspbook.com/IndexedLinks/BrushLinks.html

http://www.shadowymist.com/brushes/pspbrushes.htm

Outlook Express Stationery

Outlook Express Stationery was another topic we weren't able to cover in this book, but take a peek at these Web sites for more information.

http://members.nbci.com/aprilsplace/

http://statnook.freewebsites.com/otherlinks.htm

http://www.kiwidream.f2s.com/

Newsgroups

One final note…if you like to read newsgroups, here's a great one! You can post Paint Shop Pro questions and receive answers from other Paint Shop Pro users or even the Jasc programmers.

news:comp.graphics.apps.paint-shop-pro

C

Sample Effects

As you've already discovered, Paint Shop Pro has many powerful effects available to enhance your images, whether the image is a photograph or a drawing.

Here are just a few of the applied effects. Remember that effects can be combined for even more effects!

Original Image

Artistic - Glowing Edges

Artistic - Black Pencil

Texture - Blinds

Original Image

Artistic - Chrome

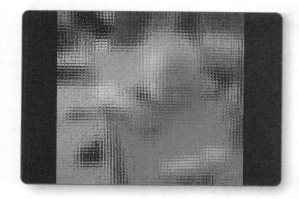

Texture - Mosaic Glass

Geometric - Page Curl

Reflection - Rotating Mirror

Illumination - Sunburst

Geometric - Weave

Original Image

Texture - Fur

Texture - Emboss

Geometric - Curly Q

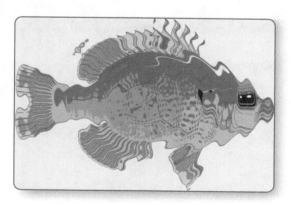

Geometric - Ripple

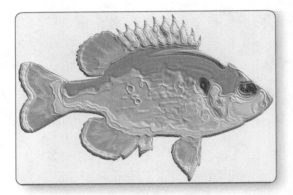

Texture - Soft Plastic

Geometric - Warp

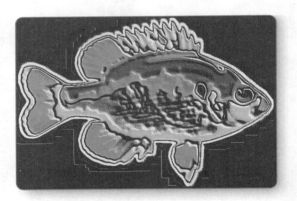

Texture - Polished Stone

Original Image

Artistic - Contour

Geometric - Twirl

Illumination - Lights (1 Up Option)

Illumination - Lights (Soft Blue Option)

Glossary

1-bit image. An image containing a maximum of 2 colors.

4-bit image. An image containing a maximum of 16 colors.

8-bit image. An image containing a maximum of 256 colors.

15-bit image. An image containing a maximum of 32,768 colors.

16-bit image. An image containing a maximum of 65,536 colors.

24-bit image. An image containing a maximum of 16,777,216 colors.

Adjustment Layer. A layer used to apply color adjustments to the layers below it.

Animation. A series of sequential images with an optional transition effect to create the illusion of movement.

Animation Shop. An application included with Paint Shop Pro to create animations.

Animation Wizard. A tool supplied by Animation Shop to assist you in creating animations.

Antialias. The smoothing and blending of pixel edges to eliminate jagged edges on curved and slanted lines.

Aspect Ratio. The ratio of width to height.

Attribute. Items that determine the appearance of text, such as bolding, underlining, italics, font, or size.

Automatic Rollups. Floating objects that open automatically as you hover your mouse in their area, but then close up again when you move your mouse out of their vicinity.

AutoSave. A feature that periodically saves a temporary version of your document.

AVI. Abbreviation for Audio Video Interlaced. A Windows multimedia file format used for video and audio.

Background. The canvas on which graphics display.

Background Color. The canvas color on which graphics display.

Background Layer. The bottom layer in many images.

Banner Wizard. An Animation Shop feature that assists you in creating animated text banners.

Bevel. A three-dimensional edge on an object.

Bezier Curve. A smooth curve with anchor points and direction handles.

Bit. The smallest unit of digital information handled by a computer.

Bit Depth. See *color depth*.

Bitmapped Image. An image composed of small squares, called pixels, arranged in columns and rows. Each pixel has a specific color and location.

Blend. To combine two layers or areas of an image.

Blur. An effect that reduces areas of high contrast and softens the appearance of an image.

BMP. File format abbreviation for a bitmapped image.

Brightness. The amount of light or white color in an image.

Browse. A feature of Paint Shop Pro and Animation Shop that allows you to see multiple thumbnail images.

Browser Toolbar. Displays useful tools when browsing images.

Canvas. The area on which an image is displayed.

Canvas size. The size of the area within an image window.

Clone. To duplicate a portion of an image.

CMYK. Abbreviation for Cyan/Magenta/Yellow/Black, which are the four standard ink colors used in printing.

Color Depth. The number of bits of color information available for each pixel.

Color Palette. Contains a selection of available colors, styles, and textures and displays the current foreground and background colors and styles.

Color Wheel. The circular color area from which you can create a custom color.

Colorize. An effect that converts an image or selection to a uniform hue and saturation while retaining its lightness.

Compression. A process applied to saved images to reduce file size.

Contract Command. Shrinks a selection by a specific number of pixels.

Contrast. The difference between the light and dark areas of an image.

Crop. To remove part of an image outside a selection.

Defloat. To merge a floating selection into a layer.

Deformation. To change an image appearance by moving data from one area to another.

Defringe. To clean the edges of a selection by removing pixels of the background color.

Digital. Information read and processed by a computer.

Digital Camera. A camera that takes pictures and stores them in its memory or on a disk.

Dithering. When a computer monitor substitutes a color it cannot display with a similar color.

DPI. Abbreviation for Dots Per Inch. A unit of measurement that measures the number of dots that fit horizontally and vertically into a one-inch measure.

Effect. A graphic function that creates a modification to an image.

Emboss. An effect that causes the foreground of an image to appear raised from the background.

Expand a Selection. Increases the size of a selection by a specified number of pixels.

Export. The process of saving a file into a different format.

Feather. The process of fading an area on all edges of a selection. Measured in pixels.

File Associations. A method of determining which files your computer opens automatically using Paint Shop Pro.

File Format. The structure of a file that defines the way it is stored.

Filter. A tool that applies special effects to an image.

Flip Command. The command that reverses an image vertically.

Float Command. The command that temporarily separates a selection from an image or layer.

Floating Objects. Screen elements appearing in the middle of the Paint Shop Pro window that can be moved to other areas of the window. Floating objects have automatic rollup.

Foreground Color. The primary color for the painting and drawing tools.

Format. The shape and size of an image or text. Also, the method a Browser uses to display an image.

FPS. Abbreviation of Frames per Second. The rate at which animations are displayed.

Frame. A single complete image in a series of images, usually animations, that indicates a step in the image movement.

GIF. File format abbreviation for a Graphic Interchange Format image. GIF images support transparency but only 8-bit (256) color. Commonly used with Web graphics.

Gradient Fill. A fill created by the gradual blending of colors.

Greyscale Image. An image that uses up to 256 shades of grey.

Grid. An equally spaced series of vertical and horizontal lines to help align objects.

Grow Command. Adds color pixels adjacent to an active selection.

Handles. Control points on vector objects used to edit the object.

Highlight. The lightest part of an image.

Histogram. A graphic representation showing the distribution of color and light in an image.

HSL. Abbreviation for Hue/Saturation/Lightness. A method of defining colors in an image.

HTML. Abbreviation for Hypertext Markup Language. A programming language used to create Web pages.

Hue. A color.

Image Window. The area in which you work on your image.

Internet. A global network of computers used to transfer information.

JPEG. Abbreviation for Joint Photographic Experts Group. Same as JPG File Format.

JPG File Format. A file format that supports 24-bit (16,777,216) color but not transparency. Commonly used with Web graphics.

Kerning. The distance between characters of text.

Layer. A level of an image that can be edited independently from the rest of the image.

Layer Palette. Lists each layer in the current image.

Leading. The distance between lines of text.

Line Art. An image composed of one color.

Logo. A name or symbol used by many businesses for easy recognition.

Luminance. A physical measurement of the brightness information in an image.

Magic Wand. A selection tool that works by selecting content rather than defining edges.

Marquee. A selection area, represented by "marching ants."

Mask. A feature that allows some portion of an image to be hidden.

Mirror. An exact copy of an image placed in reverse of the copied image.

Negative Image. A photographic image in reversed form where the light areas become dark and the dark areas become light.

Node. A control point on a vector object.

Noise. The grainy appearance in some images.

Object. A single element in an image.

Opacity. The density of a color or layer.

Overview Window. Displays entire image when zooming in to a small area.

Path. The guiding line for a vector object.

Picture Tubes. Fun little pictures that you paint with your brush.

Pixel. The smallest element in an image.

PNG. Abbreviation for Portable Network Graphics. A file format designed for Web graphics that supports both transparency and 24-bit (16,777,216) color.

Posterize. Effect that replaces areas of continuous color tone with single colors.

Preferences. The area in which each user maintains customized settings for Paint Shop Pro.

Print Preview. The feature that allows you to view an image prior to printing on paper.

Raster Image. A bitmapped image made up of pixels.

Rasterize. To convert a vector image to raster.

Red-eye. An effect that frequently occurs in photographs of humans and animals, giving a shiny or red appearance to eyes.

Replace Color Command. The Paint Shop Pro feature that allows you to pick a specific color and replace it with any other color.

Resize. The ability to make an image or object larger or smaller.

Resolution. The measurement of the detail in an image.

RGB (Red/Green/Blue). The three primary colors that compose most images.

Rotate. To turn an image or object.

Saturation. The measure of strength of a color in an image.

Scanner. A hardware device used to translate pictures and text into digital language that can be interpreted by a computer.

Selection. The outline that appears around an area to be modified.

Shadow. The darkest area of an image. Sometimes applied as an effect.

Sharpen. An effect that increases the contrast in an image.

Skew. A deformation that tilts an image along its horizontal or vertical axis.

Solarize. An effect that inverts all colors above a selected value.

Status Bar. The line at the bottom of an application window that displays help and image details.

Stroke. An outline of text.

Text Banner. Animations often seen on Web pages, usually at the top, that have text moving around.

Thumbnail. A miniature version of an image.

TIFF. Abbreviation for Tagged Image File Format. A format commonly used by scanners.

Title Bar. The bar at the top of the application that displays the Paint Shop Pro Control icon, the application name, and the name of the active image and its format, as well as the standard Windows buttons.

Toggle. To switch an item back and forth from one state to another. Frequently used to turn the display of layers on and off.

Tool Palette. Contains the image editing tools.

Toolbar. Displays tools to manage files and commonly used menu functions.

Tools Options Palette. Displays options for the currently selected tool.

Transparency. An area with no color.

TWAIN. A common computer interface between scanners, digital cameras, and computers.

Undo. The ability to reverse actions.

VCR Controls. An Animation Shop toolbar that controls viewing an animation.

Vector Graphic. An object that uses mathematics to create images. Vector graphics can be easily edited, moved, and resized.

Watermark. Embedded information in an image, used to mark an image with copyright and author information.

Web Browser. A software program specifically designed to view Web pages on the Internet.

Workspace. The portion of the Paint Shop Pro window where you work on your image.

Zoom. The process of viewing an image in a larger or smaller magnification.

Index

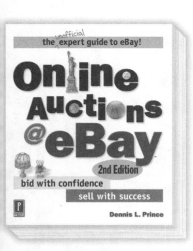
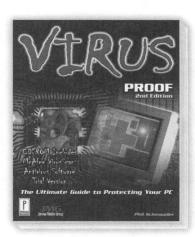
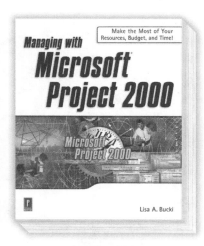

Fast Facts, Easy Access
PRIMA TECH'S *fast&easy* series

Offering extraordinary value at a bargain price, the FAST & EASY series is dedicated to one idea: To help readers accomplish tasks as quickly and easily as possible. There's no need to wade through endless pages of boring text. The unique and carefully developed visual teaching method combines concise tutorials and hundreds of WYSIWYG (what-you-see-is-what-you-get) screen shots to dramatically increase learning speed and retention of the material. With PRIMA TECH'S *FAST & EASY* series, you simply look and learn.

A Division of Prima Publishing
www.prima-tech.com

Call now to order
(800)632-8676
ext. 4444

Quicken® 2001
0-7615-2908-X ▪ U.S. $18.99
Can. $28.95 ▪ U.K. £13.99

WordPerfect®
Office 2000 for Linux
0-7615-2857-1 ▪ U.S. $18.99
Can. $28.95 ▪ U.K. £13.99

Paint Shop Pro™ 7
0-7615-3241-2 ▪ U.S. $18.99
Can. $28.95 ▪ U.K. £13.99

Red Hat® Linux® 7
0-7615-2679-X ▪ U.S. $18.99
Can. $28.95 ▪ U.K. £13.99

Photoshop® 6
for Windows®
0-7615-2850-4 ▪ U.S. $18.99
Can. $28.95 ▪ U.K. £13.99

iMovie™
0-7615-2907-1 ▪ U.S. $18.99
Can. $28.95 ▪ U.K. £13.99

Microsoft®
Works Suite 2001
0-7615-3371-0 ▪ U.S. $18.99
Can. $28.95 ▪ U.K. £13.99

Microsoft® Windows®
Millennium Edition
0-7615-2739-7 ▪ U.S. $18.99
Can. $28.95 ▪ U.K. £13.99

Family Tree Maker® 8
The Official Guide
0-7615-2998-5 ▪ U.S. $18.99
Can. $28.95 ▪ U.K. £13.99

Photoshop® 6
for Mac®
0-7615-3000-2 ▪ U.S. $18.99
Can. $28.95 ▪ U.K. £13.99

iMac™ Revised Edition
0-7615-3136-X ▪ U.S. $18.99
Can. $28.95 ▪ U.K. £13.99

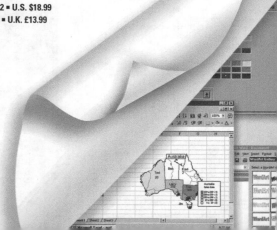